MW00981743

an introduction to teaching adult esl

Virginia L. Sauvé

OXFORD
UNIVERSITY PRESS

OXFORD
UNIVERSITY PRESS

70 Wynford Drive, Don Mills, Ontario M3C 1J9
www.oupcan.com

Oxford University Press is a department of the University of Oxford.
It furthers the University's objective of excellence in research, scholarship,
and education by publishing worldwide in

Oxford New York

Athens Auckland Bangkok Bogotá Buenos Aires Calcutta
Cape Town Chennai Dar es Salaam Delhi Florence Hong Kong Istanbul
Karachi Kuala Lumpur Madrid Melbourne Mexico City Mumbai
Nairobi Paris São Paulo Singapore Shanghai Taipei Tokyo Toronto Warsaw

with associated companies in Berlin Ibadan

Oxford is a trade mark of Oxford University Press
in the UK and in certain other countries

Published in Canada
by Oxford University Press

Copyright © Oxford University Press Canada 2000

The moral rights of the author have been asserted

Database right Oxford University Press (maker)

First published 2000

Canadian Cataloguing in Publication Data

Sauvé, Virginia L. (Virginia Louise), 1946-
Voices and visions: an introduction to teaching adult esl
Includes bibliographical references and index.

ISBN 0-19-541393-8

1. English language — Study and teaching as a second language.* I. Title.

PE1128.A2S283 2000   428'.0071'5   C99-932972-3

Cover & Text Design: Tearney McMurtry

1 2 3 4 - 03 02 01 00

This book is printed on permanent (acid-free) paper ∞
Printed in Canada

Contents

Acknowledgements / iv

Introduction / v

Section I   **Reflecting on the Task at Hand / 1**

Chapter 1   Answering Some Basic Questions / 3

Chapter 2   Understanding Your Context: Who Are the Learners? / 16

Chapter 3   Understanding Your Context: Yourself / 37

Chapter 4   Understanding Your Context: The Program / 48

Chapter 5   Understanding Your Context: The Community / 54

Section II   **Entering the Classroom / 61**

Chapter 6   Planning a Lesson / 63

Chapter 7   Planning a Resource "Stash" / 73

Chapter 8   Finding and Creating Activities that Work / 82

Chapter 9   The subject and the Subject / 94

Chapter 10   Teaching Listening, Speaking, and Pronunciation / 110

Chapter 11   Teaching Reading, Writing, and Vocabulary / 128

Chapter 12   Teaching Grammar / 142

Chapter 13   Accountability and Evaluation / 162

Section III   **Being an Educator in ESL and EFL / 171**

Chapter 14   Relationships / 173

Chapter 15   Professionalism: What It Means and Why It Is Important / 182

Chapter 16   Discernment in Developing Voices and Creating Visions / 190

Appendix 1   Sample Lesson Plans / 197

Appendix 2   Writing Intents—Answer Key / 219

Appendix 3   List of Phonetic Symbols / 223

Bibliography / 224

Acknowledgements

I would like to express my sincere thanks to a number of people who enabled this book to come to being:

Robert Doyle of Oxford University Press, now working in Chile, who offered his encouragement, inspiration, and support in the conception of *Voices and Visions*; I miss you, Robert.

Merilee Brand, whose commitment and dedication to editing this book were outstanding and with whom I am glad to share a new friendship.

Monica Schwalbe of Oxford, whose patience is just short of miraculous and whose diplomatic skills would recommend her to our External Affairs office, should she ever desire a career change.

The reviewers who read a very poor first draft of this book when my new computer seemed to delight in deleting lines without my knowledge; they made many excellent and helpful suggestions for revisions.

Yvonne MacMillan of Oxford who took over when Robert Doyle left and had to accommodate my delays; you have my apologies, Yvonne.

Phyllis Wilson for her typing of the final draft of the text, not an easy task with phonemics and other detailed non-standard text.

My former colleagues from Portals, English Language Professionals, and the Alberta Vocational College in Edmonton from all of whom I learned so much in the last twenty plus years.

Dr. Tetsuo Aoki, my teacher, professor, initial dissertation supervisor, and friend, who most of all is my mentor as an educator. I thank you for being who you are, and for allowing me into the privileged circle of your wisdom and tutelage. I also thank you for trusting me with the Korean Teacher Education Project.

Virginia Satir, a woman who opened many doors of knowledge and possibility for me. May you rest in peace knowing that you left this world a better place for your commitment to and love of people.

And last, but far from least, to the many students who have allowed me the privilege of teaching and learning from you. May you be happy and successful in Canada or Korea or wherever you happen to be.

Respectfully,

Virginia L. Sauvé, Ph.D.

Introduction

Why "Voices and Visions?"

You are about to read a book that is unlike most other introductions to teaching English as a Second Language. This book does not focus on second language acquisition theory, and although the second section is packed with practical suggestions, a larger part of the book reflects one person's experiences of teaching in this field. The series title "Voices and Visions" was chosen because it seems to me an appropriate one to capture the essence of the work we do and the decisions we make in doing it.

Language is first and foremost about *voice*. One can take that in the literal sense of speaking or in the more meaningful sense of giving *voice* to one's being in the world, namely of having power in the world through the exercise of voice. In this, I probably have stronger feelings than many practitioners. I believe that it is my role to teach the language in such a way that the learner has confidence in his or her power to affect the context in which he or she is speaking the language. While traditional forms of language teaching have cast the learner in a passive light, I prefer critical forms of language teaching which cast the learner as a participant in the ongoing creation of the world around us. These contrasting beliefs result in radically different ways of teaching language.

Vision, in this context, is that picture we have in our minds of where we are going, as teachers and as learners. Many would say that they do not understand this, that they have no particular vision when they set out to teach or to learn, and I accept that this is true. However, in my experience, vision is what empowers us to make conscious choices, to give detail first in our minds to that which we wish to create in reality. If we have no vision to guide us, we have a tendency to go around in circles, never moving far from where we started.

If, on the other hand, we assume that education is about making the world a better place, for the learner and for the society in which that learner lives, then we need to have a well-developed vision, as teachers and as learners, as to why we are doing what we are doing, and how that fits into the meaning of our lives, as individuals and as communities. We need to see where we are going and to ensure that our direction is indeed where we want to go.

I had originally intended to include a variety of people's voices and visions in this text, but I changed my mind when I began to work as I felt it might be a little confusing to one who is just beginning to work in this area. I decided instead to simply be as true to my own voice and vision as possible, while at the same time raising the kinds of questions that might call forth the true voice and vision of the reader, your voice and your vision. I have chosen to write from personal experiences, rather than in the objective manner favoured by most authors of such texts. I believe there is a place for both modes of sharing knowledge.

Purpose of the Text

There are two kinds of approaches which can be followed in the preparation of teachers. One is what I call the *recipe approach*. This method is direct, clear, and easy to use. Do what it says and this is what you will get. While this is appealing for newcomers, it leaves much to be desired. For one thing, there is too much we do not know about individuals before we begin working with them. If one does not have the ingredients for a recipe, a good cook improvises, but in order to do that, she has to know the limits of such improvisation. You cannot substitute yeast for baking powder and get the same result. New teachers, in my experience, do not have sufficient knowledge to be able to improvise and have a tendency to read the recipes quite literally. When they do, the learners do not get the quality of program they need to meet their individual needs. Such learners are expected to fit into the program as it stands and are considered failures when they are unable to do so.

An alternative approach is initially more onerous for the teacher but, I believe, is ultimately more successful. Instead of presenting the would-be teacher with only recipes to follow (and all beginning cooks do need recipes), we can present him or her with a series of good questions, ideas, and stories which will provide sufficient background to respond creatively to the learner in whatever context he or she appears. It is this approach I have chosen to follow here. The first section in this handbook is about context. The second contains a few recipes and some solid practical suggestions. The third concludes with a few chapters which explore what it means to *be* an ESL or EFL (English as a Foreign Language) educator, as opposed to exploring what an educator does.

There are many books on the market which present the ample research that has been done on second language learning and which provide suggestions for those who are preparing themselves to teach English in a variety of contexts. The purpose of this book is not to replace those texts, but to provide an alternative approach to understanding what we do and why we do it in both English as a Second Language and English as a Foreign Language classrooms.

I have written to you in a very personal manner, from my experiences. Some may find this style of writing uncomfortable. If so, I am not surprised, for our schools have repeatedly taught us to be objective. In spite of this, as a learner, I have always found that I learned much better through stories than I did through theories. If you find yourself agreeing with this experience, then I trust that you will find this a useful resource for you.

The chapters follow a common format. In a box at the beginning of each chapter is a list of key points to be found in the chapter. At the end of each chapter are some questions to think about and, if appropriate, to discuss, followed by suggestions for further reading. The questions are primarily for use in a classroom situation but may be used by individual readers for reflection purposes as well. The suggestions for further reading are given in the form of an annotated bibliography. I have placed these chapters in an order that makes a certain sense to me. However, if a particular chapter in the contents catches your eye, feel free to read it first.

Who Is the Author?

Since I am presenting a personal view in this book, I think it will be helpful to tell you a little about myself and my background. My name is Virginia. I have worked in English as a Second or Additional Language classrooms since 1968, and those classrooms have taken many forms: a head-start program for four- and five-year-olds on a First Nations reserve, evening classes for adult immigrants who worked during the day, full-time classes for newly arrived immigrants, English in the Workplace and ESL literacy classes, teacher education programs for Canadian and Korean teachers, and employment preparation programs for adult immigrant learners. I have worked in urban and rural settings, in western and central Canada, in public and private organizations, and as a teacher, administrator, and teacher educator. In addition, I have spent extended periods of time living in a second language myself and experiencing many of the joys and frustrations of that situation. In short, I have learned a lot of lessons from people of all ages from many parts of the world, and it is from the wealth of those valuable lessons that I have chosen to share a selection of my learnings with you.

In addition to teaching and administering programs, I have taken an above-average interest in policy-making, which affects the programs in which we all work. I have worked with ATESL (Alberta Teachers of English as a Second Language) in a variety of roles and likewise with TESL Canada. I have served on the Review Board of the *TESL Canada Journal* and have written some articles that have been published in that journal and in Ontario's *TESL Talk*. I see all of these activities as part of my role as a professional, to do my share to improve the work we do with learners and to improve the environments in which we as professionals (or volunteers) work.

As for my academic credentials, I have a B.A. in Sociology and Linguistics, an M.Ed. in Educational Administration, and a Ph.D. in Curriculum Theory.

As a mother, I have raised four children (a son and three daughters), all of whom I am very proud. My son was killed in a tragic accident in 1987. My daughters are now delightful and interesting companions as they go about their chosen careers—one working as a specialist in International Education, another as a printmaker, and the third as a sommelier (expert on wines).

I speak as honestly and clearly as I can with the vision that has arisen from these experiences in order that my words may call forth your own unique vision of possibility within the context in which you are preparing to teach or are already teaching. I hope that as you listen to my voice through the words on these pages, you will find your own voice chiming in, "Yes, but . . .", "Ah, I remember feeling that way. . . ." and, "No, that doesn't work for me."

Discerning What Is Important

Inevitably, the success or failure of any classroom learning depends very much upon the quality of the relationships within that classroom: teacher to learner as individual, teacher to learners as a group, learner to individual learner, learner to the group of learners, and the relationship each self finds to itself. Therefore, you will see an emphasis in this writing on the human element of our interactions with learners.

If you have never taught second language learners before, you are in for a wonderful surprise. I could not have stumbled upon a more fascinating, stimulating, and rewarding career. Through the immigrants and refugees of Canada's ESL classrooms, I have glimpsed a world I could never otherwise have seen: joy in communities unlike those we know in North America, family structures bigger than I can comprehend, war and all its agony and wasteful loss, courage that refuses to be kept down, dignity that refuses to be destroyed, and success after overcoming barrier after barrier.

Through the eyes of visiting Korean English teachers here to experience the culture of the language they teach in their homeland, I have had the mirror raised to my eyes so that I can begin to see my own culture—a feat difficult if not impossible to achieve until one is confronted with the differences between one's own culture and one that is quite different. Through the many colleagues with whom I have worked throughout the years, I have learned the importance of working out, for myself, a philosophy and teaching style that works for me. I have learned not to copy any one theory or method, but rather to stay open to many ideas and approaches, picking and choosing what works for me today, knowing that tomorrow that which worked today may have to be discarded, for which of us is the same today as we were yesterday?

ESL and EFL: The Difference

Some of you may have picked up this book wondering about the possibility of preparing both ESL and EFL teachers from the same text, while others may still be of the opinion that ESL and EFL are one and the same thing. Let me clarify by saying that English as a *Second* Language is what we call teaching English to those who have immigrated from non-English-speaking countries, while English as a *Foreign* Language is what we call teaching English to those who are simply learning the language—for travel, for academic purposes, for fun—but who are not in the process of settlement. ESL is more than language learning; it is also about the struggle to maintain and adapt one's identity in a new world. EFL is about being able to understand and communicate one's needs in an environment that is not one's own. In a sense, these two very different contexts could be seen as the extremes, while, within each, there are mini-contexts that need to be considered.[1]

In ESL, there are women's classes, seniors' classes, job-related classes, academic preparation classes, and many others. In EFL, there are courses abroad and courses taught right here; there are courses for international teachers, for students planning to study abroad, and for international business people. Since I believe that good teaching is dependent upon our understanding of and willingness to adapt to context, I have no problems with discussing both of these areas of teaching in one text. And while there are big differences in the way we teach learners in both groups, there are also some similarities. We are, after all, human beings who need to feel good about ourselves, to trust our environment, and to function successfully within that environment. If, as a teacher, I can enable learners to experience these three things, and I happen to do so in the medium of English, I am confident that the learner is going to learn much about this language.

It is my hope that you will find this text both pleasant and easy to read, and that it will provide a solid complement to the many fine second language acquisition texts and methodological texts available from the publishers.

I am happy that you have picked up this text and excited for the many

---

1 Technically, by these definitions, a teacher of English in Quebec would be an EFL teacher. However, in Quebec, the second language program is referred to as ESL.

adventures which await you as a teacher. I will do my best to honour your trust by presenting you with ideas, stories, and practical tools which will enable you to become the best teacher you can possibly be in whatever context you are preparing to enter. Good luck! Have fun!

Virginia L. Sauvé

Reflecting on the Task at Hand

CHAPTER I

Answering Some Basic Questions

In this chapter, you will have an opportunity to consider:

- the meaning of language
- the meaning of education
- the vision towards which we teach
- the relationship between our understanding of language and the way we teach
- the impact of the learner's personal experiences with the language
- the difference between *education* and *training*.

Whether we know it or not, our words and actions are always based on a set of understandings and meanings. So when we teach, it is very important that we begin with questioning our own understandings and ensuring that they are consistent with the values we think we hold.

There are three very basic questions which I have learned to pose and re-pose for myself in this work. They are

- What is language?
- What is education?
- What is the vision of society towards which I want to teach?

These questions may seem obvious or even silly to some of you, but bear with me for just a moment, and perhaps you will join me in seeing these as very important questions.

Language

When I was a student in school long ago, I was taught the *transmission theory* of language. You know the one: the sender constructs and sends a message, and the receiver, hopefully, gets the same message that the sender sends. In order for that to happen, both parties have to have common understandings of the bits and pieces of what composes language: the grammar, the vocabulary, and in oral communication, the sound system or pronunciation. Whereas you will not find this definition of language in current linguistic texts, you will find that this model is still the underlying assumption from which many language teachers work.

I have learned to understand that language is much, much more than the structures we use to describe how it works as a system of communication. Language is also the medium of human experience. It is in language that we know what is *real* and what is *unreal*. It is in language that we learn who we are in relation to the world around us. It is in language that power relationships are learned and maintained. It is in language that we create our very lives.

Even as we think we are *using* language to exist in or shape our world, language is also *using* us. Language limits what I can think and therefore, what I can see, feel, and even do. When I was a student working in the North in the sixties, I remember living in a small community called Assumption. At that time, this community was still very isolated, and for the most part, the only people who spoke English were the children. Everyone else spoke Slavee. For four months, my status in that community was as an Intercultural Education Student studying to become a teacher. When the children asked how we wanted to be introduced to the community and why we were there, we told them this, and they looked at us blankly. The children could think of no words to translate this concept. So, rather than taking the time to figure out how we could explain ourselves when we hardly knew ourselves what we were doing there, we simplified everything and told them to introduce us as "teachers who were learning about the North."

Because the Slavee culture had raised generation after generation of children by telling stories and showing The Way, they had no word for "teacher" as we know it. We certainly were not elders or storytellers. Those were the people who taught in that culture. So, they made do with their interpretation of the white teachers who had come onto the reserve in 1952 and thereafter to teach the children. Their word for teacher translated literally as "paper house man." We laughed when we heard this, but when I thought about it, I realized how totally irrelevant they saw the schooling of the white people. A teacher as we know it was no more to them than a man who worked in a house of paper.[1]

Although I had studied French for many years, this experience in Assumption was perhaps the first experience I can remember of having

---

1 The early teachers were all priests and, therefore, men.

that insight into the ways language shapes everything. I could not tell these people who I was or why I was there. Nothing I could think of to say would have made sense to them. To the children, it may have, a little, but not to their parents and grandparents. They were still living in a world where a photograph was a deliberate attempt to steal someone's spirit. They had yet to know the torturous path of integration, which had just begun.

If you speak another language already, perhaps none of these ideas will be new to you, so you may want to skip ahead to the next question: education. If you do not speak another language fluently, I would like to say a little more so that you understand what I am trying to say because our understanding of what language *is* influences profoundly how we set out to teach it to another.

Other small "lightbulbs" that went on for me very close in time to that first one in the North, were two experiences I had when I went to Quebec to study French for one of my university summers. The program was very intense. More nights than not, I went to bed in tears because I felt so stupid, so incapable of retaining all the information that was thrust upon us everyday. I was tired of the red ink all over my papers and the very nice professor who kept correcting my "r" in the language laboratory. (Mine was the Gaelic variety which rolls off the tongue, and he wanted that lovely guttural Parisian one that slips off the uvula in the back of the throat.) In the midst of all this, I had two relatively profound experiences. One occurred on the morning when, halfway through the course, I woke up, looked out the window and thought, "Quel beau jour!" It was the first time I had noticed myself thinking something in French first, and I was so excited. That small moment gave me hope that maybe I could learn something after all.

The second experience happened the night before we left. The facilitators of the summer school had organized a big bonfire, and it seemed that all the French-speaking summer students had also come to enjoy the fun. The evening's planners had dressed up as voyageurs with their red sashes and toques, and had arranged for us a wonderful evening of entertainment. Can you imagine hundreds of people singing in French around a giant bonfire two storeys high beneath a warm, starry sky? My whole body tingled with the energy of these French Canadians who were sharing with us the best of their culture, their energy, their joie de vivre. I suddenly realized that the word "ambiance" in English did not mean the same thing as the word in French, the language from which we had borrowed the term. The experience we were having just was not possible in an anglophone gathering. I cannot explain it. It was just—different.

It is in moments like these—and I hope you have the opportunity to experience such moments—that we come to understand why language is not altogether translatable. Language is inextricably bound to the culture in which it resides and can only express the experiences of that culture. Translations and interpretations are, at best, approximations of meaning.

Language has evolved as the way in which we, as human beings, contain our experiences. In naming something, we give it boundaries, and the boundaries are very different from culture to culture. Language reflects the environment in which it is spoken. I remember asking a Chippewyan youth to say something to me in his language so I could hear the sounds. He said, "What do you want me to say?" I said, "I don't care. How about 'the dog jumped over the fence'?" He scratched his head and said, "Well, I can't just say that." I asked why. He explained that he needed to know if it was a wild dog or a pet, what the fence was made of, and if there was water on the other side. He had given me, if not a translation, a wonderful sense of the mystery of language and the worlds it both reveals and hides, according to one's depth of understanding within it.

So what, you ask, does any of this have to do with teaching English? A lot! If I believe that language is about grammar and vocabulary, that is what I will teach. If I believe that in order to know a language, all I have to know is the grammar and vocabulary, then all I need are some good texts and workbooks to teach those things. That is how English is still taught in many parts of the world. That is how I was taught French in public school. Students who learn in this manner tend to go blank when they are asked, by a speaker of the language they are learning, any real question such as "Excuse me, do you know where the washroom is?" A person can have studied the language for six years and be totally unprepared to answer that question. First of all, he can't understand it because he has not heard anyone speak the language correctly before, and secondly, what we in Canada call "the washroom" may well not have been in his vocabulary books—which did mention "bathroom" in the chapter called "Rooms of the House."

However, if I see language as the medium of human experience, then that is where I am going to begin, with people's experiences. I am going to begin by being who I am with the learner, which means respecting that person for who he or she is, not concentrating first and foremost on what he or she does not know, i.e., English. This means that I will start by introducing myself and hoping that the other will see me as a friendly being who does not pose a threat to his or her existence in this foreign and therefore frightening environment. It means that I will be more concerned in the beginning with meaning, than with form. I will only attend to form when it gets in the way of understanding and, even then, I will do it in a respectful manner which offers assistance rather than "corrects" in the all-too-frequently condescending manner of expert to novice. It means that, in respect for the other and his or her situation as learner, I will open myself to learning from the other not only to understand him or her better, but also because that person has something of value to teach me.

Understanding that language is the medium of human experience puts me in a position of beginning to understand that while I may be the expert in this language at this place and time, the learner is the expert in his or her life. If I am going to figure out how this particular learner learns, I had better listen more than I speak, and watch more than I perform. (Which is not to say that teaching English can't be very dramatic. The more fun you have in the classroom, the more fun the learners will have; the more fun the learners have, the more likely it is that they will forget to be nervous and just absorb what they are learning—in English!)

Part of understanding the mystery and complexity of language is in knowing that one cannot teach just language. When, as native speakers, we teach language, we are teaching our culture, and that means our values, our power structures, and more likely than not, our social class too. How often I have heard ESL students meeting a teacher after a one- or two-year interlude, and making the comment that the teacher spoke much better English than the people with whom this person now works. More often than not, such a person, regardless of their background in their own country, is working in an entry-level job where the majority of speakers use double negatives, speak in fragments, and swear frequently. One who speaks "correctly" in this situation may not be seen merely as a foreigner, but as a snob. What sense is the typical language learner to make of all these differences between and among native speakers of the language? What *is* correct? What *is* important? How *should* he or she speak in that context? And more to the point, *what* should we be teaching, to whom, and when?

I am not suggesting that we teach people to use double negatives, swear, or speak in fragments, however, it might be a good idea to prepare some of our learners for these situations so that they understand why others speak that way. Then, they will not only understand non-standard forms of communication, but feel free to be themselves wherever they are.

One last thing about language. Because we are as human beings so deeply rooted in our language and culture, the associations we have with a language can either be helpful or totally problematic, depending on whether they are positive or negative. If you are trying to teach learners whose associations with English are horrific or otherwise unpleasant, you are not going to make much progress unless you can create new, pleasant associations with the language. That is not easy because the learner has to be open to it, but it is possible. Let me give you a couple of examples of what I mean by associations.

I have noticed that many refugees have more difficulty learning the language than many immigrants do. I have wondered why that is and have too easily assumed that perhaps it was because many refugees have less formal education than their immigrant counterparts. Refugees also have not chosen to be here in the same way as immigrants have, but they have been allowed to be here because their lives depended on not being where they were before. While those factors no doubt play a role, I think there is more than that. There is also the factor of resistance. Those refugees who come from countries where they belonged to political groups which saw North America as the enemy (such as certain people who came here from Chile and saw the Americans as responsible for the overthrow of Allende), associate English with oppression and interference. For some, this association is not even at a conscious level; for others, it is very conscious.

When I started investigating what I wanted to do for my Ph.D. research, I did some exploratory research interviewing people who had been identified either as good language learners or as poor language learners. I was interested in what it was that made a "good" learner good and a "poor" learner poor. I had asked teachers to identify learners who fit into either of these categories, and I then asked the individuals if they would be willing to give me 15 minutes of their time to help me better understand how people learn. I had a questionnaire and a tape recorder. One learner, a refugee from which country I do not remember, who had transited through Turkey, gave me one of those epiphanies I shall never forget, and it happened, of course, when I was turning over the tape on the tape recorder. He had just told me that he had spent two years in Turkey, and that he had learned English from a battered old dictionary and grammar book someone had given him. Amazed at the quality of his English because he had only been in Canada for three weeks, I commented casually, tape in hand, that he must have really learned a lot of Turkish in that time.

I was totally unprepared for the eruption that followed. His words exploded from his mouth as he told me how he hated the Turks, how they had raped the women, and robbed and terrorized the people in the camps. "I did not learn one word of Turkish," he said most adamantly, hate burning in his eyes. Ah-ha!, I said to myself. So, language learning is not just about intelligence or technique or good materials. He associated English with freedom and with hope, and he was thankful to the country which had brought him here and allowed him to study, and had given him a start. He associated the Turkish language with pain, suffering, and despair. One language he learned with ease; one he refused to learn. So much for the immersion theories I had studied.

Education

Everyone knows what education is, right? Well, not exactly. Because "education" is a common word, we all think we know what it is and, therefore, we think we know what someone else means when they use the word, too. Unfortunately, people have very different understandings of what most important things are. Common understandings around education would include schooling, instruction, and teaching/learning. If these are the limits of the understandings with which we set out to teach someone else, we may in all probability fall into the *post office metaphor* which describes a good deal of our own learning. In this metaphor, the teacher (or the government) prepares these great curriculum *packages* and *delivers* them to the students who, in order to be successful and get the *stamp* of approval, have to follow the instructions inside to the *letter!* (And no one is happy unless the carrier gets it there *on time.)* Is this the most appropriate metaphor for the one who wants to learn what it means to *be* in another language?

The *Oxford Dictionary* lists four definitions for education, which range from the nourishing or rearing of children to the common understandings I have listed above. I am more interested in going back to the root of the word *education* and, from that, distinguishing it from its partner, *training*.

Education comes from the Greek "educere," which means to lead or call forth. The image I have of this word is considerably different from the image I get from the word "training," which comes from the Greek root "trahere" meaning to pull or drag, the same root that gives us the word "tractor."

I love the idea that my good teachers have done their best to *call forth* my potential, to recognize what was already present within me, and to invite its emergence. I laugh at the image of those teachers who pulled me kicking and screaming to places where I did not want to go. (For me, Physical Education and later Statistics were like that. What were your unchosen destinations?) Now to be sure, there are limitations as well as value in retracing our roots like this. I see both education and training as being very valuable approaches to teaching and learning. The question we want to ask here is, which approach is most conducive to second language teaching and learning and in what contexts?

I believe that training is an appropriate approach when one is learning a straightforward skill, such as driving a car, flying a plane, or performing a tonsillectomy. In training, one knows clearly what the necessary end is and, through experience, has identified the most efficient route to that end. If the learner does what is asked and understands the concepts and procedures, in all likelihood, he or she will be successful as a learner in this context. Language training, therefore, may be an appropriate approach when working with well-educated, psychologically sound, healthy individuals who can keep the pace, understand the concepts, and have the supportive skills (for example, literacy or study skills) in place to learn the new skills. This type of language learning would not, however, be appropriate for learners who have never been to school in any language, and/or who have been traumatized in their experience of leaving their country or arriving in this country, and/or who are totally preoccupied with survival needs even more basic than learning the language such as money, shelter, and food.

Let us suppose that you know whether training or education is the best approach for the context you are in. Exactly what does that mean for how you are going to teach? If training is an appropriate mode, it may mean that you can predict fairly accurately how much time will be needed, which resources will be most effective for your curriculum, where you want to begin, how you will proceed, and when you will consider yourself "finished." It means that the learner's progress can be relatively easy to measure at the end of the program. This is a good mode for many EFL programs, for academic English programs, and for many English for Special Purpose Programs (ESL/Accounting or ESL/Computer Skills). Training also means that, with care, you can probably find some very good texts and workbooks to use for your program. The essence of training is that, compared to education, it is relatively predictable and can be applied to large groups of learners with few adjustments. It also means that there will be casualties who fail.

Education, on the other hand, is totally dependent on the actual learners who are in a given class. Since you are starting with these learners where they are and taking them where they want and need to go, it means there are limits to how much preparation you can do before you meet them. It means that you do not know how fast they will learn, what they will want to learn, or how they will most easily and effectively learn. (In some cases, it even means that you do not know if you have the skills and knowledge to find out where they are, much less lead them to where they want to go!) Education is, I believe, the only way to go when you are working with people who are illiterate or semi-literate in their first language, who are not adapted to the context in which they are living and are having difficulty with the basics of existence, or who are desperately in need of healing the woundedness of their pasts. These are the learners who, when placed in training situations, most often fail to learn.

In a school where I worked some years ago, we called those learners who seemed to make little or no progress "terminal zeroes," a dreadful term, especially when translated into some other languages. These men and women had life priorities that were simply not on the curriculum. We did not know how to deal with them, and they certainly did not know how to deal with us. Our curricula, or learning programs, must be in harmony with the real-life priorities of those we teach. To put this in simple terms, it makes no sense to teach primarily grammar to someone who is hungry because they sent their last bit of money to family members who are hungrier still in a refugee camp somewhere.

We have to build our programs around the lived priorities of the learners within them. It makes no sense to assign five pages of homework to someone who is still trying to figure out how to hold a pencil without having it flip around like a wayward chopstick in the hand of one more accustomed to a fork. When we engage learners in an educational program, we must be willing to listen, to learn, to see the world through their eyes and, step-by-step, to offer our hand where they do not know the road and we do, being careful to let them choose the journey. We must honour their choices.

I have done, and am reasonably comfortable doing, both training and education, but I prefer the educational approach. It is by far the most challenging and is the most exciting in terms of my own growth as a human being, as well as in its capacity to meet the individual where she or he is. It is also tremendously rewarding to participate in the learning of someone who has never before experienced himself or herself as capable of learning, or who has never before had the chance to learn in a formal setting. The joy such a one feels is contagious, and the progress is so visible. But, we cannot predict how long such a journey will take, and we cannot pressure people to move faster than they are able. Nor can we *measure* the self-esteem, courage, account-ability, and other traits that are the foundation stones of that learning journey. In our society, it is far easier to be a trainer than an educator.

A Vision of the Society Towards Which We Teach

This may be the most difficult of the three questions with which we have struggled in this chapter. (No, that is not a rhetorical "we." I am struggling to communicate ideas I see as paramount, and many of you, no doubt, are struggling to figure out when I am going to get to the how-to material. Actually, I would like to digress on this subject for a moment. The world of science and technology has led to the hurried "How?" as its favoured question. Of what good is asking *how*, when we have not very carefully determined the *what* and *why*? If I were merely to tell you that were you to do A, B, and C, you would be successful, that would be dishonest, and I would be treating you like a robot. I don't want you to treat your students that way, and I have no intention of treating you that way. I far prefer to take some time to reflect with you on things you know a lot about, but you may not have taken the time to reflect upon. I don't intend for you to struggle to memorize what I am saying; rather, regard the words as water in a stream flowing over you, refreshing you. Let the ideas glisten like the bubbles in the stream as they catch the sun and reflect its rays back out to the surrounding banks. What you need and can handle will stay with you; the rest will flow on leaving no burden upon you. What you need to remember will return to you in the future when you need it.)

Back to our question: what is the vision of society towards which we teach? I have posed this question to many teachers in our field and, for the most part, they look at me quite skeptically. They do not understand what I mean. Perhaps we are conditioned not to question who we are, but if we do not, we are automatically doomed to be reproducing students who are, to some degree, like us. Is it our job to reproduce ourselves or to enable individuals to be the best selves that they can possibly be? In that we are working across cultures here, I think it is extremely important to be very clear about the values that are implicit to our teaching.

Take time, for example. Yes, it is important to teach newcomers that employers in North America place a major value on punctuality and respect for the time of others. However, it is different to *share* that information with someone than to *impose* it upon them by humiliating them when they return to class late because they have been conversing with someone in the hallway at break time. We cannot assume that our values are the best values or the only acceptable values. When we are irritated by the behaviour of our students, we need to ask ourselves where that is coming from. People behave in ways that are logical to them. If they have different values than we do, their behaviour will most certainly be different. If they are preoccupied with priorities of which we know nothing, they will most surely have difficulty conforming to our agendas. In such situations, we have to make a choice. Do we as teachers use the authority of our role to impose our values and ways of being on them because we assume that is our role? Or, do we take a moment to question whether or not the values and behaviours the other has presented may, in fact, make our world a happier, healthier place to be if more of us were to take them on?

Some of us will no doubt take a firm position that immigrants come to our country to become like us and, therefore, it is the teacher's job to do everything necessary to facilitate that transition. If we were to speak to the learners, however, I think we would find that this is not their perspective, although they may or may not feel safe sharing that idea, depending on their perception of who we are and how much power we have over them at the time of our asking. I do not take this position. For me, our country is still very much in transition. I like diversity! I enjoy what I have learned from those I have taught, and I have no wish to see us freeze the culture we have now. There are many things I do not like about Western culture: the violence, the loneliness, and the individual-comes-first attitude, for example. I see in the lives of learners, qualities and values I admire and would dearly love to see added to our culture: a deep understanding of community, an abiding balance that comes from centuries of being knocked off-balance, a simple joy that is not dependent on material wealth, and the list goes on.

My vision of the society towards which I want to teach is one that is constantly changing and growing, and this reflects upon each new idea, behaviour, and value as it appears. Our culture is often made visible by its inherent conflict with differing ways of being which appear in our classrooms. I want to continue to see waves of people coming from all over the globe. Such migrations have enriched us enormously. Most of all, I see my country as a kind of workshop for the world; if we who have such racial, ethnic, linguistic, religious, and other types of diversities cannot create peaceful ways of being together and creating health and abundance for all, who can? The multicultural vision I seek is one that serves not only newcomers, but each and every one of us and, ultimately, the world.

This stands in direct contrast to the vision held by many which states that North Americans know the way, and only our way is valuable and good. Those who hold that vision will impose their understandings on others believing that it is right. They will not approach the learners with the essential human respect each person deserves just for being born. They will, inevitably, be "the expert" teaching "the one who does not know." I ask you, what is your vision of society? Are you content with how things are, or do you think they could be better? And, if you agree with me that they could be better, would you also agree that six heads are better than one, and that if those six heads come from six different cultures, this situation creates all the more possibilities for hope and peace for this planet?

Vision is a concept equally relevant in preparing to teach both ESL and EFL. The vision will, however, be shaped by the context. In teaching English as a Foreign Language, we consider the reason the students are learning and we mold our vision to serve that end. If a student is likely to come abroad to study, we need to consider the best possible experience such a learner could have. I would hope he or she would not only become more fluent in English, but would make friends with native speakers, come to experience and understand how we live and why, and have memorable dialogues that enrich that learner's perception of his or her own potential to expand human consciousness. There, that's a broad vision to be sure. It is also one that guided my teaching of the Korean English teachers for six years. In that time, they and I had deep, rich experiences that continue to shape my life and, I hope, many of their lives. It was a vision of a global society to which we all bring our gifts and take what we need, no more, no less.

Many would argue that we do not need a vision of society to teach English. The reality is that we all have one whether we know it or not and, if we cannot name it, then it probably means that we value the status quo. If that is the case, our teaching will most certainly reflect that. We have a choice. Let us be conscious about that choice.

Questions to Think about and Discuss

1. What concrete situations can you think of in which English might limit your thinking and understanding of reality as compared with what another language might do in that same situation?

2. Looking back on your own experiences as a learner, what falls into the category of "training" and what into the category of "education"? How do both types of learning contribute to the person you are today?

3. If you could envision the ideal society, what would it be like? How would it differ from society as you know it today?

4. Think of some of the people you know from cultural backgrounds different from your own. Can you think of character traits or customs in those individuals which you would be happy to add to those typical of our own cultural experience?

For Further Reading

Ashworth, Mary. 1985. *Beyond Methodology: Second Language Teaching and the Community*. Cambridge: Cambridge University Press.

Mary Ashworth has been called the mother of ESL in Canada by many of us who have appreciated her wisdom through the years. *Beyond Methodology* shows us how language learning is contextualized in the communities in which we live, and she explains how recognizing this can benefit all concerned. The text includes a special section on EFL. This book speaks to our vision of the work we do.

Sauvé, Virginia. 1991. *Windows of Meaning in Adult ESL*. Unpublished doctoral dissertation. Edmonton: University of Alberta.

For those interested in working with learners who are illiterate and semi-literate in their first languages, this dissertation may be of interest. Through a participatory research process, the teachers come to see the ways in which their own hidden meanings around language, education, and power affect the curriculum of their classes. As their own meanings are revealed to them through their stories and discussions, they have new choices in their teaching practice.

Stevick, Earl W. 1990. *Humanism in Language Teaching*. Oxford: Oxford University Press.

Stevick is one of my favourite theorists in ESL. In this book, he takes us beyond linguistics and explores the role of feelings, social relations, responsibility, intellect, and self-actualization in learning. He also introduces us to the work of Gail Moscowitz (self-esteem), Charles Curran (Counselling-Learning, community language learning), and Caleb Gattegno (Silent Way).

The following references, not written for ESL audiences, nonetheless have much to teach us.

Giroux, Henry A. 1983. *Theory and Resistance in Education: A Pedagogy for the Opposition.* South Hadley, MA: Bergin and Garvey Publishers.

This is a good, although semi-heavy, introduction to theories of critical education and resistance in education.

Gusdorf, Georges. 1965. *Speaking (La Parole)* Translated by Paul Brockelman. Evanston, IL: Northwestern University Press.

A fascinating introduction to the phenomenology of language for those who are comfortable reading philosophical text.

CHAPTER 2

Understanding Your Context: Who Are the Learners?

In this chapter, you will learn about:

- factors in the learner's experience which will affect his or her learning
- where to begin when the learner knows no English
- what kind of English to teach in what context
- matching your teaching style to the actual learners
- working with racial differences in the classroom.

Some of you will be going into the classroom (or are already there) with a curriculum and materials in hand and with the benefit of some classroom training, while others may be going in ready to learn on the spot. When I began working in ESL, I had been trained as a French teacher and had a degree minoring in linguistics. I knew I would have to make adjustments, but little did I know how many. My training as a French teacher was more appropriate to the teaching of EFL than to ESL as both were foreign languages. Neither type of teaching involved settlement issues. When I was sent into my first adult ESL classroom, I had had no coursework in teaching adult ESL, the textbooks had not yet arrived, and there was no curriculum. In hindsight, I am very glad because it meant I had to think things through for myself rather than blindly following someone else's idea of what was appropriate to this context.

My first class was a delightful group of students from all over the world. They studied at night and worked during the day. I learned from them even as they learned from me. The most important thing they taught me that year was that language is not learned in a vacuum, it is learned in the context of one's daily life. The Czech refugee who had arrived in Canada only three months earlier, having lost everything when her family fled the Russian tanks in 1968, had immediately been sent by the government counsellor to work as a dishwasher. She had been an accountant in her country and was suffering not only the loss of all her belongings and the settlement challenges of her whole family, but her hands were bleeding and raw from the dishwater. She did not like to wear gloves because she found she tended to drop the dishes when she did. She cried a lot in the beginning of the class because she found it very depressing to be working as a lowly dishwasher when she had been a successful professional in her country. These daily experiences shaped the context in which she experienced language learning as a necessity. They both distracted her and motivated her.

The German student in that class was a young woman who had come to Canada for adventure. She was a qualified special education teacher in her country, and would be returning there one day, but she wanted to learn English and experience living in a new country. Here on a work visa, she was working as a nanny and enjoyed the opportunity to get out and meet new people in the class four nights a week. The learner was very unhappy in her job as nanny, feeling that she was not valued by the family, neither with material returns nor appreciation. She was frustrated because she felt powerless to say "no" when asked to work weekends and many evenings in addition to her 12-hour days. She also felt taken advantage of when her employers deducted half of her meager wages as room and board charges. She was homesick and missed her own family. This was the background against which she tried to learn English.

I could present you with similarly unique scenarios for each of the men and women in the class. Those two examples have come to mind 30 years later, because I became involved in the lives of these two women and they in mine. The Czech woman and I became friends after the class, and I attended her daughter's wedding and her 50th wedding anniversary, and later comforted her after the death of her husband. Two months after finishing the class, the young German woman left her employment as a nanny and moved in with us for several weeks until she could sort out what she wanted to do next. While living with us, she taught my own infant German nursery songs that we still remember with a smile.

You can understand why I have not forgotten the early days in which I knew these students. In any case, I do not need to present you with stories for each one. I simply need to give you some understanding of the elements of context which affected my teaching decisions then as they do now.

Where Do You Begin?

When teaching ESL or EFL, you begin by getting to know the individuals you are teaching, not as students, but as human beings. "My name is . . . What is your name?" "I am Canadian. Where are you from?" "I speak English and some French. What languages do you speak?" In doing this, I am not just teaching the learners questions and answers. I am establishing a relationship of trust and mutual liking which will enable them to let me get to know them, and which will motivate them to get to know me—all of which will happen in the medium of English.

I cannot emphasize enough the difference between teaching language as a subject and teaching people in the medium of language. When we do the latter, learners are so intrigued with the people they are getting to know and the activities we are doing, that they forget they do not know the new language. We forget to be nervous when we are having fun. We forget all the notions of our failures in school, and we are caught up in the moment. In short, we learn in spite of ourselves.

Language learning has to be enjoyable. At the same time, it has to be sensitive to the painful experiences people bring to the classroom. One does not ignore bleeding hands or wounded hearts. One must respond to them, also in the language, for what choice do most of us have? If I do not speak the language of the learner, then I must reach out to him or her with the only language I have, the language that person has chosen to learn.

When we read about bleeding hands and wounded hearts, those among us who draw pleasure from being helpers in the world may fall into the trap of becoming bleeding hearts! A person who is struggling with his or her own weakness does not need someone to emphasize that weakness by performing a rescue mission! Such a person needs to be acknowledged and supported in making his or her own decisions. He or she needs the information to enable informed decision-making and the skills to follow through on the decisions made. While there are instances wherein a person is so far removed from that possibility that one does have to intervene and act on his or her behalf, for the most part, it is better to take the time necessary to support that person in taking action alone rather than to take the action for him or her. There are many good-hearted people teaching ESL. Not all of them understand that what appears to be helping someone in the short term can, in fact, be crippling that person in the long term.

If we look again at the two brief descriptions offered at the beginning of this chapter, we can see that one's health and one's psychological state, one's financial security, and one's family are all part of the context in which he or she learns. Here are some of the factors that influence a person's learning and, therefore, our teaching.

1. Education

The amount of formal learning a person has had and the degree to which the person has experienced success in that learning may be the two most important factors one needs to understand in planning a curriculum or a lesson. If your learner or learners are well-educated and confident in their learning abilities, it will be important for you to find out how they learned and to take advantage of that.

Many of our European students, for example, came from very formalized learning situations in which concepts were taught, analyzed, and practised in highly structured ways. Such students may not be able to speak the language, but they have a good understanding of grammar as a concept, and they relate well to instruction that is very systematic and objective. They may not be interested, however, in singing songs and painting pictures. Because they have been taught in groups where the individual simply had to go along with the group, their expectations of you will be to teach authoritatively. If you ask them what they want to learn, they may tell you, but they will probably also say that you are the expert, and it is up to you to decide what to teach them.

In my experience, it is best to go with the flow, even when you disagree with the learners' pedagogical ideas. There is enough that is disturbing in language learning that you do not also need to challenge their ideas about what it is to learn and to teach. They have a set of successful learning experiences, and we can draw on those experiences to make it easier to teach them now. Such students often like dictations, spelling tests, and grammar quizzes. If so, give them that. I find that if I honour what an individual thinks he or she needs, that person will feel acknowledged and will, more often than not, respond by trusting me enough to then try out some things which he or she may not have experienced before. Most people are willing to compromise.

On the other hand, students who have never been to school, or who, for whatever reasons, did not succeed in school, will not relate to such an approach. It overwhelms them, and they shut down for self-protection. I love teaching these students; they are so open. With these students, the only way to teach them is to be yourself and be open and authentic. They will learn in whatever manner you teach *if*, and it is a big if, you have first proven that you respect them, that you believe in them, and that you will support them, no matter what. With these students, the first thing you can do to support their learning is to minimize the amount of paper you give them. Remember, these students do not relate to paper; they relate to people and events. And they don't know a lot of English words, so even when you do give them a paper, a few words go a long way.

2. Learner's Relationship to the World of Work

Here is a big difference between immigrant learners and EFL learners. The immigrant learner in a full-time classroom most often has one main thing on his or her mind: finding a job! These men and women have families to support in their new country and often in their homeland or in a refugee camp as well. They do not want to waste their time. They insist on learning what is relevant to their lives, and they want you to be efficient in getting them where they want to go. These learners welcome information that will help them to understand and to access the labour market in their community. They want to become independent but are, at the same time, struggling with their fears. Will they be accepted by those with whom they work? Will they make friends? Will their skills be marketable here, or do they need to learn more?

Immigrants who are in evening or other part-time classes and are already working, are frequently tired. This affects the speed with which they learn. When they are tired, they absorb less, and they do not have time to do homework like full-time students do. You will have a few highly motivated students who will do all you ask and want more, but there will be others who feel like failures because they are already overloaded.

When I teach, my response to this situation is to give a lot of choices. Most homework is optional, and I try not to make people feel guilty about not being able to do assignments. I want them to see assignments as options. Some students want and expect the teacher to pressure them. (And they want and expect the teacher to pressure everyone!) Whereas I am willing to negotiate with an individual regarding what works best for him or her, I am not willing to impose that on others. Sometimes, that causes resentment from those who expect the teacher to be demanding and who believe that is what produces results.

Some learners, both immigrant and EFL, are looking for a particular kind of English, the English that is related to their work. We call this English for Special Purposes (ESP) or English in the Workplace (EWP). EWP is taught in the workplace, whereas ESP can be taught anywhere. It is very rewarding to teach a group of learners who do similar work because it is so much easier to teach material that is equally relevant to everyone. It is difficult, on the other hand, to have only one person in a class who needs plumbing vocabulary, another who needs to know how to get qualified as an engineer, and still another who has no job experience at all. This necessitates a lot of individualized work, in some cases, as well as a lot of imagination. For people with highly specialized needs in a class, I like to keep extra books on hand that I can lend out. I also give these individuals their own homework assignments.

When everyone is looking for work, this too is an advantage because you can teach what has come to be known as *Language through Content*. By teaching employment preparation, for example, people are learning English, but they are also learning the information and processes they need to find and sustain appropriate employment. (If you are teaching EFL, some of your students may want Academic English so that they can study abroad, or they may want Business

English so that they can transact business in an English-speaking context.) The important thing for us as teachers to realize is, that if work is the priority, then this area should take priority in language teaching. Do not waste the learners' time on that which is not of interest because they as less likely to learn under those conditions.

The other implication with regard to work is the *register* of language you want to teach, and by that I mean the kind of language most appropriate for the workplace. This is tricky because a lot of workplaces do not use standard English (i.e., "correct" English). Whereas we do not want to teach learners to use non-standard English, we also do not want them to alienate, or feel alienated by, those with whom they work. If a man is going to be working in a working class job with other men, he is probably going to hear profanity, double negatives, and a lot of sentence fragments. While I would have difficulty with the notion of teaching students to speak in that manner, I have no difficulty whatsoever with teaching them that this is a reality in many workplaces, which means they need to understand the meaning and intent of what is said to them or about them. Learners need to know if they are being insulted or talked down to, and they need to know what to take seriously and what to regard as meaningless.

3. Gender

Gender has been recognized as an important factor in many learning contexts. Are your students male or female or both? What difference does it make?

I have found that gender makes a lot of difference in some situations and not much in others. In groups where students are well-educated, accustomed to being in mixed groups, and from a society in which men and women are treated *relatively* equally, I find it makes much less difference than when those factors are not present. In situations where there are learners who come from cultures where women are very oppressed or from home situations that are abusive, it is very important to provide a learning environment which allows them to feel both safe and free to speak. In other words, women's programs are very necessary for some learners.

If you have a mixed class in which some men try to dominate the discussion, answer all the questions, and demand all your attention, you will have to make a very deliberate effort to get the class to assist you in taking responsibility for ensuring that each member has an equal opportunity. This begins with your own awareness as to which students are very accountable for their own needs, and which learners find that accountability is very difficult to achieve. The first group you applaud for taking care of themselves in the classroom, and the second group you encourage to do likewise. At the same time, you encourage learners to take some responsibility for each other and to be patient with those who find it more difficult to speak out.

There are some topics for which you may wish to separate the men from the women, again depending on the context. If you have in your class a group of Arabic-speaking women who are very traditional in their religion, they will not likely ask questions about Pap smears and breast examinations in a mixed classroom. (In fact, many women would not.) It may be appropriate to share that information when the women can be together without the men. Similarly, most men would be very interested in the vocabulary for parts of the car, whereas the majority of women may not be. Perhaps teachers could cooperate so that there are some times when groups are formed by gender and/or interest to address different topics.

Gender may become a factor in husband-wife combinations in the classroom. Some schools try to prevent this from happening because, in most marriages, one partner dominates while the other follows. This is especially true in language-learning situations where one partner may have had more exposure to the language, and the other partner has developed a pattern of dependency with the other. If you have no choice but to have the husband and wife in the same class, at least point out to the couple in private your reasons for wanting them to sit separately in the classroom, and ask if they would be comfortable with this.

4. Family or Other Significant Relationships

Some learners are single people out for adventure, while other singles are very lonely and preoccupied with sadness. Some learners are married with supportive family members who are very happy they are learning the language. Still others may be married but feel burdened by their responsibilities as husbands and fathers, or wives and mothers. The degree of support the students get, both in life and as a language learner, can affect the speed and quality of their learning a great deal.

Singles who are out for adventure will make an effort to meet people and speak the language. They make friends, and soon they have picked up many things you would not think of teaching in the classroom. The more immersion a person has in the language, the faster they generally learn and the better they tend to learn the kind of language they need to cope with life. (This also means, by the way, that if you are teaching EFL while learning the language of the learners yourself, you do not do the latter during class time. Your learners need to hear English from you; bilingual instruction is not normally the way to go, unless you have tried every other means to communicate.)[1]

---

1 Some argue strongly on behalf of bilingual instruction. I have found it useful in situations where all the learners speak the same language and have little confidence in their ability to learn the new language. I also believe, and strongly, that learning is much slower in a bilingual context and that it should serve only as a bridge to immersion.

Singles who are shy and lonely and wish they were not in this situation at all, need first to become at home with the people in the classroom, with you, and with themselves. They need a lot of acknowledgment and generally respond well to light humour. If they feel happy in class rather than self-conscious and embarrassed, that will go far in enabling them to feel a little more outgoing elsewhere.

In an ESL teaching situation, when a man or woman is married and has a lot of duties or worries in his or her family, you cannot have the same expectations for homework that you would of a single person. In addition, such a learner is usually most grateful for any information or support you can give which will lessen the burdens of dealing with all the family's problems. For example, if you know of a free income tax clinic for immigrants, let them know. If you have a friend who is looking for a mechanic, and your student is a former mechanic working as a cleaner, you may wish to put your friend together with this learner.

If you are working with adults who have been in the country for some time and who have children who have learned the language quite well, do not assume that they will be supportive of their parents and help them. Some do and some do not. Settlement can play havoc with family relationships. Some children are ashamed of their parents' lack of fluency in the language and resent them for the embarrassment they feel with friends or teachers. Some even make fun of their parents. Other children, fortunately, may be tremendously respectful of their parents and be quite willing to support them in any way they can. Just do not make assumptions.

There is also the danger of having an attractive student who is unattached to anyone romantically and who is quite attracted to the teacher. This happens often. I know several ESL and EFL teachers who have ended up marrying a former learner. While there is nothing wrong with this, be very careful to draw a clear line for yourself should you find yourself in this situation while that person is in your class. If you do not, the other students will be shortchanged, and they will resent it. We need to be conscious of our own ethical guidelines *before* we start to teach.

5. Ethnic Mix of the Classroom

Another big difference between the average ESL and EFL situation is the ethnic mix. In the typical ESL classroom, you will have a good variety of cultures with no one culture dominating the others. In an EFL classroom, you are most often working with one culture and language. It is very, very different.

I had my first experience of working with a mono-ethnic group of learners after I had had many years of teaching in multicultural classrooms. I was unprepared for the challenges this new reality posed. In a classroom of mixed ethnicities, each learner or group of learners has different expectations of the teacher according to how teachers teach in their country of origin. However, because the group is mixed, people take their cues from the teacher and are much more open to negotiation.

When only one culture is represented, as is the case in most EFL situations, the group quite unconsciously imposes their way of learning on the teacher and, until the teacher becomes aware of what is going on, there is going to be great frustration for both. Even when you as the EFL teacher realize why things are not going the way you think they should, you still have quite a lot of work to do to bring all of this into the consciousness of the learners and negotiate what you want to do about it as a group.

Perhaps the easiest way of explaining this is, once again, by way of example. When I taught my first group of Korean teachers, I was totally exhausted at the end of the first day because my teaching style did not meet their learning style, and initially, I could not understand why. I simply lacked sufficient understanding of their learning culture. For example, I asked open-ended questions and was not getting any answers. Little did I know that in Korea the teacher does not ask a question until the answer has been taught. Questioning is a way of checking understanding of taught material, not a way of assessing what people know to begin with. To ask a question a student cannot answer causes that student to lose face, and a teacher in Korea should not do this. Students consider it unfair.

In addition, when the questioning begins in an adult context, the teacher is supposed to ask questions in respect of the order of authority of the learners; thus the oldest man would be first and on down to the younger men, then, and only then, would one ask the women. This I was taught by the supervisor after two days of my feeling enormously frustrated, and the students feeling totally confused and uncomfortable with my unorthodox style. (I should point out that successive groups of Korean teachers did not have this problem, for two reasons. One reason was that I was more aware of this cultural difference, and the bigger reason I believe, was that successive groups had been oriented in their country that this was how things were done in Canada and not to take it personally. Successive groups seemed to find it amusing that their orientation had been correct!)

The most obvious difficulty of a mono-ethnic classroom is the ease students feel in speaking their own language with one another. While it can be helpful to have learners who can assist one another with difficult concepts in their first language, it can also be frustrating if learners lack the self-discipline and insight to see the value of persisting in using the language they are learning.

6. Age and Life Experience

While related, age and life experience are also different. By age, I mean biological years. Age affects learning in different ways. Seniors cannot generally learn as quickly as younger learners, in part, because they do not retain new material as easily. On the other hand, if they are not preoccupied with basic issues of survival, older learners are often open to learning in a way that younger learners are not.

A few years ago, I worked as a consultant for a seniors' ESL project. One of the insights we wanted to glean from the project was whether or not the seniors would find it beneficial to be taught in gender-specific groups. While those women who were taught in women-only groups said they preferred this type of grouping, most learners said, "We are old. Same same, man woman." We understood that to mean that by the time they reached their ages, the gender differences they had wrestled with as younger people no longer mattered. They had faced life and the certainty of death, and come away from that appreciating each day for what it was. They valued some learning experiences I did not expect. They wanted to learn everything and were so happy to do so. They wanted to tour the newspaper plant and learn how newspapers were assembled. They wanted to visit a greenhouse, City Hall, 911 Central,[2] the university, and so many different places. In each locale, they soaked up the experiences, laughing at what they did not understand and celebrating what they could.

Life experience, on the other hand, while certainly connected to one's age, is not necessarily parallel to it. For example, a couple came to their new country 30 years ago. In that time, the man has gone out and worked, and learned the language. He has made friends in the community and feels like he belongs to this country. His wife, however, has stayed home to raise the children, and then, when they had left home, felt like she could not face the world because she did not speak the language. She has no friends, no family save her children and her husband, and no connections with a broader community. It is as if she has lived in a bubble, out of touch with the community around her. It is very difficult for that woman to then decide to come to school. She is embarrassed when other students ask her how long she has lived in Canada, because she thinks they will think she is stupid to have lived here this long and yet not be able to speak English. Her language experience in Canada has not extended with her age.

The learner who is well-travelled and who already speaks several languages, does not have the same struggle with culture shock as the

---

2 911 Central refers to the place where the emergency calls come in. The city police in many urban centres give tours showing people how the system works.

learner who has only lived in one place and heard one language all his life. The learner who has worked in many different kinds of occupations and met many different kinds of people, is much more relaxed about the learning experience than is the person who has only worked in one kind of job and known one kind of people. The person who has seen death and destruction and has managed to rise above it to experience joy in the present, is not as likely to be rattled by the stresses of language learning as one whose life was relatively peaceful until war blew it apart, or until an adventurous husband decided to uproot that settled life and bring the whole family to the new land. All of these examples are samples of what I mean by the relevance of life experience and the extent of life experience which a learner has.

7. Health

A person's health affects every aspect of his or her life and that includes their time in the classroom. What I'm referring to is physical, mental, emotional, and spiritual health.

a. Physical Health

If a person is in constant pain, it is difficult for that person to learn. The reality is that, as teachers, we will have learners who have unresolved health issues. I remember a Chilean man who was always glaring at me. After two weeks of my best efforts to win him over, I finally expressed my observation about his seemingly angry looks only to hear his enormous surprise. He said he had a very bad toothache but could not afford the root canal the dentist had told him he needed. He was planning to finish his English course, get a job, and then get it fixed. Needless to say, he was not learning anything at all. When I found money for his root canal, he was very grateful and, free of pain, he was now able to learn.

You may have people with chronic pain problems in your class. This is very difficult because, in many cases, there are no obvious solutions, or the solutions that would be available for a person with money are not available to a person with no money. I have no answers to this dilemma other than to suggest that we be present to such learners in whatever ways we can, providing laughter in abundance and being understanding of their situation when we cannot provide money. It is an unjust world in which we live, and this has been one of the greatest frustrations in my career—to see people for whom there is a solution, if only there were the money to provide it.

b. Mental and Emotional Pain

If you teach refugees, you will undoubtedly have many learners who are in enormous anguish. They have been through experiences you and

I could not begin to fathom. They did not choose to be in their new country, rather they took advantage of the only choice available to them if they were to stay alive.

Many of these learners put on a brave face and, knowing that we can neither understand nor do anything about their situations, keep their burdens to themselves. Unresolved trauma is a great barrier to learning. Larger urban centres often have centres for trauma victims where they can get support in dealing with their issues from people who understand. In other places, there are settlement agencies with counsellors who speak the language of the person and may or may not have an understanding of their issues.[3]

There are other forms of mental pain not associated with trauma. Immigrants and refugees experience the pain of loss of one's country, one's language, one's extended family, one's career, and much more. There is the pain of the individual who has lost a family member in an untimely manner. There is the pain of losing hope, of facing oneself in the mirror every day, no longer feeling the dignity and self-respect one had in one's own country.

Many teachers think they are being helpful when they ask learners to talk about what it was like in their countries, to bring in pictures of their families and their homes, and indeed, some EFL learners are usually very happy to do these things. Refugee learners, however, are often angry at being thrust into the pain of what they have lost. We need to be sensitive to when it is appropriate to do these things and when it is not. If you think it appropriate, ask learners what they think of this activity and watch for faces that seem hesitant.

c. Spiritual Health

Spirituality is not to be confused with religion. There are those who are spiritually healthy but not religious, and those who are religious but not spiritually healthy. Religion and spirituality are not the same thing. Spiritual health is a comfort with oneself and the world around one. When one is spiritually healthy, he or she has a good sense of balance and meaning in their life, of being okay with all that is, of being able to go with the flow.

One of the pleasures for me in working with some of the Vietnamese people who came here as refugees in the late seventies, was the sense of strength and deep inner peace that many people I came to know

---

3 In referring students to agencies, we need to be aware that a common language alone does not mean the client and the counsellor can relate to each other. Histories and political rivalries within an ethnic group may mean that they see one another as enemies, no matter what the agency says their policy is.

attributed to their Buddhist background. This attribute enabled them to accept the unacceptable and to get on with life. Their spiritual health was nourished by their beliefs and customs.

On the other hand, I have taught fundamentalists of different religious backgrounds who were obsessed with converting others to their own beliefs. These learners were definitely not okay with accepting others as equals, and this created a lot of barriers to their settlement, their language learning, and their relationships with those who were not members of their religious group.

The best way I know to nourish spiritual health and well-being in our students is by nourishing it in ourselves. If we are acceptant of others and balanced in our approach to life, it is likely that learners will feel accepted and relaxed in our presence.

8. Personality

Personality influences each and every setting we are in. The attitude of individuals towards their learning, the maturity and social skills they bring to their interactions with the group, and the self-confidence they possess all have an impact on the outcomes in the classroom. There is just one word of wisdom I would leave with you here, and it was something Virginia Satir said to a group I was in years ago:

> Every person does his or her best under the circumstances, and if it does not appear that way to us, then we are just lacking sufficient information to understand it.

Try to understand what it is individuals are trying to gain from their behaviour. Respond not to the behaviour itself, but to your understandings of where it is coming from. For example, if an individual is dominating the scene, is it because they need attention or power? If so, try to identify positive ways of allowing them to experience that. Sometimes, you can successfully recruit such a person to help you get others more actively participating.

Because we are all different, some learners will shine in one area and wither in another. This is one reason it is so important to vary your classroom activities. Someone who is very weak analytically and suffers accordingly when it comes to grammar work, may be very artistic, thus gaining a lot of admiration from the group when there is any kind of artistic expression involved. I have found it to be very healthy for a group's dynamics to provide an opportunity for everyone to look good in some way or other. Then, when the learners have one another's respect, they will be more likely to work together as a group with mutual trust, and to take mutual responsibility for the learning of each member of the group.

9. Culture and Language

Many teachers would put culture and language first on their list of factors influencing how a student learns a second language. While these areas certainly play an important role in the classroom, their import in determining what goes on in the classroom has a lot to do with the approach you take to your teaching. If you teach a class informed primarily by linguistics, then for sure, the particular languages represented in the classroom are going to play a significant role in determining the work which goes on. If, on the other hand, you facilitate a participatory style of learning, these factors are no more significant than any others and are even less important than some. (In an EFL class, it is appropriate to attend to the differences between the learners' language(s) and English.)

Some teachers would separate culture and language in this instance; I would not. To do so adds to our belief that they can be easily separated in our thinking, and I do not believe that is so. Culture speaks itself in language; language lives out of and reproduces the culture.

Language per se influences the classroom most when the class is a homogenous group of learners who speak one language. Then, the differences between the two languages become the stumbling blocks that mark the points of major instruction. Such points of confusion are less obvious when the class is composed of many languages because one cannot afford to concentrate only on the hard contrasts between any one language and English.

But language and culture together also play an important role. As I mentioned earlier in relating my first experiences with the Korean teachers, because they were a group and I was just one, their culture took actual priority over mine by weight of sheer numbers. If, in their culture, the oldest man was to answer first, there was no way I could ignore that. I had either to succumb to the custom or to bring the group to a conscious decision around it.

Actually, the first decision we had to make in that group was what to call one another. It is my custom in the classroom to ask to be called Virginia. It was theirs, as students, to be called Mr. Lee and Miss or Mrs. Park, for example, which was as foreign to me as my use of a first name was to them. They dealt with this conflict by calling me "Professor Virginia" or "Virginia Sir." When I pointed out that "Sir" was reserved for men in this language, and that if they must use some honorific, which I would prefer they did not, they would have to say "ma'am." Henceforth, I was addressed as "Ma'am Sir." For them, the honorific was in the "Sir," and no matter what else went in there, it just did not feel right to them unless they added the "Sir." It became a big joke, but one that was repeated nonetheless. If you are curious as to what I called them, I compromised. The younger ones I called by their first names, with their permission. The older ones, I called "Mr. or Mrs. _____" as they were just too uncomfortable with the North American informality.

What is important in dealing with these cultural factors is, I believe, negotiating them with learners rather than imposing our ways upon them. The imposition of anything, whether consciously or unconsciously, is disrespectful. Disrespect destroys self-esteem, which is of singular importance in learning a new language—a process in which the learner inevitably experiences moments of failure that are hard to take unless they are balanced with a healthy self-esteem. It is not difficult to identify the points of intercultural conflict and to negotiate ways around them. Learners will most often want to do what the teacher is comfortable with, knowing that they are there to learn both the language and the culture. However, it makes it so much more palatable when the teacher has recognized the position learners are in, and takes the time to acknowledge the difficulties they may be experiencing.

10. Race

In many cases, too little attention is paid to the racial differences in our classrooms, primarily because most ESL/EFL teachers are white and have no idea of the pain racial difference has led to for so many in English-speaking countries. As a Canadian, I would dearly love to see the day when racism no longer exists, but I have long ago passed the point where I deny its frequent presence in our society. The fact is, that it is a handicap to be dark-skinned for the majority of those so born in North America. We can deny that by citing all the examples to the contrary, but all it takes is just one or two experiences of racism for the average victim thereof to feel outraged, hurt, and helpless to do anything about it. Racism happens in the workplace. It happens in the community. And yes, it even happens in the classroom.

While I am far from an expert in this area and often feel helpless myself to know what to do, I do feel that we owe it to the learners of colour to, first of all, become aware of their reality, and to do our best to understand it and acknowledge it to them in appropriate ways. For example, when we are preparing learners to enter the labour market, they need to know that there is a probability, if their skin is dark, that some people are going to have a problem with that. Some coworkers feel threatened; some are simply ignorant.

In other cases, it is not the workers who are the problem, but the residents of the nursing home or the customers of the business. As one businessman said to me when I asked him to explain his preference for hiring white staff, why should I add to the discomfort for existing staff and clients when I can find what I need in the white population? While this attitude not only jeopardizes the human rights of the black population, but of other races as well, it does seem to be more prevalent for members of the black race. While such attitudes are unacceptable and illegal, they are real and our teaching needs to enable learners to deal with that reality.

In dealing with racial difference in the classroom, we have to become aware not only of how the learners experience those differences, but also of the ways in which they have chosen to respond to those experiences. Some learners have become very bitter and intolerant, while others are still in denial. In my experience, the best way to prepare for all eventualities is to ensure that we ourselves treat everyone with respect and that we do not "lose it" when a learner, out of his or her own pain, acts less than respectfully towards us. Again, we have to remember that a person's actions make sense to that person, even when they do not make sense to us.

When I am teaching any learner who experiences herself or himself as powerless, I teach the principle of *accountability*. Accountability is the opposite of blame; it means searching for and using the power one *does* have in a situation to make things better for oneself. This idea has been surprisingly controversial to some of my colleagues who have seen this principle as accepting injustice.

I do not see it that way at all. I see accountability as a powerful way to support people in surviving day-to-day existence. The political battles must be fought, and fought hard, to gain social justice for everyone. But while we are fighting those battles, we still have to go to work and raise children and live in neighbourhoods. Teaching people the power of taking accountability for one's experiences is *not* the same as blaming the victim. It is the opposite. In accountability, one blames no one; rather, one says, what is it that I can do to make things better for myself in this moment and in the future? This is an empowering position to take in situations which feel anything but empowering.

11. Degree of Integration

Integration is a factor in ESL, not EFL, programs. Coming to a new country is a tremendously unsettling experience, if you will forgive the pun. Not only are these learners struggling with the language, but in addition, all the assumptions which grounded their existence are suddenly up in the air. When one enters into a new culture, one does not know what is the same and what is different. This is called culture shock, and whereas it affects people differently, there are some well-known stages, one of which is depression.

Those learners who have lost the most in terms of their status, in my experience, suffer this period of adjustment with the greatest difficulty. When a person was respected and powerful in his or her own country and is suddenly viewed by many people in the new country as "an immigrant," it is humiliating and frustrating. The individual may spend a lot of energy trying to show others who he or she really is: the certificates and diplomas, photographs taken with important people or when receiving awards, résumés with varied job accomplishments listed, etc.

When faced with this painful threat to the learner's identity, the educator's job is not an easy one. On the one hand, we must be able to demonstrate our respect for that individual without making someone else feel less respected by comparison, but we must also be realistic in not creating false expectations. Whereas I am a firm believer in being able to create what we want if we want it badly enough, I also know that one seldom jumps from a position of status and money in one country into that same position in Canada without a good deal of hard work and disappointment in between.

I had a charming and well-educated learner from Poland who had worked in international banking. She had been told by our immigration officials that she would have no problem doing the same work here. While her knowledge of the language was moderately good, her pronunciation was far too heavily accented to be readily understood by native speakers. She was still translating everything in her head as she spoke, which slowed down her communication to the point of requiring some patience on the part of her listener.

The student had only been in the country for six months and was still heavily invested in impressing us with her status. She entered a job training program as a way of gaining some credentials and of finding her way into the system here, a realistic decision for her. However, when her job placement supervisor at a bank offered her a teller position, which elated us, she was incensed and turned it down. She felt it was beneath her and, in spite of our assurances that this was the way to get her foot in the door and move up the ladder, she insisted that taking this position would hurt her. I met this learner four years later, and she was still unemployed and hurting, but was definitely more realistic. She had considered returning to her country permanently, and did so for a visit, but realized she did not want to be there anymore. Now, perhaps, she can move on.

Her story illustrates what I mean by "degree of integration." Often, only time will enable a person to accept some sad realities and to begin to make realistic choices within those realities. A person who is well-integrated also knows how to use the systems that are in place in Canada, and is not normally preoccupied with what to do when one cannot pay the whole phone bill that month.

12. Intelligence

I am hesitant to use the term "intelligence" due to the baggage that normally goes with it, but something akin to intelligence is most certainly a factor in determining one's teaching. My hesitancy to speak about intelligence[4] comes from my experience in settings wherein "slow" learners had a tendency to be written off by instructors who had no idea how to "locate" them in terms of their learning style and ability, or who just assumed these learners were incapable of learning. The moment someone had a such a label, that was it; the problem was suddenly his or hers rather than ours. I do not accept that. Each learner is equally entitled to the best of what I can give and, as an educator, it is my responsibility to find that learner where he or she is and come up with strategies which are effective in meeting those needs and abilities.

An intelligent learner is one who knows him or herself well, and who probably has an effective set of learning strategies in place which work well for that individual. A less intelligent learner may not find it easy to know (or to say) what he or she knows, to determine what he or she wants to learn, or how to go about doing so. As a result of frequently feeling confused in life, such an individual is often seriously lacking in self-confidence, which exacerbates the problems that would otherwise be present in learning new things. Therefore, building self-confidence is where we start with learners who are challenged in this manner. This means providing ample acknowledgment, and setting tasks which can be easily accomplished by the learner. It means that every stage of learning must be made as transparent as possible; we cannot assume anything.

The other consideration for classroom success for such individuals is humour. It is so important to laugh and have fun because, in that state, we are relaxed and are more open to learning.

13. Religion and Politics

In most situations, religion is not a big factor, but when it is a factor at all, it is a big one! Religion is the institutionalized structuring of a person's most significant belief systems about the world and his or her place in it. When a religion dictates that men and women have separate roles to play (which normally translates as men having power and women not), that individual is automatically at a disadvantage in both the classroom and the workplace in North America. For individuals such as these, women's classes have been a great bonus. It is not our job as educators to dictate the values of learners who come to our classrooms; it is our job to give information in such a way that learners can make informed choices about their new context.

Religions also play a major role in how we interpret the meaning of

---

4 I am coming to the realization that what we have called "intelligence" in the past probably has more to do with access to quality learning opportunities, than it does to anything in our gene pool.

events around us. If we believe, as do Buddhists, that life is about suffering, we are going to accept our suffering in life in a different way than would a Marxist who believes that religion justifies suffering and ensures its continuity.

Similarly, I believe that those who have very strong political views can also be at a disadvantage in our classrooms. Like the strong religionist, the strong politician spends a lot of his or her time trying to persuade others to his or her way of thinking. The stronger one's views, the more one believes those views are the only views, and that any other views are to be pitied or scorned. These positions create tensions in heterogeneous classrooms wherein a great diversity of beliefs, values, and assumptions are present. The individual holding those views can be alienated from the rest of the group, a fact which seldom bothers that individual. However, this learner's political agenda can be distracting and confusing to others who are trying to focus their energies on both the basics of learning a new language, and getting along in a new culture.

Again, I would emphasize that it is not, for the most part, our responsibility to impose values; in fact, I treasure what I have learned about the values of learners through the years. However, I do not hesitate to use my authority in the classroom when I see an individual imposing his or her values on those not able or willing to stand up for themselves. But my authority can only be a temporary solution. Individuals must learn to stand up for themselves, and the classroom is a great place to begin that learning. (If you have not noticed the irony, I have just imposed a value, namely that of standing up for oneself. Some learners do not want to stand up for themselves; they believe it is my job to control what goes on in the classroom. While I understand and respect the place from which that view comes, I must, at some point, insist on being myself and saying what I am willing and not willing to do, and why. True respect for another human being means also that I am authentically myself. In my view, to be otherwise is disrespectful.)

Questions to Think About and Discuss

1. Imagine that you are offered a class of ESL women or ESL seniors. Both classes contain mixed ethnicities and mixed educational backgrounds. What differences do you anticipate in teaching these two groups? Which one would you choose and why?

2. Imagine that you are offered a choice between an EFL class for Japanese businessmen preparing to come to North America for business purposes, or an EFL class for young Chinese men and

women who must pass the TOEFL prior to coming to North America to study. What differences do you anticipate between the two groups? Which one would you choose and why?

3. Imagine that you have just been told that the married couple in your class saw their parents butchered before their eyes in Cambodia or Bosnia. What difference might that make, if any, in the manner in which you would teach these learners English?

4. If you're a white teacher wanting to become more sensitive to racial issues for black and Asian learners in your classes, what might you do?

For Further Reading

Canadian Congress for Learning Opportunities for Women (CCLOW). 1996. *Making Connections: Literacy and EAL Curriculum from a Feminist Perspective.* Toronto: CCLOW.

Rather than list the number of fine resources on gender theory in relation to ESL, I will refer readers to this excellent and unique resource, if for no other reason than the excellent bibliography of text and video resources it contains. This truly national project drew together women from all sorts of venues across the country. All were committed to the notion of women's education. It was field tested as a teaching resource right across the country. Highly recommended.

Dalton, Harlon L. 1995. *Racial Healing: Confronting the Fear Between Blacks and Whites.* New York: Doubleday.

I have read a wide variety of texts on the subject of racism. Some are biased in ways that I consider helpful to no one; others are so filled with anger that, as a reader, I cannot get beyond the vitriol. This book strikes what I find to be a good balance between telling it like it is, and still respecting that members of the white race have a role to play in resolving the problems. This text went a long way towards helping me to understand how our black brothers and sisters experience life in North America. I highly recommend this book.

Helmer, Sylvia and Catherine Eddy. 1996. *Look at Me When I Talk to You: ESL Learners in Non-ESL Classrooms.* Toronto: Pippin.

Written with K-12 instructors of ESL learners in non-ESL classrooms in mind, this book has a good discussion of the role of values and beliefs in the classroom.

Lightbown, Patsy and Nina Spada. 1993. *How Languages Are Learned.* Oxford: Oxford University Press.

These two authors are applied linguists, and the book reflects their background. However, they have combined linguistic learning theories with some other insights as to what affects language learning. This book is much more readable than many similar texts.

Moskowitz, Gertrude. 1978. *Caring and Sharing in the Foreign Language Class: A Sourcebook on Humanistic Techniques.* Rowley, MA: Newbury House.

When this book first came out, it was like a breath of fresh air. It was one of the first signals that ESL was willing to move beyond linguistics and into humanism. It is a sourcebook of practical teaching tips, many of which are for building self-esteem in the classroom.

Satir, Virginia. 1976. *Making Contact.* Millbrae, CA: Celestial Press.

Virginia Satir is one of my two significant mentors. She represents the best of the human potential movement of her time and, as a psychotherapist who pioneered conjoint family therapy, she shows us how to promote self-esteem in those we care about and in ourselves. Satir was an inspired educator who taught workshops all over the world to people of many languages and cultures, and always managed to make herself understood. I believe she touched our universal soul. This is a small book with some very big and wonderful ideas.

Wallerstein, Nina. 1983. *Language and Culture in Conflict: Problem-Posing in the ESL Classroom.* Reading, MA: Addison-Wesley.

A relatively radical book when it was published, I still find that Wallerstein comes from a place of understanding the relationships between language and power in our society. It is insightful in its approach, and very practical for anyone interested in learning more participatory forms of teaching.

Zukav, Gary. 1990. *The Seat of the Soul.* New York: Simon and Schuster.

Zukav is a physicist who, like so many others, discovered that the new physics is "discovering" what the mystics have known for centuries about time, space, and "the precious moment." *Seat of the Soul* is an excellent read for anyone interested in the spiritual dimension of life—and education.

CHAPTER 3

Understanding Your Context: Yourself

In this chapter you will learn about:

- legitimate and illegitimate reasons for teaching ESL/EFL
- the need for commitment *and* boundaries
- discernment
- avoiding exploitation of the learners
- making the most of *your* personality in the classroom
- seeing your own culture for the first time
- social class as it affects the classroom
- knowing your own limits.

This may seem like a very strange chapter to include in a text for beginning language teachers. We have traditionally been taught that who the teacher is should be immaterial. Curriculum and materials developers have gone to great lengths to ensure that their work is "teacher proof," which means that the teacher who follows the directions will have the desired results. I believe this is a great myth. Just as it matters very much who the learners are in the classroom, it matters very much who the teacher is. Just as we explored factors in the learner population that will affect the classroom experience, we are now going to explore factors in the teacher's life, your life, which will also impact the classroom. Some of those are the same and some are different. I offer this discussion to you as a tool for reflection, believing that when we are conscious of that which is within us, we are free to make choices in regard to it. As long as we remain unconscious of much of what is going on within us, we have no freedom to control or to change those things that may be in contradiction to what we think we believe and value.

1. Motivation for Teaching

In a place of stillness and solitude, be honest with yourself: why have you decided to become a teacher? If you simply say, "because I like teaching," then keep asking, "Why do you like teaching?" If you say, "because I like helping people," keep going and ask yourself, "Why do you like helping people?" If after all your asking, you discover that the classroom is one place where you have power, then be conscious that you are treading on dangerous ground. This may be a very honest answer for many teachers, and I commend those with sufficient self-insight to recognize it.

Traditional classrooms have given all the power to the teacher. Learners continue to give that power to the teacher. The bottom line, however, is that we cannot teach others to have power over their lives by perpetuating their experience of powerlessness in the classroom.

If we feel good about having the power the classroom gives us, we do not need to use that experience to have power over others, but can choose to use it to inform ourselves as to the human need to feel power over one's own life situation. If we like the feeling power gives us, can we not see also how necessary it is for learners to feel that same sense of power? This can begin in the classroom. Programs which develop with the learners genuinely at the centre of decision-making are called *participatory education*. This means that learners have power over what they learn and how—a very different situation from traditional classrooms where all that is decided before the learner even enters the classroom.

2. Extent of Commitment

Many ESL teachers are among the most highly committed teachers I have ever known. In fact, many of us are burned out by being *over-committed*. ESL is a field which calls forth every bit of energy we can muster. While I applaud those who go above and beyond the call of duty in this field, I also believe it is important to have boundaries, and I have been no expert on that point. Because the needs of our immigrant and refugee newcomers are so pressing and so fundamental to their survival and well-being here, it is very easy for us to get drawn into these problems and their resolution to an extent where our own families suffer and so does our own health. No one expects this. No one has a right to expect this. I would encourage teachers to ensure that they maintain activities outside their ESL or EFL circle. It is a way of staying in balance. It is also a good check against solving problems for those who would be better served by learning to solve those problems themselves.

EFL teachers abroad are likewise drawn into the lives of learners. Teaching overseas is interesting and exciting and, often, the teacher knows no one in his or her new context outside of those he or she meets at the school. If you are working with adults in this context, you welcome the opportunity to do things with people in your new country and to make friends. Here, it is easy to confuse commitment with taking care of one's own needs. While it is legitimate to care for oneself in any context, it is problematic to change the nature of the teacher-student relationship for that reason, a relationship which must remain professional in order to ensure that all learners have equal access to the teacher's time, resources, and attention. Furthermore, the teacher must be seen to be fair in giving equal access. Sometimes, perception does not equal reality, and when that is true, it is perception that counts. If a group of learners know that you are socializing with one student outside class hours, they may well resent that regardless of how careful you are to not let it interfere.

3. Ability to Discern

Discernment is a wondrous gift. It can be purely intellectual, or it can run much deeper into second sight. Discernment refers to the ability to distinguish something from something else. The teacher must discern when it is appropriate to intervene and when it is appropriate to remain silent, when it is appropriate to advocate for someone and when it is appropriate to patiently allow that person to make his or her own mistakes, and so on.

The teacher who is delivering a curriculum package sees little need for discernment. He or she simply stands in front of the class and delivers the program. It is up to the learners to take from it what they are supposed to. For the teacher who embraces the mystery of the classroom as a joint project with the learners, discernment is an art to be developed and cherished.

How do we know when to correct a person and when to listen respectfully, without interruption, to what that person is saying? The answer to that question lies in discernment. Some learners *think* they want us to correct their errors, but are devastated when we do. A discerning teacher learns from that experience and changes their approach with that learner in future.

How do we know when a person's stated priorities are, in fact, his or her real priorities? Most, if not all, students will tell you that they are in the classroom to learn English, period. In fact, many night students come to class because they are lonely, or because they are unhappy at home and enjoy the experience of being somewhere else. The teacher's ability to discern this in those students for whom it is true will stimulate her to put much more emphasis on joy in the classroom than will the teacher who thinks that all the students in the class are only there to prepare for the TOEFL examination (the Test of English as a Foreign Language which is used for university entrance).

Discernment is that quality which enables us to distinguish fact from desire, belligerence from the need to be acknowledged as a human being, and many other behaviours which present themselves as apparent contradictions in the classroom.

4. Support Systems

Some of us have wonderful personal support systems in place: parents, spouses, children, friends, people who love us and care about our well-being. Some of us do not experience such support. In the case of teachers, we cannot compensate by drawing on the learner population to meet those personal needs; this is unfair to the learners whose human nature reaches out to take care of the teacher, when they really need to be taking care of themselves.

5. Personality

Each one of us has a distinct and, indeed, a unique personality. None of us is perfect. Most of us put some energy into portraying ourselves in a positive light. There are certain personality traits to which we would be well advised to pay attention, as we may otherwise be unaware of the impact these have on our teaching and the lives of the learners with whom we work.

You have probably all heard the adage that children learn from who we *are* as parents rather than from what we *say*. The same is true in the classroom. We may think we are teaching grammar and vocabulary. The learners may be conscious of learning many other things. Some of these may serve them very well in life; others may have the opposite effect.

I remember one teacher I worked with who was very authoritarian in the classroom. Her adult students complained about it, and she was startled. She did not intend to be authoritarian. She simply knew no other way. It was the way she had been taught, and she was simply acting out of what she knew. But she had an even greater problem in my eyes. She was not a happy person, but she did not realize that. She had so masked her own unhappiness from herself that she was totally unconscious of its effect on the students with whom she worked. Group after group of learners seemed depressed in her class. They yearned to be with a teacher who manifested energy and joy because they themselves wanted to experience those feelings. This teacher's own emotions were calling forth the learners' negative emotions, and it was from those feelings that they wanted to escape. Try as she might to be lively in the classroom, this teacher could not. Because it was an act; it was not her. The only way her demeanour would change would be if she were able to deal with her own issues and change her own inner feelings about life.

Energy is a significant factor. The most successful teachers I have seen in ESL and EFL classrooms were those who had a lot of focused energy and were able to use that to generate energy in the learners.

Attitude is another. When the teacher has a very positive attitude about life and possibilities, the learners absorb that. If I am optimistic, my students are more likely to be so. If I am cynical and angry, I should not be surprised if my students become cynical and angry about the same situations. We do not just teach what is in our curriculum guides and textbooks. We teach who we are. We teach what it means to be a Canadian or an American. We teach what it means to be successful.

Maturity is another factor in personality. A mature person has learned from his or her own life experiences and chooses his or her battles more selectively than a person who sees every challenge as a personal one. A mature person has learned that conflict is a necessary part of living and that nothing is resolved by avoiding or suppressing it. A mature person has learned that one has to let go of yesterday and let today be a new day. A mature person has learned to throw out the garbage of life on a daily basis rather than letting it store up until it becomes an insurmountable problem. While there is an obvious correlation between maturity and age in terms of possibility, I have met several young people who manifested a lot of maturity and a number of older people who were still quite childish in their reactions to life. Maturity is learned and chosen. We learn from our mistakes, and we choose to take time to be reflective so that we are aware of what our choices are. To do the latter is to *respond* to situations rather than *react* to them. *Responding* most often produces much more favourable results for all concerned than *reacting*.

One's social skills can be an asset in the classroom. A teacher has to be able to work with all kinds of people: good and bad, wise and foolish, old and young, quick to learn and very slow, educated and uneducated, confident and abused. We need to have a large enough set of social skills to be able to establish meaningful relationships with all of our students because it is in relationships that people learn. There has to be trust, and that means we have to know and respect one another. We cannot assume that it is the learner's responsibility to make that happen. It is our job to make it happen, and when the learner is able to cooperate and even go beyond our skills, that is a bonus.

6. Languages and Intercultural/Interracial Experiences

It has long been recognized that one's experience with other languages (or lack thereof) is a factor of some significance in the classroom. What is less often recognized, perhaps, is why that is important. A traditional linguist would say that the more languages you speak and understand, the more likely you are to understand the kinds of contrastive difficulties a learner will experience in learning a new language. While that is true, it goes much deeper than that.

What *is* language? What *is* culture? There are many understandings of both, and I would suggest to you that the deeper and less superficial you are willing to go with these questions, the better chance you have of reaching meaningful understandings of who the learners are and what it means for them to be in the second language classroom. In Chapter 1, we explored several meanings of language.

What about culture? The *New Shorter Oxford English Dictionary*, Volume 1, lists a very long column of definitions of the word, the 7th of which reads, "The distinctive customs, achievements, products, outlook, etc., of a society or group; the way of life of a society or group." If we return to the root of the word, "cultus," which means to worship, we have a deeper understanding of the significance of culture to a people. The anthropologist Edward Hall speaks of three levels of culture: primary, secondary, and tertiary. The last level fits the Oxford definition and pertains to what can be readily perceived by outsiders. The second refers to those things that are less obvious, but that can be understood with a little help from insiders, and the first refers to those elements of a culture which are so unconscious that, normally, even insiders are unaware of them until they are transgressed.

In my experience, the biggest advantage to jumping headfirst into another culture is not in what you learn about *that* culture so much as it is what you suddenly become aware of in *your own*. We cannot truly know ourselves without having that mirror of difference thrust before our eyes in which we suddenly see ourselves as if for the first time. Things that we have always taken for granted are suddenly choices; some appear attractive and others unattractive. When second language learners come to our country, these are the experiences confronting them at every turn. When a learner has a conflict with an individual, he does not initially know if it is cultural or personal because he lacks the experience to discern that. The learner looks to the teacher for guidance, assuming that the teacher represents the new language and culture of the group. By ourselves having had these kinds of experiences that thrust us into confusion and self-doubt, we can understand so much better how the second-language learner feels in those environments in which we are comfortable, but he or she may not be.

And then there is race. When we live in an environment where race is either not an issue or where we are of the dominant race and are unconscious of the pain of belonging to the race or races which are denied access to the corridors of opportunity and power, we cannot begin to understand the added dimension that poses for a second-language learner. Such a learner is not only struggling to cope with a new language and a new cultural milieu but also finds herself at a serious disadvantage due to her race. In some regions, the racial barrier is frightfully obvious. A visit to Atlanta years ago was enlightening to me as I realized that, while the signs indicating "Whites Only" or "Blacks Only" were gone, the reality of difference between White and Black was still very present. The people had simply found other ways of excluding one another from belonging. Change takes a very long time. We are not, however, immune to racism in Canada; far from it. Racism is, many believe, harder to recognize here because its perpetrators reject the other with a polite smile on their faces, and find other excuses to exclude the one who is seen as different and, therefore, to be feared.

For a language educator, this means that settlement education or preparing an international student of colour for North American culture means far more than teaching a person how to speak English and how to set the table for dinner. It means preparing a person for the realities he or she will face in the community and giving that person strategies for overcoming the barriers he or she will inevitably meet. It means acknowledging the person's inherent strength and dignity even when that person feels those qualities have long ago deserted him or her. In order to do this, it means we must be open to discovering within ourselves the unpleasant and unconscious ways in which we have absorbed racist elements in our language and culture from our childhood onwards.

I am still horrified to recall that as a child, I loved to eat "Jap oranges," "nigger babies," and "nigger toes." I have since learned that these are mandarin oranges, licorice candies, and Brazil nuts but as a child, I thought nothing of the implications of what I was hearing and saying. Those expressions are fairly easy to eradicate from our speaking, but what about words like "denigrate," which we understand to mean "to put down?" If you look closely at the word, it means exactly what it says, "to treat one like a nigger." Words like these have become such a commonly accepted part of our language that most of us use them with no consciousness. I wonder if I would be equally unconscious if my skin was black? Somehow, I doubt that. Overcoming racism is everyone's business and it involves a lot of soul-searching and hard work.

7. Social Class

While as familiar as any Canadian with the terms "working class, middle class, and upper class," as a liberal-minded individual, I have never paid too much attention to those concepts, believing that I am open to all and acceptable to all. Yes, that is rather naive, isn't it? We can see clearly in countries such as India, with its de facto caste system, and England, with its nobility, the effects of social class on the lives of people in those cultures. It is less easy for us to see the effects in North America and even less easy to see social class as it plays out in the ESL or EFL classroom.

In most ESL classrooms, learners are seen as "immigrants" in need of the language and some cultural information. Too often, we have not seen the men and women who were among the cultural elite of their countries, in spite of the energy they give to trying to get us to recognize them in the manner to which they were accustomed. We have not recognized the dignity of the father who, as the patriarch of a large family, was responsible for everyone's well-being. Instead, we see a wrinkled, poorly dressed old man unable to remember the vocabulary from one day to the next. We have had a tendency to reduce everyone to the same status, defined not by who they are but by what they do not know. This attitude has a devastating effect on those individuals who are struggling to cope with all they have lost.

This lesson was most poignantly brought home to me when an international student invited me to a dinner party with his aunt who lived in our community. Without thinking, I wore the same clothing to the dinner that I would wear in the classroom, and it was not until we drove into the circular driveway in front of their very large home that I began to get this sinking feeling in my stomach that I was about to make a huge social faux pas. As the double doors opened onto a quartet playing Bach and a beautiful woman in a long satin gown beckoned us enter, I knew I was in for an evening of profound embarrassment in my cotton blouse and flowered skirt. Like people of culture everywhere, no one in that home of sixty elegant guests gave me even a clue as to what they may have thought of my tasteless and inappropriate response to their invitation. They were all unfailingly polite and gracious. Until that evening, I had had a picture in my mind of what the Korean immigrant was like, and my limited experience with that group had never caused me to question that image, until then. I am grateful for that evening in many ways. I actually had a very nice time, but more importantly, I learned to pay attention to more than a learner's pronunciation problems and his need to understand the grammar and vocabulary of the language. That night, I added "social class" to my list of valuable-to-know information about a learner.

8. Life Experience

You may be very young or very old. In any case, whatever experiences you have had in life are yours to ignore or to use as you approach the teaching of second-language learners. It is not enough to have had experiences; we need to reflect on what those experiences mean to us, and on what they teach us. I love the expression "There are no failures in life, just learning opportunities." For every mistake I have made in my life, I can either choose to feel stupid, guilty, or foolish, *or* I can choose to be thankful for what it taught me. For every painful experience I have had, I can either choose to feel sorry for myself, or I can choose to be thankful, when I encounter others in distress, for the compassion that my experiences have made possible.

Good teaching happens when, as teachers, we are able to find or create our common ground with learners. A senior citizen is more readily able to teach seniors in the classroom because she knows, and they know she knows, what it feels like to face one's end, what it feels like to get up with stiff joints in the morning, what it is like to keep forgetting things. They have a silent understanding between them that requires no defence, no explanation. Likewise, I was able to find my common ground with many refugee learners when I shared with them the death of my son in an accident. They knew I understood a little of their loss. By using our life experiences to find our common ground, we open the way for trust and safety in communicating with the learner.

Sometimes, that common ground is not there and we have to create it, not only with ourselves, but amongst the learners themselves, who sometimes tend to see their differences more than their similarities. A party or an outing in which people can eat together, dance together, play baseball together, and get to know one another as human beings can provide that common ground where we see one another first as people, and second as learners or teachers.

9. Training and Experience: Knowing Your Own Limits

Teaching inevitably comes with power and sometimes, in our attempts to live up to the responsibility that comes with that power, we take on things that are beyond us. We give advice that is not supported by reality. We offer hope when there is no possibility that we can deliver what we have promised. Never be afraid to say, "I don't know" or "I'm sorry, but I can't help you," if that is what is true. Such statements, while possibly disappointing initially, will only build your credibility in the long run as learners come to trust that you are honest and know your own limitations. I am not talking about grammar questions, the answers to which, if we do not know, we should most certainly be able to find. I am talking about people who have serious problems with their health, the law, or finances, for example. Trusting us, they ask for help. Wanting to help, we are sometimes tempted to take on more than we can manage. Take the time to know what resources there are in your community to help people with problems when they have little or no money to pay for such services. Refer people to those services when you lack the expertise or time to help learners yourself.

Questions to Think about and Discuss

1. Aside from wages, what do you expect to get out of teaching in an ESL or EFL classroom?

2. What kind of boundaries do you foresee needing to set for yourself in this work?

3. What kinds of intercultural and interlanguage experiences have you had which will inform your ability to teach English to speakers of other languages?

4. Do you have the courage and self-confidence to confront another teacher if you believe that teacher to be behaving in a way which is harmful to his or her students?

5. For those readers of the white race, how can we work at discovering and changing those aspects of our language and culture which deny access, and/or cause pain to those of other races? For those readers who are people of colour, how can you continue to draw attention to racist behaviours as you encounter them without coming across as having a chip on your shoulder? For all of us, how can we ensure that people of all races in our classroom are treated with dignity and justice by all?

For Further Reading

Hall, Edward. 1983. *The Dance of Life: The Other Dimension of Time.* Garden City, NY: Anchor Press/Doubleday.

_____. 1973. *The Silent Language.* Garden City, NY: Doubleday Anchor.

_____. 1969. *The Hidden Dimension.* Garden City, NY: Doubleday Anchor.

I have included three of Hall's books on this list for those who are interested in a foray into anthropology's description of culture. *The Hidden Dimension* is a cross-cultural analysis of space, *The Silent Language* deals with the ways in which we communicate our manners and behaviours non-verbally, and *The Dance of Life* provides an analysis of time, across cultures. These books have been very helpful to me throughout the years in coming to understand the huge breadth of possibility scanned by the cultures of the world and, therefore, by the students who come into our classrooms. It is humbling to acknowledge how little of that breadth is covered by our own culture, and how much we have to learn from those of other cultures. Hall also gives us a vocabulary to talk about those aspects of culture we encounter in our classrooms. A must-read for anyone who wants to enter into cross-cultural appreciation and understanding.

Nozick, Robert. 1989. *The Examined Life: Philosophical Meditations.* New York: Simon and Schuster.

This book is a touching collection of philosophical meditations on the key aspects of human experience: dying, creating, nature, sexuality, love, happiness, selflessness, faith, and many more. For the person who wants some touchstones against which to reflect on his or her own life, this will be a pleasant read. I find this to be a deep but very readable book, even for the novice philosopher.

Sennett, Richard and Jonathan Cobb. 1973. *The Hidden Injuries of Class.* New York: Vintage Books, Random House.

While this book does not address issues of social class cross-culturally, it is a good introduction to the presence of social class in North American society. It discusses the ways in which those class realities work to subtly, and not so subtly, force workers to measure their own value against the values assigned to them in various ways by the society in which they live. Because many of our students would be considered by sociologists to be members of the working class, it behooves us to attempt to understand what that term might mean.

West, Cornel. 1993. *Race Matters.* Boston: Beacon Press.

Like Dalton's book listed in the bibliography of the previous chapter, Cornell's is respectful of the reader, regardless of race, without sacrificing the painful honesty of racism's insane cruelty to its victims. He presents a reflective analysis of contemporary racism in the United States interspersed with personal experiences that are very helpful in understanding what he is talking about.

CHAPTER 4

Understanding Your Context: The Program

In this chapter, you will learn about:

- considering and pushing the parameters of your program
- respecting the priorities of the program
- accountability structures and their effect on curriculum
- working with a supervisor.

Examining the Parameters of an ESL or EFL Program

In Chapters 2 and 3, we examined elements of the life experiences of the two people at the heart of the fundamental relationship within the classroom: the learner and the teacher. The next part of our contextual reflection concerns the program itself. By "program," I do not mean just the content of what is to be taught but also the parameters of the program, those limitations which are set by whatever authorities have the power to set parameters, of which content may be only one.

I. Constraints

The most obvious parameters of an ESL or EFL program are those concerning time, money, resources, and the facility. Someone has decided that this particular language program will start on this day, finish on that day, and operate for X hours in between. In addition, a budget has been allocated for the program, and there may or may not be flexibility in terms of how those figures may be redistributed between categories. There are a limited number of resources in place—physical and human—and the facility itself has its limitations in size, temperature, etc.

The key to making the most of your opportunities in regard to these constraints lies in seeing that one side of the line is a constraint, but the other side of the line as a possibility. The trick is to determine where the line *really* lies as opposed to where it first appears to lie. In other words, we make assumptions which may or may not be true. For example, we may assume, because of our own experience as learners, that all the classes have to take place in the classroom. This may or may not be true. It is quite possible that field trips would be a welcome idea if they were well planned and carefully executed.

Likewise, programs always have limited budgets, but who says you cannot bring in volunteers to help you with tutorials or small group projects? You will never know unless you ask. You may have a resource room with texts and workbooks and a couple of video tapes or audio-tapes, but the best resources are often those found in your own home and community. We will talk more about that in Chapter 7, "Planning a Resource 'Stash.' "

If your classes go from 9:00 a.m. to 3:00 p.m. with an hour for lunch, five days a week, has anyone said you could not organize a camping trip to the mountains or the lake on a weekend? You will never know until you ask. And lest you think I am assuming that you will spend a lot of overtime on your job, I am not. Some of us have families, and it is important to establish our own personal boundaries around work and home. However, those of us who are single may welcome the chance to get to know a group of very interesting people by doing some social activities with them. Or, some of us might welcome the chance for our children to meet those same people from many cultures. All I am saying is that real constraints are not always clear. We have to feel our way along, not presuming that we can do what we want, but certainly seeking permission to do things out of the ordinary when we believe it is in the best interests of the learners to do so.

If you engage learners in social activities outside of class time, be sure you include the whole group in your invitation and planning. Choose activities which are religiously and politically neutral. It is not appropriate, for example, to invite students to your church or to campaign for your favourite political party. It is also not appropriate to invite students to those parties where someone is trying to sell something, be it ladies' wear, makeup, or insurance. Our students feel pressured to support our causes, and we must be very careful not to put them in that position.

2. Priorities

Every program has its priorities, expressed and/or unexpressed. It is helpful when these priorities have been articulated in some sort of philosophy or vision statement, mandate, or mission statement, but even when they have not been articulated, they are there and you need to find out what they are.

Every program is based on some sort of philosophy or understanding as to what good education and/or training is about. The majority of these goals are said to be "delivered," which means that materials are developed and gathered according to a set of assumptions as to who the students are and what they need, and who the teachers are and what they are capable of. An extreme example of this are some of the private schools in Japan that set a rigid curriculum which all the teachers are supposed to follow, even to the point of telling teachers the very expressions they are to use in greeting the students. The teachers are told exactly what to teach every day and are expected to use the resources provided for that purpose, whether the learners like them or not. Those with authority in such programs obviously have little confidence in the abilities of the teachers they hire to determine what and how the learners need to learn. They see the teachers as parts of a machine to be plugged in to the system they in authority have designed. If you find yourself in such a situation, you have my sympathy, as do the students paying money to learn in such a setting.

At the opposite end of the continuum would be the participatory classroom in which learning moments are negotiated and then recorded after the fact, with learners taking a lot of responsibility for deciding what they want to learn and how. In some such instances, learners have had a role in hiring staff.

In comparing these two extremes, one can see that the priorities are very different. Both schools no doubt want the students to learn, but what? Authorities in these schools have made very different assumptions about their learners and about their teachers. I suspect that the Japanese school is concerned only with the teaching of a subject, English, in order to make money. Whereas the participatory school is most concerned with the teaching of human beings, in the medium of English, in order to improve their lives. Whereas teachers can exercise some personal latitude in acting out of their own values, beliefs, and assumptions, it is important to find a context in which the values, beliefs, and assumptions of the host program are somewhat similar or at least open to your own. To do otherwise is to find yourself in constant conflict with authority and to become very tired very quickly.

3. Degree of Flexibility for the Teacher

In some ESL and EFL programs, the teacher is very closely monitored and is controlled by the program documents and the supervisory structures of the school. In other programs, however, once the teacher is in the classroom, there is a minimum amount of supervision and control. As a new teacher, I wanted a lot of guidance, but I also wanted the freedom to try out things and the trust that it was okay to make mistakes and learn from them. As an experienced teacher, I prefer to be told clearly what the parameters are, and then to be given the freedom and the trust to do what is best within those parameters.

When you are new in a job, talk to the other staff and ask them how much freedom they have to do what they think is right. When you are not sure, ask your supervisor. It is better to ask, than to presume and make a mistake. As an administrator, I tended to leave the teachers largely alone in the classroom. I read their reports, and as long as they appeared to be doing what the students found valuable, I did not intrude unless I received complaints. I had one experience of a teacher who had taken her students to a weekend gathering organized on their behalf at her church; she had not asked to do so. I lost trust in that teacher for she had, in my eyes, gone beyond the bounds of what was acceptable. Because of the power learners accord the teacher, many of them would not have felt comfortable refusing that invitation, even though they may have felt very uncomfortable accepting it, given the fact of their own diverse religions.

I believe we have no right to impose our religious or political values on our students. That is an abuse of power, and we must not be seen to put our students in positions where they are forced to make such uncomfortable choices. The teacher, no doubt, thought she was providing an opportunity for the learners to speak one-on-one with other native speakers, but there was another agenda there that the students certainly did not miss. This is where the ethics of our work come in. We have an obligation to teach, to inform, and to support learners in learning what they want and need to learn to be successful in our society. We also have an obligation to respect their choices, especially when it comes to religious beliefs and political stance.

4. Accountability Structures

Any program of substance has some sort of accountability structures in place. Depending on what these structures are, they can play a large or small role in determining the day-to-day choices the teacher makes.

In Korea, I learned that the ultimate goal of their English program was to have students pass the Grade 12 examinations, which would determine their eligibility for entrance into Korea's universities. The primary goal for these EFL learners was not to become fluent listeners and speakers of the language, or even to become good readers or writers in the language. It was simply to score well on those final examinations. So, in spite of mixed messages from the authorities that they wanted to move towards a curriculum which put more emphasis on listening and speaking skills, all teachers knew what the bottom line was, namely, to pass tests which were largely based on grammatical ability in writing. In that Korean teachers are placed in schools and regions according to the results their students get on tests, teachers were unwilling to heed new guidelines when they knew that they would suffer the consequences if their students did not do well on the tests. That is one form of accountability.

In North America, there is a strong push towards "measurable learning outcomes." These outcomes take various forms, most of which are quantifiable. When a university-bound learner wants to pass the TOEFL exam, we want to know the scores that the students get on practice tests. However, there are other instances in which the most important outcomes for learners are not so easily measurable. When a learner with very low self-esteem coming out of an abusive relationship begins to believe in herself and her possibilities as a result of her learning program, that is a very significant outcome. But how does one demonstrate that to the computer? When a man in a workplace program who has worked for 18 years sweeping stairwells because he was afraid to ask for a different job assignment asks for and is given that assignment, how does one predict that as a measurable learning outcome?

Educators who see their work as affording people new and better choices in their life are struggling to find acceptable ways of demonstrating success to those seeking efficient accountability structures. While needing to demonstrate success by whatever measures are given to us in a program, we must remember what is really important in education. Education is about making people's lives better and that means different things to different people.

5. Your Supervisor

Last but not least, your supervisor is part of the context of your program—an important part. You may like or dislike this person, but the fact is that you have to find ways to work successfully with him or her. Believe it or not, like yourself, your supervisor is doing the best he or she can based on what he or she believes to be true. You can respect him or her as a human being even if you disagree with what he or she believes and/or does. Your supervisor can make your life easier or more difficult. To a large extent, that is up to you.

Whatever you do, do not get caught up in office politics in which someone is trying to sabotage the existing authority structures by undermining the supervisor, or spreading rumours about him or her. If you have accepted to work in a place, you have accepted to work under certain authority. If you cannot at some point do that, you should seek another place to work unless, of course, that person is clearly in violation of the legal or ethical provisions of his job. In that case, you have an obligation to confront this individual and, if that proves ineffective, to report him or her to his or her supervisor.

Getting along with your supervisor does not mean buying gifts or buttering him or her up with false compliments. Most people can see right through that, and you will not only lose the respect of the supervisor, but that of your colleagues as well. Simply be respectful, honest, and pleasant. What goes around comes around!

Questions to Think about and Discuss

1. Imagine that you have a student in your class who is much slower at her learning than the others, but who is totally committed to that learning and works very hard. Knowing that she will not finish the course by way of understanding the curriculum within the allotted time, how might you ensure that she makes the best possible use of her time?

2. Imagine that you have a one-year contract with a private school in Japan to teach English to a number of small groups. After six months, you know a lot about what your students like and do not like about the curriculum and the materials you have been directed to use. Some of these materials are so irrelevant that the students actually fall asleep in the classes. What can you do about this situation?

For Further Reading

Boud, David, Rosemary Keogh, and David Walker, Ed. 1985. *Reflection: Turning Experience into Learning*. London: Kogan Page.

This somewhat unique book draws together theories of reflection. In that reflection is acknowledged to be a necessary component of such learning, this text is especially useful to educators who believe in designing experiential learning opportunities for students. Topics covered include reflection in relation to skill learning, autobiographical reflection, and the politics of action research.

CHAPTER 5

Understanding Your Context: The Community

In this chapter, you will learn about:

- the importance of having a sense of possibility in a community
- the need to belong to a community
- the openness or closedness of certain communities to immigrants
- English-speaking peoples as oppressors, historically.

In considering community as context, we can look at many levels of community: local, provincial or state, federal, and global. Traditionally, people have prepared to teach ESL and EFL by studying linguistics because that was the field of academic study which led us to an understanding of what language was about, how it was constructed, and how it was learned, in the case of applied linguistics. That field, however, has done little to prepare us to understand the historical, political, and economic impacts which affect a person's learning of a language.

In Chapter 1, I related the story of the refugee who had transited through Turkey and learned not one word of Turkish in two years, despite his having been identified by his teachers here as an exceptional language learner. I had concluded, from what he told me, that his emotions towards the Turks he encountered in the camp had effectively precluded any possibility of his learning that language, whereas his desire to be at one with Canadian society, however, had ensured that he absorbed every opportunity to learn English that came his way. This story not only shows us the power that a person's experience in a language can have on his or her desire and ability to learn that language, but also points us to the relationship the learner had, has, or will have with a variety of larger communities which communicate in that language. It boils down to whether or not the learner can see himself or herself belonging to that community or not.

1. The Local Community

Just as the experiences learners bring with them to the classroom affect their ability to learn, so do the experiences they have while they are studying, and the experiences they anticipate having after they have finished their studies. To begin locally, a person either feels a sense of possibility or a sense of impossibility. Will I get a job or not? Will my family feel comfortable and at home in this community or not? Is there a religious community into which we can comfortably fit or not? Is the economy such that it inspires confidence in the future, or fear? Are the educational opportunities in the community commensurate with what my family needs or not, and are these opportunities accessible to us or not?

Some immigrants and refugees feel immediately at home. Their neighbours or coworkers are welcoming, accepting, and eager to learn from them, as well as to help them adjust. Other newcomers feel foreign for years. I remember a woman telling me how for ten years she and her husband said good morning to the next door neighbour only to get no answer whatsoever. They felt invisible but were not about to compromise their own integrity by returning what they were getting in kind. They persevered, believing that things would change. One day, to the woman's shock, the man replied in a very friendly manner, "Good morning, lovely day, isn't it?" The two families now enjoy barbecues and long conversations together. I don't believe I know anyone else who would have persevered that long under those conditions, but that family is glad they did.

Communities vary considerably in their treatment of newcomers in general, of immigrants, people of colour, particular ethnicities, etc. I did not know what a prejudiced neighbourhood I had lived in for years until I started bringing students to my home for field trips. Suddenly, I saw a nastiness in many of my neighbours that I would not have imagined to be there. There was no tolerance for difference in that neighbourhood.

How does this impact the classroom? Only in the sense that the classroom should prepare people for the real world around them, not just the language, but the experiences that language mediates. I have long believed that what we call ESL in Canada should be called *settlement education*, which describes much better what we are doing.

Likewise, when we are doing EFL, we need to know the reasons our students are learning the language so that we can prepare them for whatever realities await them when they use those language skills. If, for example, students in Latin America or the Far East are learning English to study in a university or college in North America, part of our job must also be to teach them the academic culture of where they are going because, like anything else, that varies considerably from culture to culture.

I remember the first time I taught graduate students from China and solicited opinions by asking open-ended questions of the group. Much like the Koreans, they were shocked because I was asking them questions for which I had not yet given them the answer. They were afraid to speak for fear of giving the "wrong" answer. When I explained that in our culture, we encourage people to think for themselves, to be critical of what they have read and heard, and to express their opinions and ask their questions openly, these learners were amazed, as that had not been their experience of learning in China. Many international students say that it takes them a good year of adjustment before their listening skills pick up, and their cultural know-how adjusts enough for them to be able to participate in graduate programs the way in which they are expected.

2. Provincial or State Community

When someone comes here from another country, they tend to see Americans as Americans and Canadians as Canadians. It takes those of us who live here a while to realize that in some ways Texas and Alberta have more in common than do Texas and New York, or Alberta and Ontario. Many factors impact the development of regional differences within our countries. The oil industry has given wealth to Texas and Alberta that other states and provinces have not enjoyed. This financial reality has shaped the economies of these two areas such that they require particular kinds of individuals and not others. New York and Ontario are more established regions which are heavily dependent on industry and finance for their economic well-being. They need immigrants, and lots of them, to prosper. Thus, it is not surprising that immigrants often feel more welcome and more optimistic in Ontario and New York areas than they do in other provinces or states.

The economy of a region is also very important. In a state or province where the economy is down and there are no jobs for anyone, people may see immigrants as a threat and may be more highly intolerant of immigrant newcomers than usual.

3. National Community

The politics of a country determine the immigrant and refugee policies of that country, as well as the settlement policies, to a large extent. In Canada, immigrants have traditionally fared better under Liberal governments than they have under Conservative ones. That this is seen to be changing in recent years has more to do with a general right-wing swing throughout the country, than with changing political views on the value of immigration to our country.

If those who immigrate are to enjoy their democratic freedoms and exercise them responsibly, it is up to educators to ensure that they understand how the systems work and understand and feel confident that they can learn to participate responsibly within them. For the past 12 years, I have been working with an English in the Workplace program located in a large garment factory. At one point, we did a survey in which over 90% of the operators in the program said that they were citizens of Canada, and close to 50% of the workers said they had never voted in an election. They went on to say that they were not interested in learning anything about citizenship.

Puzzled by this apparent incongruency, we did another survey which did not use the word "citizenship" but instead asked questions about interest in learning about the community, and about participating in the community. There was a much more positive response to that survey. People had equated the word "citizenship" with passing the test, not with the act of being a participating citizen of the country. I felt very sad to think that after several years in the classes, many people still lacked either the confidence, the skill, or the incentive to get out there and vote.

The classroom should reflect the country's stated myths about itself. When a country stands for justice and liberty for all, that should be the experience learners have in the classroom. When a country stands for multiculturalism, as Canada claims to, classes containing students from many different cultures should experience respect for all of those cultures in the way in which decisions are made in the classroom, and in the demeanour of the teacher towards the learners as a group. In a multiculturally oriented program, Islamic students would not be expected to come to school the last day of Ramadan, nor the Asians on their New Year celebration.

4. Global Community

Last, but not least, more and more, we live in a global community where news is instantly transmitted, not only over short-wave radios and CNN, but over the Internet as well. It is becoming impossible to impede the flow of instant information from one place to the next. When learners have family members at risk in their own countries, they often know about it the same day. What happens in one place, affects us all one way or another. For example, when the environment is threatened, it is in all of our interests to understand why, and what we can do about that. Our air, our water, our rain forests, our land—these are common resources we all need to survive. It is in everyone's interests to see ourselves as one big family sharing this planet, and that can begin in the classroom with recognizing and honouring one another's humanity and dignity, no matter where we are from or why we happen to be where we are.

We might also want to examine the role English-speaking peoples have played throughout the world. Whereas we feel fortunate to be able to travel to most countries and find people who speak our language, not everyone in the world views English amicably. Many see it as the language of the oppressor. We are not far from times of genocide and slavery, such as happened in Africa and Latin America, not to mention to our own First Nations peoples. (There was once a tribe of indigenous people called the Beothuk in Newfoundland. They are there no more.) Even now, many nations in the world are economically dominated and oppressed by English-speaking countries. These deep-seated resentments will need time and openness to heal. As educators, we owe it to ourselves and our students to familiarize ourselves to some degree with these realities, in order to better understand how we are seen by others and how our language is experienced by some.

Making Connections

The best ESL programs I have seen throughout the years are those whose teachers have gone out of their way to enable learners to make connections with the broader community. They have paired students off with community members to allow both the opportunity of getting to know one another. They have introduced students to people who work in the same field as the learners did in their own country, in the hopes that these community members might help them to find appropriate employment. These ESL programs have organized social events to which community members and students have been invited to enjoy one another's company. They have invited guest speakers, including former students who are now successfully employed, to come into the classroom and talk to the students.

It is natural for human beings to want to be in community with other people. The fact that many of our students come from environments where communities are close and people help one another in times of need, makes coming to North America all the more lonely and difficult. Anything we can do to mitigate that harsh reality is welcome.

Questions to Think about and Discuss

1. It is not easy for us to overcome historical hatreds. Can you think of a group of people that your parents or grandparents just flatly disliked because of some experience they (or their parents) had had with people of that same language, race, or culture?

2. What can you do to enable learners to feel more at home in your broader community?

3. Is there anything you can do in an EFL classroom to give learners a sense of English-style community (e.g., campfires, potluck meals, a Christmas celebration, etc.)?

4. If you are aware of discriminatory attitudes in your community towards any of the groups of learners you teach, what might you and possibly others do to address that problem?

For Further Reading

Ashworth, Mary. 1985. *Beyond Methodology: Second Language Teaching and the Community.* Cambridge: Cambridge University Press.

(See notes at end of Chapter 1.)

McKay, Sandra Lee. 1992. *Teaching English Overseas: An Introduction.* Oxford: Oxford University Press.

This book is an informed and very interesting exploration of the kinds of contexts in which English is taught abroad that includes case studies to illustrate the author's points. In addition, we see the implications of these different contexts for the teacher. This text would be excellent for anyone preparing to teach English in a non-English speaking country.

SECTION II

Entering the Classroom

CHAPTER 6

Planning a Lesson

In this chapter, you will learn about:

- how to make a lesson plan
- how to write three different kinds of intents
- five sample topics to work on
- how to choose appropriate resources and activities
- how to evaluate as you go
- the value of anecdotal records.

If you are new to teaching, you may feel a little overwhelmed at this point. Please don't. For one thing, learners are remarkably understanding. When they know you are doing your best, they will most often support you all the way. For another, you do not need to remember everything you are reading here. What you are ready to remember, you will remember, and as for the rest, questions will present themselves to you in your planning. Pay attention to those questions.

It is time to begin. A lesson plan itself can alleviate a lot of the initial jitters one feels when going into the classroom for the first time. It is like a crutch; you use it when you need it and abandon it when you don't. Not everyone would agree with that. For many people, the plan is everything and you follow it no matter what. I disagree with that. The plan is based on what I know before I go into that classroom. The moment I begin to interact with the learners, that begins to change. I learn new things about them. Through them, I learn new things that are going on in their lives and in the community. If I am to be authentic to their needs, I must be willing to change my plan and, occasionally, to abandon it altogether. Nonetheless, I need a plan to begin with, and more often than not, that plan will prove to be appropriate to the needs of the moment.

On page 64, you will see a diagram which reflects the thinking that goes into either a whole curriculum plan or the lesson plan for the day,

Table 1: Curriculum Plan/Lesson Format

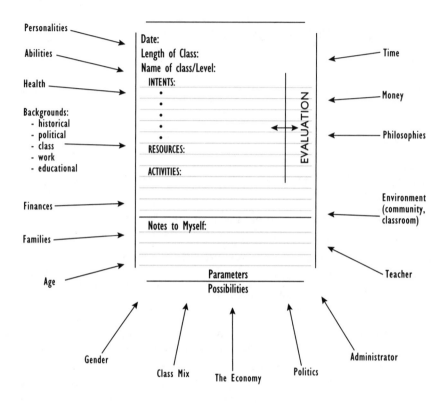

for the components differ only in scale. First, you will note that the lines bounding the components are not connected in the corners. This indicates that parameters are seldom as fixed as we think they are, and it is up to us to test the limits of those parameters. They are also open to change as conditions change.

Secondly, you will notice the arrows pointing at the model. These arrows indicate the forces which affect and are affected by what goes on in the classroom. These elements have been discussed in some detail in the first five chapters.

The model has four components, all of which are to be regarded as dynamic rather than fixed: *intents, resources, activities,* and *evaluation.*

Intents

You have most often heard the words "goals" and "objectives" when it comes to planning. I still use those words in the classroom, but I use them when learners are planning their own personal goals. I prefer the term "intents" for planning purposes because this word implies a direction rather than a fixed end. The word "intent" acknowledges that I do not yet have all the information. With the information I do have, however, I can determine the general direction in which I want to move, always being open to change if the lived priorities of the classroom appear to be elsewhere.

Teacher Intents

We also have the choice to word our intents as *teacher intents* or *learner intents*. Both have their advantages. For a lesson plan, I prefer teacher intents as they tell me clearly what I am doing from moment to moment. In the following examples, you will notice a number of different types of intents:

1– To introduce learners to the use and form of the present perfect tense and enable them to see the connection it makes between two points in time.

2– To anticipate, present, and explain sufficient vocabulary so that learners are able to express the feelings and emotions evoked in looking at 10 laminated pictures of various local (or regional) scenes.

3– To introduce and practise the telephone dialogue that would be needed to answer the phone and take a message for someone at home.

4– To enable learners to understand the culturally acceptable do's and don'ts around accepting a dinner invitation to the home of one's employer or supervisor.

5– To elicit from learners their ideas as to what they most need to learn in the next 12 weeks and what kinds of activities they find most useful in enabling that learning to take place.

As you read these five examples, you can see that each one differs in its focus. The first is a *grammatical* intent. The second is a *lexical* intent (intended to teach new vocabulary). The third is a *functional* intent, which would enable someone to do a particular task. The fourth is a *situational* intent, which would enable the learner to understand what is appropriate and act accordingly in a particular situation, and the fifth is a *participatory* intent.

These intents do not belong to the same lesson, nor would they be appropriate for the same group of learners. However, the way we work with them to develop a lesson is similar and, after considering the process which follows, you may wish to have a look at the intents of the sample lesson plans given in Appendix 1 (pages 197–218).

Learner Intents

Teacher intents are not appropriate to give to the learners. I like to give the learners the intents of their curriculum so that they know what to expect and can make suggestions if what is planned is not what they think they need. For the learners, intents need to be worded not in terms of the teacher's behaviour (to introduce, enable, or elicit, etc.), but in terms of the learners' behaviour. The five teacher intents given earlier, if written for the learners, might then read as follows:

1–To understand and begin to use the present perfect tense of some common verbs.

2–To fully express the emotions I feel when I look at 10 local (or regional) scenes from Alberta.

3–To be able to answer the phone and take a message for someone at home.

4–To understand what is culturally appropriate when I accept a dinner invitation to the home of my employer or supervisor.

5–To say with confidence what I want to learn in the next 12 weeks and to tell the teacher what helps me to learn.

These intents may have to be worded differently, depending on the level of the learners for whom they are written.

Intended Learning Outcomes

In view of the types of accountability measures being imposed across the continent, it is good that you know how to write intents in one other manner, namely, as *intended learning outcomes*. Learning outcomes describe in precise detail the desired outcome of the lesson and can, because of their precision, be assessed for the degree of success present at the end of the lesson. I might use this style of writing when I am doing a proposal for a funder and know that I will have to provide quantifiable data to demonstrate success in the program upon completion. The downside of these "intents" is that they cannot legitimately be called intents in that they are fixed. If one promises these goals, one is expected to deliver these goals—a conundrum for the teacher who recognizes the importance of learners' defining their own learning goals and processes.

On the other hand, because these intended learning outcomes are so precise, you do have a lot of time to do more than what has been defined, as long as you can demonstrate that what you have committed to teach has been learned.

The five examples of intents given previously, rewritten as learning outcomes, might thus be changed as follows:

1–Learners shall understand that the present perfect tense is used in reference to something that was true at some point in the past and is still true, and the learners shall be able to correctly use the tense, verbally and in writing, in describing:

- the length of time they have been in the country,

- the amount of time they have studied English,
- the length of time they have been married, and
- the length of time they have lived in their current apartment or house.

2– Learners shall be able to describe their emotions in regard to 10 pictures provided by the teacher in such a way that at least seven different adjectives are used appropriately in relation to the set of pictures (e.g., happy, sad, sentimental, sorry for, peaceful, hopeful, contented, frightened, excited, worried, angry, curious, depressed, upset).

3– Learners shall be able to take a telephone message which correctly conveys to the intended recipient the time of the call, the caller's name, the caller's number, an accurate, legible message, and the name of the message-taker.

4– Learners shall know the following cultural information with regards to accepting a dinner invitation to the home of an employer or supervisor:

- It is appropriate to arrive on time or up to 15 minutes late, but not later and not earlier.
- If one is unavoidably delayed beyond 15 minutes, it is appropriate to telephone the host or hostess and let him or her know when you will arrive.
- It is considered thoughtful (but not necessary) to bring flowers, wine, or some other small gift.
- Unless the person giving the invitation is from the same culture as the individual invited and that culture is one in which inviting a person is the same as inviting the whole family, one never brings others unless those others have been expressly invited (e.g., spouse, children, relatives, friends, etc.).
- One does not begin eating until the hostess does so, unless invited to do so.[1]
- It is generally considered impolite to slurp or burp at the table.
- It is considered polite to speak to other guests at the table.
- In terms of knowing which utensils to use for which foods, it is appropriate to watch the hostess and do what she does.

5– Learners shall have identified at least five goals for their collective learning and at least one goal for their personal learning for the next

---

1 These cultural do's and don'ts might be considered strange or even controversial by some. Cultural norms are dependent on rural and urban settings, social class, and cultural background. In Korean households, slurping is expected and is the only way to eat noodles without making a mess. Male burping is quite common and is often viewed as an expression of enjoyment of a meal. Traditional middle- and working-class Koreans do very little talking at the table and consider it rude to do so. This is why any such ESL/EFL lesson should be tempered by the context in which it is given.

12 weeks, and will have prepared a list of at least five activities that the majority agree are helpful to their learning. (This goal-setting should be done with as little prompting from the teacher as possible.)

As you can see, the list of intended learning outcomes is by far the most detailed and lengthy of the lists of intents thus far. It is also the most bounded and the easiest to measure, as all of these items are readily testable. You may have no choice but to prepare your curricula and lessons in this manner. In any case, it is a useful skill to have. Whereas there are many ways of developing similar intents, the format should have some consistent characteristics.

> Useful Format: To enable the learner to distinguish between "should not" and "must not" in giving and receiving simple directions.
>
> Example: *You should not be late for dinner.* (Someone will be unhappy.)
> *You must not be late for work.* (You could get fired.)
>
> Not Useful Format: To make the learner use "should not" and "must not" correctly.

The statement above is not useful on two counts. To begin with, it is not our job to *make* anyone do anything but rather to enable learners to exercise new choices should they choose to do so. Secondly, the statement is ambiguous and much too large in its scope. The first statement is more specific and gives examples for clarity. In the examples, we clearly see the difference in consequences between "should not" and "must not".

Exercise

Here are five topics along the same lines as those provided. Write a teacher intent, a learner intent, and then an intended learning outcome for each, and then compare your answers to those in Appendix 2 on pages 219–221. These topics are very general, and you may narrow them as you see fit.

1. Asking information questions (who, what, when, where, and why).
2. Using appropriate vocabulary to describe the location and circumstances of a persistent headache to a doctor.
3. Refusing to do work that is dangerous.
4. Questions one does not ask a new acquaintance.
5. Deciding which candidate to vote for in an election.

Resources and Activities

Once you have decided what you are trying to accomplish in your lesson, you are now ready to begin to consider two other questions:

- How can I best achieve these learning goals in the time given?
- What resources would best serve me in doing that?

In that Chapters 7 and 8 deal at length with these two topics, I will not go into a lot of detail here. What I will do at this point, is give you some things to think about as you make these decisions.

1. Are the activities and resources you have chosen appropriate for the age, background, and abilities of the individuals you are teaching?

   Some activities which are excellent for children or teenagers would be considered very childish for adults and downright dangerous for seniors. Some materials designed in California might be excellent for learners there, but quite irrelevant for learners in Manitoba, or vice versa.

   Learners who are literate in their own language, can handle paper in learning a second language; learners who have never been to school or who have only a little education, are easily overwhelmed by paper and just get depressed when they are given too much of it.

2. Are you prepared to discern from the learners whether the activities and materials you have chosen are appealing to them or not?

   Learners most often try very hard to please the teacher. Just asking them if they like something will not be effective if they think you want to hear a particular answer. Instead, watch their faces. See what excites them and what bores them. See what motivates their participation and what they merely tolerate.

3. Is there enough variety in the kinds of activities and materials chosen to keep the learners interested?

4. Is there so much variety in the lesson that the learners feel confused and off-balance?

   We need to find a balance between creating a comfortable routine and providing sufficient variety to keep people's energies high.

5. Are we expecting too much or too little in what we ask people to do in the classroom?

   Each learner is different, and learns at a different pace and in a different way. Remember that not everyone learns as we do. We have to be very perceptive in determining how best to enable each individual to be successful in the classroom. Nothing motivates like success, even when the success is a small one.

6. Do the materials dignify the learners and help them to see themselves as belonging?

A lot of materials on the ESL/EFL market show white faces doing white middle-class activities, and this portrayal neither reflects the realities of the multiracial, multicultural environments in which most of us live and work in North America, nor does it recognize the realities for the immigrant newcomer. Learners need to find faces with which they can identify. Learners need to see workers doing jobs like those they will do, or are doing. They need to see lifestyle choices they can afford on low incomes, if that is their reality. Choose books which include rather than alienate learners. Choose materials that dignify learners by being attractive and interesting to them, books in which they learn more than just grammar and vocabulary.

Evaluation

Most people think of *evaluation* as something you do *after* the lesson or after the program has finished. That is only one kind of evaluation. Please think of evaluation for what it really is—the *valuing* of what is happening. Evaluation includes many things:

- the process of a learner's valuing himself or herself and what he or she is capable of
- the valuing of our own teaching
- the valuing of the curriculum, materials, and program
- the valuing of the progress which has been made by the learner
- the valuing of what has been learned about learning, about teaching, about all aspects of the program.

This process of evaluation should be a part of everything we do, with an attitude of questioning as we go, and of encouraging the learners to do likewise.

One simple but potentially inspiring activity I have done in some teaching situations is to save five minutes at the end (or beginning) of each day to ask, "What did you learn today (or yesterday) that mattered?" Initially, students will say what they have been conditioned to say: vocabulary, grammar, English, etc. Those answers do not wash. If they say vocabulary, I ask, "What words did you learn?" When they identify a word, I ask why it matters? When will that word ever be important to them? After a while, this process of valuing what they are learning becomes automatic, and they start to formulate what they are going to say as the day goes on. In the process, they come to take accountability for what they are learning. You will occasionally be surprised by their answers. I remember one woman saying, "I learned cooperation." I thought she meant the word. She did not. She meant the act of cooperation. This concept was for her something new and she liked it. I was, needless to say, thrilled.

At the beginning of this chapter, you will see the format for what could be a lesson plan or a whole curriculum document. The last item you will note in the plan document is "Notes to Myself." I write notes at the end of a class for two reasons. One is to remind me of things that need to happen in the next class. It might be notes about what I did not finish or things that came up in class that need to be addressed either in future lessons, or in private sessions with a student. The other use for this section in one's lesson plan is to make a note of significant anecdotes or incidents which show clearly that meaningful outcomes are happening—outcomes that may not be measurable, but that can be accounted for.

The first time someone initiates a question, for example, is a milestone for that person. The time someone comes to school and tells a classmate that her husband's place of employment is looking for someone with that student's job skills is an indication that a sense of community is building in the class. When a mother excitedly reports that she no longer needs her children to accompany her to the doctor because she can now go by herself with confidence, that is an achievement for her. These anecdotes are infinitely more valuable to me than any number of test scores, because they speak to meaning, and that is not quantifiable. In programs that I administer, I ask teachers to turn in their most significant anecdotes at the end of each session as markers of the success of the program. In time, these provide a record of what a program means to the lives of a group of learners. (Beware of assuming that you will remember these incidents or events at the end of a class. You may remember a couple, but if you do not take time to write them down on a daily basis, you will forget many significant happenings.)

Have a look at the lesson plans provided in Appendix 1 on pages 197–218. Note that the left-hand margin indicates the amount of time that you think will be needed. Note also that there is an extra activity just in case you move along faster than you expected. In my experience, new teachers typically move much faster through material than do experienced teachers because they have not yet learned how to seize the moment and do mini-lessons around opportunities which arise in the class.

If you are a new teacher, remember to provide more to do than you think you will have time to do, and more importantly, remember the importance of review. Review does not mean doing the same thing again. It means approaching the same concepts from several different directions until they become familiar and comfortable to learners. The biggest mistake new teachers make is to approach teaching in a *linear* fashion instead of in a *spiral* fashion. Go around again and again, each time adding something new, but still reviewing basic concepts. Before you know it, your intents will have become habits for the learners.

Questions to Think about and Discuss

1. Of the three types of intents (learner intents, teacher intents, and intended learning outcomes), which type do you prefer and why?

2. If you are given a book to use in your class which is clearly less than appropriate for your learners in that it reflects a lifestyle which they could never attain, how can you use that book critically to the value of the students in the class?

3. If you prefer classroom activities that the students do not like, and the students prefer classroom activities that you do not like, how can it be decided which activities to use and which to abandon?

4. How will you know from beginners whether they are finding value in the class or not, when they do not have the language as yet to tell you?

For Further Reading

Robinson, Julia and Mary Selman. 1996. *Partnerships in Learning: Teaching ESL to Adults.* Toronto: Pippin.

> The strength of this handbook for beginning teachers lies in its simplicity and organization. The authors present an easy-to-follow alternative for organizing units and lessons in a program.

CHAPTER 7

Planning a Resource "Stash"

In this chapter, you will learn about:

- developing a good picture collection
- collecting good teacher references
- using found objects in the classroom
- creating context-appropriate collections
- using texts and workbooks critically.

While there is no substitute for a good library of the latest texts and workbooks available from a wide variety of publishers, I have found it very useful through the years to build my own personal collection of resources for any occasion. At the top of my list are pictures and from there, the list is endless. I will share with you some of the resources I have found particularly useful through the years, that are easy for anyone to put together. Some of these resources are specifically designed for the activities that go with them in the following chapter, so if you are left wondering what on earth one would do with *that*, check the next chapter before you scratch your head.

Pictures

In ESL/EFL, a good picture is invaluable. One picture can be used in dozens of ways. For each individual who sees it, something different is seen. A picture can elicit emotion or be used to tell a story. It can illustrate a verb tense we are teaching or be used for teaching vocabulary and colours to beginners.

In EFL, pictures can have an additional value: they're intensely interesting to learners when they also reveal the culture and geography of places with which learners are unfamiliar, thus providing the context in which English is spoken. Pictures can be used for the whole class or for individuals. In fact, I have found them so valuable, that I am amazed that publishers have not gone into building good picture sets for us. I would most certainly buy them as it takes a lot of time to collect good pictures. Furthermore, few pictures are big enough for a whole class to be able to see and many are only useful in small group work.

The most useful pictures are those that are big enough for the whole class to see if they are held up. In other words, look for full-page magazine pictures or pictures from old calendars. I suggest you get a box or filing cabinet and organize these pictures into categories such as the following:

A. Vocabulary

- household objects and furnishings
- recreational activities
- medical/dental
- foods:
  – count (e.g., eggs, potatoes, oranges)
  – noncount (e.g., sugar, flour, rice)
- emotions
- occupations
- clothing
- parts of the body
- animals
- nature scenes (e.g., waterfalls, jungle, forest, plains, rivers, lakes, streams, mountains)
- weather and climate
- seasons

B. Verbs

Look for pictures which illustrate the following tenses. Here are some possibilities:

- present continuous (*He is shaving.*)
- simple present (*She starts work at 8:30 a.m.*)
- simple past (*The baby fell down.*)
- past continuous (It *was raining* when the baby fell down.)
- future (*Canada Day will be next week.*)
- present perfect (*We have been married for fifty years.*)

C. Stories[1]

D. Cultures

E. Famous personalities

F. Geography

---

1 Some pictures imply the possibility of one or several stories. For example, a woman looking with terror at a dent in the new 4-wheel drive, as her husband comes out the front door, could trigger a wonderful story as we imagine why she was driving his new car, what he is going to say when he sees it and, of course, what happened.

G. History

H. Politics

I. Religions of the world

J. Science and technology

K. Employment and the world of work

L. Food

M. Healthy lifestyle

N. Social issues (e.g., poverty, racism, injustice, ecological issues, crime)

O. The Arts

P. Sports

Q. Holidays and celebrations

Some of these categories may be inappropriate for your purposes, while others may be more appropriate than what is given here. These categories are offered as suggestions only. Pictures serve many uses and, in the beginning, you may not want to sort them at all. But as your collection builds, you may find it difficult to locate what you want unless you have organized it.

I mount these pictures on construction paper and then run them through a laminator. If you do not have access to a laminating machine at your place of work, you can get them done at a printer, and it is well worth the cost since the pictures will last much longer and stay nicer looking if they are laminated. In addition, I suggest that you put a label on the back of each picture so that you will remember how you have filed it. Most pictures would fit into several categories.

Smaller pictures are useful in making flash cards, games, and question and answer cards for individual and pair use. They can be kept in envelopes in the classroom and used by students when they are waiting for the class to begin, or when they have finished whatever activity is going on. See the next chapter for some suggestions on how to use pictures in the classroom.

A Good Grammar Reference

The more education your students have had, the more they will ask you *why* something is true. They are not content to know *that* it is, but need to know *why*. I understand this. I do not easily accept anyone's word for anything either, but if I understand *why* something is so, then I have a means to remember it and a reason to do so. You need a good grammar reference. You can get references that look like large Bibles or slim references that fit easily into your briefcase. In any case, try out your reference book before you buy it, because if it is so complex that you do not know how to look up your questions, it is not the book for you. The texts which are available for ESL learners are not detailed enough for what you need unless you plan only to work with beginners. You need a comprehensive grammar reference text. I actually use a combination of texts since different authors use different terms to name things, and your students may come from a school of thought quite different from the way you learned grammar yourself. See the bibliography at the end of this chapter for a few suggestions.

A good grammar reference is particularly valuable for EFL teachers in that EFL learners are typically more informed on grammatical points than on usage and, therefore, put a lot of value on grammatical explanations. Woe betide the teacher who can't answer their many questions—you lose a lot of face!

A Good Dictionary

Whereas your students will need a good dictionary appropriate to their level of learning and literacy, I find that I need a dictionary that not only contains almost any word I would care to look up, but that also gives me a good etymology of words. I now use the *Canadian Oxford Dictionary* (1998), a wonderful addition to my library because in it you can see how Canadians use English. Before this dictionary was written, it was at times frustrating to have to choose between an American dictionary and a British one, neither of which was consistent with common usage in Canada. American readers will want a good American dictionary; many like Webster's. In addition, you will need to choose a learner dictionary appropriate for the level of your students. Teachers I have worked with like the *Oxford Learner Dictionaries*.

A Good Thesaurus

I find a thesaurus useful not only when I am writing, but also when I am preparing exercises for learners or trying to explain to them the parameters of words which their bilingual dictionaries say mean one thing, when I know they mean something else. The hardbound *Bartlett's Roget's Thesaurus* is a good choice. Students would want a small paperbound version.

The ESL Teacher's Book of Lists (distributed by Pearson Education in Canada)

I came upon this resource at a conference and promptly bought one for my daughter to use in Japan. This text is exactly what it says it is—a book of lists—and it is very handy when you are trying to come up with examples to illustrate a point, and your mind suddenly goes blank. It has lists of mass nouns, count nouns, irregular verbs, regular verbs, past participles, and all kinds of other things in one handy place. And much of it is legally copiable! (Many other activity books are also available from which games and activities can also be photocopied. See bibliography for publishing information.)

Household and Found Objects

You may wish to simply gather these items as you need them for a particular lesson, or you may wish to keep some collections in shoeboxes for fast use when you need them. A couple of publishers now have good picture dictionaries, which save the need for bringing in a lot of found objects, but I have still found it useful to have the real objects for various kinds of activities (e.g., following commands, giving commands, making polite requests, etc.). Objects are also a good way to build confidence when a student has a passive understanding of the language, but is not yet ready to speak. He or she can follow instructions and feel quite proud of his or her success, without ever saying a word.

When you teach clothing, it is infinitely more helpful to actually have clothing samples there that people can try on and laugh about. Putting on a floppy toque ensures that people will remember it much more than simply seeing a picture of it. Better yet, let people dress up in whatever they want and then take photos, which can then be used to write stories. This kind of humour is not for all students. But there are many learners who love any excuse to laugh and will learn much more when they are laughing than when they are serious. (I would remind the reader of my suggestion to invite rather than compel learners to participate in activities. None of us likes to feel embarrassed or awkward, and what some learners would regard as fun would be humiliating for others.)

Maps or a Globe

When you have learners coming from all over the world to a class, it is especially important to have a map so that people can see where they are, where they have been, and where everyone else came from. Do not expect that all learners will know how to use a map. This is a learned skill, and those learners lacking in formal education will see only a multicoloured piece of paper with a lot of irregular shapes on it. Literacy learners must be taught how to use a map and to understand the concepts underlying it, in which case, a globe is more practical.

Cassette Tapes

Depending on who your learners are, cassettes with easy singalong music may be welcome for both ESL and EFL learners. Not all learners want to sing. Some feel silly or childish doing it, while others enjoy singing and find it an easy way to learn rhythm and stress. I have had some classes that loved to sing and others whom I did not even ask, as I knew that was not their style. Students I have taught have often enjoyed songs sung by The Carpenters, which are easy to sing along with, or by Roger Whittaker. Some students will have learned some traditional English songs in their own countries.

Some ESL students want to learn the national anthem. Others want to learn Christmas songs.[2] Christian students who sing the same carols in their own language will really enjoy these, while ESL learners who have no experience of Christmas in their cultures may not. However, some of them will want to learn these songs, as they know their children are learning them at school.

Games

Commercial games such as *Scrabble*™ or *Pictionary*™ are very popular with some language learners while teacher-made games such as Go Fish using homemade pictures and words are also very popular. You can make elaborate board games or very simple games such as Marketplace, where students use play money to negotiate prices in an imaginary market for items which are on the tables.

I do not use games much in my classes, but that is just my personality. You have to find the tools that work for you and for your students and if games work, by all means use them.

Context-Appropriate Collections

Your classroom should be filled with resources that are appropriate to the class you are working with. If you are doing academic preparation, a number of different TOEFL manuals would be good to have on hand. If you are working with a group of mothers whose children are in the childminding centre down the hall, you might want to have recipe books and cooking facilities available, along with a sewing machine and information about the public school system, the children's library, and the zoo. If you are doing an employment-preparation class, hang posters on health and safety and Labour Standards for your province or state. A literacy class should have lots of easy readers for learners to

---

2 Carol singing is very controversial. Because we frequently are teaching people of many religions in ESL classes, many students may learn these songs because the teacher is telling them to, but may resent it. Once again, this should be an optional activity for those who want it, and should be balanced with choices of other kinds of music.

pick up and browse, or to borrow to take home. Many students love to read stories by and about other immigrants and are often motivated to write their own stories when they read those of others. *Voices* magazine out of Vancouver is a lovely resource for this group. (See bibliography.)

Language Masters

A Language Master is not something you need, but this device is a handy resource to have if you are teaching beginners in need of individual work. A Language Master is a machine that reads magnetic strips on which sounds are encoded. You could have a picture of someone riding a bicycle, for example, and the student looks at the card, says, "The man is riding a bicycle," and then listens to the card as it passes through the machine. The learner compares his or her answer and pronunciation to the recording, and adjusts it accordingly. You can buy commercial sets of cards, or you can buy blank cards and make up your own for individual students. Language Masters are available from commercial audio-visual supply centres.

Texts and Workbooks

There are so many texts and workbooks on the market, that I will not even begin to recommend which are good and which are not. For one thing, some texts are good for one context and not for another. In general, though, I find most students want to have a text and/or a workbook because it gives them the sense that they are progressing in a particular direction, a sense which they may not get from using handouts. If at all possible, I suggest that you have a selection of choices and let the students choose as a group, which text and/or workbook they prefer. (Unfortunately, EFL teachers are seldom given a choice.)

Teach your students some critical reading skills, first of all, so that they do not just judge a book by the price or the picture on the cover. In addition, make sure that you yourself feel comfortable with the texts or workbooks chosen. Consider the following guidelines:

- Is the material appropriate to the language level of the learners?
- Is the material attractively presented and easy to follow in its formatting? Does it dignify the learner both in its form and its content?
- Can the learners find themselves in the material? *Does it reflect their lifestyle and their realities?*
- Is the language of the material consistent with the country and region where it is to be used? (There is no point reading about "lorries" when the students see "trucks," or learning to say "sodas" when the students drink "pop.")

- Is the size appropriate for the amount of time the learners have in the class, or will they be able to use only 2 or 3 chapters out of 20?
- Is it a book the students will want to keep, or is it best purchased as a class set which can be used by other students later on?
- Are there ample opportunities in a workbook for learners to practice the material, or is too much information given too fast?
- Are the explanations clear and easy to follow with lots of examples given?
- Is the material in any way condescending or racist in its tone?

In addition to the many books on the market, there are listening programs with tapes, video programs with workbooks, and a burgeoning market of ESL software. However, all of those things cost money, and frankly, I have found no single resource available for purchase that is as valuable as my ever-growing picture collection.

Questions to Think about and Discuss

1. Consider *National Geographic*, a magazine that most North Americans have read at some time. How was your experience of reading an article about a place you have visited different from your experience of reading about a place you have never been to, and to which you will never go? What does this difference suggest about the importance of matching your teaching resources to the context in which you teach?

2. Consider the varied appearances of women throughout North America—old and young, rich and poor, skin of many colours, attractive and less so, healthy and unhealthy, neatly attired and casual in appearance. How do you suppose all these different women feel about advertising which predominantly displays wealthy, very healthy, and beautiful young women in their ads? Now compare that to ESL and EFL workbooks which write about ski trips, nightclubs, and dining in fancy restaurants? Whereas these resources might be very appropriate for a Japanese or Taiwanese student bringing considerable financial resources into the country, how appropriate is it for seniors, for poor people, and for those with chronic health problems? How do you think such people feel when they are obliged to use materials in which they do not see themselves, either as current reality or as possibility?

3. How can you structure your curriculum to accommodate the needs of some enthusiastic students who are willing to do three to four hours of homework per night to learn quickly, while at the same time meeting the needs of other learners with several others to feed and take care of each evening?

For Further Reading

Celce-Murcia, Marianne and Diane Larsen-Freeman. 1983. *The Grammar Book: An ESL/EFL Teacher's Course.* Rowley, MA: Newbury House.

This is not so much a reference book as it is a map through the complexities of English grammar for the teacher who lacks confidence either in his or her own knowledge of this critical area, or in ideas for how to communicate that knowledge to learners who need to know it. The authors use a transformational approach to grammar.

Kress, Jacqueline E. 1993. *The ESL Teacher's Book of Lists.* West Nyack, NY: The Center for Applied Research in Education. (Distributed through Pearson Education.)

An excellent resource for any teacher but especially for beginning teachers who want nuts and bolts information about what to teach, this text contains many reproducible handouts for use in the classroom. American teachers will also appreciate the lists of US publishers, associations, and resource centres at the back of the book.

Quirk, Randolph, Geoffrey Leech, Sidney Greenbaum, and Jan Svartvik. 1985. *A Comprehensive Grammar of the English Language.* London: Longman.

This resource has been considered by some to be the Bible of traditional English grammar. It is definitely not for use by the average student, but it does serve as an excellent reference for those difficult questions that come up from time to time.

Voices. Issue 18. V. 8, No. 2, Fall 1997. Available at leegee@radiant.net

This is the last issue of what was a magazine by and for ESL and literacy learners. This issue only is bound like a softcover book, and is very popular with learners as a resource because it contains a variety of stories with which they can identify. Voices is nicely presented and available from the editor, Mr. Lee Weinstein, in Vancouver. He asks that you e-mail him at leegee@radiant.net for purchasing information. I include this resource here, in part, so that readers will be inspired to produce their own books of stories with learners.

Wright, Andrew. 1984. *1000 Pictures for Teachers to Copy.* London: HarperCollins Publishers.

This collection of small, simple, and photocopiable pictures would be very useful to teachers making their own materials.

CHAPTER 8

Finding and Creating Activities that Work

In this chapter, you will learn about:

- basic guidelines for planning classroom activities
- some of my favourite activities with beginners
- art in the language classroom
- setting up role-plays
- problem-posing
- using pictures
- creating photostories
- field trips and guests.

Language learning is a holistic activity. It involves every part of us: body, mind, emotions, and spirit. Although we try to divide it up into various skills for the ease of organizing instruction, that does not reflect how we learn the language. We learn a combination of what we most need and want to learn, and what we have the opportunity to learn, regardless of the category into which such learning falls. The following are some guidelines for planning activities.

Basic Guidelines

1. Know the learners and choose activities which are appropriate to their age, gender, life experiences, cultures, abilities, and interests. Better yet, involve the learners in choosing activities they like. Children and adults alike feel respected when they are given choices.

2. Choose activities which you yourself enjoy and feel comfortable doing. What works for one teacher does not work for another, and one way to ensure that learners enjoy learning is for the teacher to enjoy it too. If you are bored, they will be. If you are intimidated, so are the learners likely to be. Try out a variety of things until you find a good collection of activities which work well for you.

3. Consider the context, and don't try to impose activities from one context into another where they do not fit. For example, you can do things with 12 learners in a class which would be totally unwieldy if there were 40.

4. Activities that involve all the senses tend to produce more positive results than those which involve only one sense. This is why TPRs (Total Physical Responses) were so popular. Asher's methodology gave three dimensions to what had been previously a two-dimensional experience. If learners do not only listen, speak, read, and write but also move, smell, feel, make, and do, their experience is fuller and is more likely to capture their personal learning modes.

5. Read up on various learning theories. We do not all learn in the same way. Some of us, for example, are very concrete and analytical in our learning while others are abstract and experiential. It is tempting to choose classroom activities which appeal only to our own preferred learning modes, but we have to learn to present learning opportunities which appeal to a variety of different learning styles. As a small example, some learners like the theory first and then the examples, while others get nothing at all out of a theory until they have a concrete example. Some learn through detailed explanations while others learn better through stories. Men tend to have different learning styles than women, and although our culture has structured educational systems to fit men's learning styles, many women have comfortably adapted to that. When we add on the dimensions of race and culture to those differences within our own systems, we have even more things to think about.

6. Do not try to teach too many things at a time. The learner gets overwhelmed. For example, if you are introducing *quantifiers* to a group of beginners (e.g., a bunch of, a cup of), don't teach *mass nouns* (rice, meat, milk, spaghetti) and *count nouns* (bananas, carrots, buns, eggs) together, as that is very confusing. Give learners the chance to absorb one pattern before you go to the next.

7. *Do lots and lots of review!* Just because people can do something one day, does not mean they understand it or will remember it. Build review into every lesson, adding a little more complexity into it each time.

8. Ensure that each and every activity you do adds to rather than detracts from the dignity of the learner. Language learning is humiliating enough without asking people to do things that make them feel foolish.

9. Remind learners often of the *Rule of Invitation*. This means that any activity someone is uncomfortable with, he or she is genuinely free not to do. What is humiliating for one person, might be good fun for

someone else. You don't need to be serious all the time. In fact, the more humour there is, the better, but there has to be choice.

10. Enjoy yourself. Laugh at yourself. Don't be afraid of making mistakes. If you can laugh at your mistakes, it is much easier for the learners to laugh at their own.

Favourite Activities of Mine

The Mystery Box

One of my favourite activities to use with beginners is what I call the Mystery Box. It is just a shoebox with big question marks drawn on the sides, and the contents of the box change regularly. In addition to being a very helpful technique for teaching vocabulary, the Mystery Box is a great way for learners to choose either when they are ready to speak, or to be successful at just following directions.

I begin by putting about a dozen simple objects in the box, usually following a theme such as "classroom," "kitchen," "small repair kit," "tools," etc. Suppose that we were doing "classroom." I might start with a pencil, pen, eraser, ruler, notebook, and dictionary. Each of these objects takes an *article* (*a* pencil, *a* pen, *an* eraser, *a* ruler, *a* notebook, and *a* dictionary). I would begin by picking up each object in turn and saying, "This is a _____" with the name of the object. I would do that a few times encouraging the learners to fill in the name before I said it, and then I would ask for volunteers to come up and I would say, "Please give me the _____." I would make sure that the learner succeeded by gesturing to the article I wanted if there was any hesitation.

The next day, I might bring in more than one of each of the objects so that there were different colours of some things. (This is an example of *spiralling*. You are reviewing the objects, but also introducing colours and word order.) I would repeat the previous day's exercise, only this time I would ask if anyone wanted to be the teacher and come and make the requests. As people are confident, they want to do this, and they feel good about doing it. When everyone knew the names of the objects, I would then ask, "What is this?" and they would say, "It's a (or an) _____" or later, I would ask, "What are these?" and they would say, "They're _____."

Only when all of that was comfortable, would I then bring in those objects which did not fit that pattern: chalk, scissors, scotch tape, masking tape. These objects take no indirect article. Instead, we could learn *a piece of* chalk, *a pair of* scissors, *a piece of* scotch tape, etc.

When you are first doing this activity, be sure you go through the commands, questions, and answers for each item you choose, because otherwise, you will have some very confused students as they struggle with which nouns take what, and when.

You can also use the Mystery Box to teach prepositions of place: on, under, beside, in, in front of, and behind. "Please put the _____ on the _____, etc."

Because we are using not only sight and sound to teach language, but also touch and movement it is easier for many learners to remember because their body is learning as well as their mind.

Posters

At the very beginning of a class, I often invite people to make posters to help them to learn the words they need to talk about things which are important to them. The first poster I would do has four segments, which I would draw on a flipchart paper: "My Life Before," "My Life Now," "My Life in the Future," and "How I Feel at this Moment." The learners fold their papers in half and in half again, and then help themselves to an assortment of markers, crayons, and magazines, in case they prefer to cut and paste rather than draw. I always do my poster first, and since I cannot draw much other than stick figures, the learners see quickly that they could not possibly do worse in the art department than I do. They can also generally tell what I am after from the pictures and my body language when I talk about it, even if they do not know what the words at the top of each segment mean. By understanding mine, they understand what I expect of them in the exercise.

You learn a great deal about your students from this simple exercise. Who uses colour? Who does not? Who makes bold, bright statements and who draws small, scared-looking drawings? Who can see a future that is brighter than the present? Who sees no future at all? Many learners portray a beautiful past and a somewhat bleak present, unless they came from war, in which case, that is evident in their pictures too. When everyone is finished, they hang their pictures up around the room, and each person walks around and looks at them all. Then we sit down and, one-by-one, people are given the opportunity to talk if they wish, and only if they wish, about what they have drawn. I encourage the learners to ask for vocabulary if they have drawn something and do not know the name. I write such words on the board, and people can write them down in their personal vocabulary lists.

Another poster which I have found very fruitful in terms of getting to know people is the "I like, I don't like, and I want" poster. For this activity, the learners divide their paper in three sections and again, they can choose either to draw or to make a collage of pictures. I encourage the latter as it enables the learners often to say a lot more than their drawings would, unless they are good artists.

I will never forget the result of the first time I did this exercise. It was a class of mostly women, about half Chinese-speaking and half Latin

American. In the "I don't like" column, most of the Chinese women had cut out pictures of cigarettes and alcohol, while the Latin American women had managed to find every ad for toilet bowl cleansers in the pile of magazines. In talking about their pictures, the Chinese women laughed as they described their husbands coming home at night to smoke and drink and do nothing. The Latin American women spoke with tears about how they did not want to be cleaners in their new country, but wanted to do the jobs they had done in their country of origin. This one small exercise taught me so much about what the lives of these women were like, and what their education needed to encompass.

In talking about the posters, the learners get a lot of speaking practice, new vocabulary, and spelling for words they may need in their writing later. They may also get to show skills in a new area; the one who may have terrible pronunciation or be very shy in speaking, may turn out to be an incredible artist and get a lot of acknowledgment for that talent. This encourages him or her to feel safe trying out other things in the classroom. As with all personal sharing, participants are acknowledged for their contributions by everyone's enthusiastic clapping.

Dress-up Bag

A bag of various hats or smocks or other items associated with work, can be a useful way to learn to talk about occupations. For example, if we have a nurse's hat, a carpenter's apron, a small wrench, a cook's apron or chef's hat, a cloth tape measure, and a toilet plunger, we also have a nurse, a carpenter, a mechanic, a cook, a chef, a seamstress, and a plumber. With one small symbol, learners can ask each other these questions:

Who are you?	I am a nurse.
What do you do?	I help sick people.
Where do you work?	I work in a hospital or clinic.

From this activity, it is much easier for the learners to then ask of one another, "What did you do in your country?" and "Where did you work in your country?"

The students can also be very creative. I will always remember a class I had the day we were studying wedding vocabulary. They said, "Let's do a wedding so that we can learn all the words." So, a wedding we did. The "bride" borrowed a large shawl from one of the other women. The groom made a bow tie out of another woman's scarf and then ran to the washroom to bring back a long "stole" of toilet paper for the priest. Two chairs became the organist's bench, and the Kleenex box rapidly produced flowers for the bride and her three attendants. I will never forget that lesson, and I doubt if they will either. (The Spanish-speaking "bride" and the Polish "groom" actually did marry six months later, and the whole class was invited to the wedding.)

Role-Plays

Role-plays can be very, very simple or very complex, depending on the level of the class and the willingness of the learners to participate in this kind of exercise. The important thing is to ensure that people have what they need to be successful with the role-plays, whether it is vocabulary, grammar, or understanding of the context. I usually use these activities in one of two ways: as an introduction to something new if I have a volunteer or higher level student who can do it with me, or as a way of practising something we have just been learning.

Suppose we were working on telephone calls, for example. One could first demonstrate a call for someone who is home, then write it up on the board, and then ask for volunteers to come and practise the dialogue. Then everyone can practise it in pairs. Next, one student could make it a little more complicated by leaving first an easy message, and then a somewhat more difficult message.

Or, if you are working with international students who are going to travel to an English-speaking country, you could do all kinds of role-plays to get them ready: ordering in a restaurant, asking for directions, checking in at a hotel, going to an emergency clinic, or shopping. Again, give the learners the vocabulary and structures they need to make the role-play work, before you ask them to do it. Afterwards, you can try changing the details. For example, someone has ordered what they want in a restaurant, and the waiter in the second role-play says, "I'm sorry, sir. We are all out of that. Is there something else you would like?" It is important to try the role-plays in several ways because life seldom goes as we expect it to, and we need to prepare ourselves for the unexpected. Again, do not ask anyone to do this until he or she is ready and, if the learner is never ready, that is okay too.

Problem-Posing Activities

Problem-posing activities can be done in a couple of ways, with either you introducing the problems or with the learners introducing the problems. When I do it, I might have several problems written on cards, and I ask pairs to choose a card they would like to develop into a dialogue in which they address the problem. Here are some examples:

- You have just bought a pair of shoes. When you get home, you discover that the two shoes are different sizes. You go back to the store to correct the problem.

- You go into a washroom in a restaurant and find that smoke is coming from the waste receptacle.
- You have just received a notice saying that you are late paying your power bill, and your power will be cut off if the bill is not paid in two days. You did not receive any other bill. Your paycheque is five days late. You phone the power company.
- The waitress comes to ask you how everything is. You have just found a half a caterpillar in your broccoli.
- You give the clerk a $20 bill to pay for a $6 item. She gives you $4 change and says, "Thank you. Have a nice day."
- You have been waiting in line at the bank for 20 minutes to deposit your cheque. Just as it is almost your turn, a woman cuts in front of you in line and smiles. (She is not old. She does not look sick.)
- You are working as a cleaner. Your supervisor is very mean to you. You have just washed the floor and she says, "What is the matter with you? Are you blind? Do that floor again." You think the floor is very clean.

As you can see, these scenarios vary considerably in difficulty. This can be good, in that learners can choose the one they want to work on. They may not choose one particular situation over another because it is easy, but because it has happened to them, and they wonder how they could have addressed the problem.

You can do these problem-posing activities orally or have the learners work out written dialogues first, depending on your purpose. There is a lot of cultural information inherent in these problems. Another use for these scenarios would be to videotape them and then let the students themselves decide whether they are happy with what they have done, or think there is a need for change. When people do not understand the presenters, they know there is a need for change. You do not have to tell them. If you do use the camera, use it respectfully, not to criticize the students, but to offer the tape to them as a tool for their own learning. Let them ask you for what they need to make the changes they want.

The best way to do problem-posing, however, is not to present the problems, but to have the students present real problems that they have encountered in shops or the workplace, for example. This is where the learners will come out with their stories of injustice, of racism and discrimination, of pain and frustration. When they trust you enough to share these stories, knowing they will be listened to and supported, your class will become more meaningful as a result. In response to these situations, do not be judgmental. Rather, listen and give information. The decisions to be made are theirs. *Your agenda is to give them the tools they need to be accountable for creating positive results in diffi-*

cult situations. We also have a lot to learn from the learners, and they have much to teach one another as well.

Using Pictures

In the last chapter, I said that pictures were possibly the most valuable resource you can have, other than the learners themselves, of course. As we mentioned, pictures can be used to

- teach vocabulary
- teach grammar
- play games
- tell stories
- evoke memories and feelings.

It is important, however, that in using pictures or photographs, we do not impose our "seeing" on the seeing of the learner, for what we see is very much a product of our own experiences. I remember showing a picture of the proverbial husband raiding the fridge to make a submarine sandwich, as his wife comes around the corner in her curlers and housecoat to bawl him out for breaking his diet. Or so I saw. I was much enlightened by a group of students who generated the following details about this same picture:

"It must be Sunday."

"Why?" I asked.

"Because he is wearing pyjamas."

"Yes," I said, "He is, but that is because it is nighttime."

"But if it is nighttime, why is he eating? And why does his wife look angry at him?"

"But if it were Sunday, why would he be wearing his pyjamas?" I asked.

"Because he is relaxing at home," they replied.

(I was later told, on a visit to a Chinese-Vietnamese family's home for Sunday dinner that the Chinese-Vietnamese men often wear only their underclothing on a Sunday, and that this is not seen as underclothing, but as "relaxing clothing.")[1]

When I explained to the students my interpretation of the picture with all the details about how wives often worry about their husband's cholesterol and blood pressure, they showed no comprehension whatsoever. I concluded that it was unthinkable, from their point of view, that a wife should interfere with what a man wanted to eat.

---

1 In reporting this incident, I am not assuming that all Chinese-Vietnamese men wear underclothing at home on Sunday, visitors or no visitors. I have no idea how widespread this custom may or may not be.

It was one picture, but it told as many different stories as there were cultures and possibly individuals looking at it.

I recommend that instead of asking only very specific questions to elicit the answers you want, you begin by asking, "What do you see in this picture?" Only then will you begin to understand what the learners see.

Another use of pictures is to elicit speaking. To the question you asked first, you can add, "What do you feel when you look at this picture?" or "Does this picture remind you of anything?" In my experience, a lot of stories will follow this kind of questioning, and in trying to tell these stories, learners will often need help to find the vocabulary they need to say what they want to say. They will stretch as far as they can to communicate in order to tell their stories.

When you use pictures to elicit speaking, I suggest that you have a number of pictures and that the individual be allowed to choose the one he or she wants to talk about. Some pictures will elicit very negative memories for some students, and we do not want to put people on the spot by asking them to recall something unpleasant.

Photostories

Creating photostories is one of my favourite activities. Done properly, this is one of the most participatory activities one can use in a classroom. By "properly," I mean that the learners control both the process and the outcomes of this activity. They take the pictures, which means deciding what is photoworthy and what is not, decisions, which I can assure you, will be different from the ones you or I would make. The learners choose how to group the pictures in order to make the stories, and they choose which groupings they want to write about. When a computer or typewriter is available, it is also desirable for them to prepare the final copy, make the photocopies, and bind them with an Ibex machine or other type of binding. Photostories are ways for learners to prepare their own texts, and these texts become treasured memories which, from what many students tell me, they read again and again. You can use photostories with any level of learners in any context where you have the freedom to use a camera and a photocopier. The school may or may not pay for the pictures, but I would not let that be an obstacle.

With literacy learners, I started doing photostories by bringing a camera to tea time and letting the learners take pictures of us trying out different foods that I and others would bring to class. I would spread these foods out on the table, and they would pick the ones they wanted to write about. One time, for example, I was biting into a very green apple and making a sour face. Someone took my picture and later wrote. "Teacher no like apple. Too sour. Very funny face." In order to write that, she had to mimic my face and ask me what the word was for "sour" and for "face." I glued these stories onto construction paper and laminated them, and we used them for reading practice. Then, I typed the stories with corrections and made them into a booklet which, by then, they could read and answer questions about.

With the Korean teachers I mentioned earlier, we used photostories to capture our experience of travelling together to the Rocky Mountains. The first time I did this, we were rushed for time and, to save time I thought, I spent the evening grouping the photos on flipchart paper so that the teachers could get right to work on the stories the next day. This proved to be very interesting, however since my groupings did not make sense to some of those who had chosen to work with them. The only way they could connect the three or four pictures in the grouping was to write an exotic fairy tale with dragons and princesses. At first sight, I was lost and asked why they had written a fairy tale instead of telling the real story. They looked surprised and asked me: What real story? They had done the only possible thing to make sense of non-sense; they had made it up! In future years, I made sure the teachers had time to choose their own groupings.

The term *photostory* as it is used in participatory education means something different from what I have related above. Photostories are used in popular and participatory education as a tool for enabling participants to become more conscious of the nature of their reality and more able to give names to their experiences, especially those experiences which devalue or oppress them in any way. The purpose, then, is to take charge of one's experiences as a community and to act in ways to change that which is not just or desirable. For more information about how to do this type of photostory, I refer the reader to the book *Getting There* as described in the bibliography at the end of this chapter.

Field Trips and Guests

Taking field trips and inviting guests to the ESL classroom are both useful for a variety of reasons, but it is as important to prepare for these activities as it is to prepare for any other. Too often I have seen teachers go on a field trip as if it were a diversion from class, rather than an integral part of it. By that, I mean there was no preparation and no follow-up. It was "a treat." Often in such cases, however, I find learners resenting the time it took out of their learning. To prevent this reaction, I make the following suggestions:

1. Involve the learners in field trip planning. Ask them to decide which trips to go on, when, and how.
2. Go on trips which are relevant and important to people's lives, or very interesting.

3. Prepare for the trip by discussing what to expect, and by providing vocabulary the learners will need to ask questions and/or to document their experience.

4. Follow up on the trip when you return to the classroom.

You may have taken photos on the field trip. If so, that is a great way to follow up with vocabulary, questions, and experiences. If not, find some other way to debrief the excursion. Some teachers give an assignment for learners to do when they are on the field trip. This activity may or may not be appropriate. You do not want people to feel embarrassed or awkward, which is already difficult when they are travelling in a group.

The least helpful field trips are those where students have to listen at length to a guide who has no idea how to speak to second language learners, and sounds much like a tape recorder on high speed. If you inadvertently get caught in a situation like this where the students cannot possibly understand what is being said, excuse yourselves and either do the guiding yourself, if that is possible, or cut the trip short. The best bet is to go yourself first, or find out from others who have gone to the field trip site and found out what the personnel are like.

The same sorts of suggestions are true for inviting guests to your class. The guest must be able to communicate with second language learners, and must have something worth communicating if that guest is a speaker. If the guest is a visitor or volunteer, you may wish to put him or her on the "hot seat" and get the students to ask questions. This can be refreshing for students who are eager to hear a new voice and to get new ideas about life in this new country.

Questions to Think about and Discuss

1. Why is the Rule of Invitation an important one when you are doing any classroom activity?

2. How might the activities selected for a group of international high school students be quite different from those selected for a group of business people from Asia?

3. Imagine that you have invited a guest speaker to address your ESL class. That speaker turns out to be a very intolerant person, who makes it quite obvious that he believes that immigrants should not be allowed into the country unless they are fully fluent in English to begin with. This man is an elected representative, and you had hoped that by introducing him to some refugees, he might open his mind somewhat. But that is not happening. What can you do about the obvious upset he is causing with his words and attitude in the classroom? Your classes are funded by the government of which he is an elected representative.

For Further Reading

Barndt, Deborah, Ferne Cristall, and dian marino. 1982. *Getting There: Producing Photostories with Immigrant Women.* Toronto: Between the Lines Press.

This book has long been one of my favourites. Not only does it give us a methodology for producing photostories with our own learners—a popular activity in participatory education programs—but it also reveals much about the life experience of immigrant women as they set about their lives in a busy urban environment in which visual media do not even acknowledge their existence.

Bell, Jill. 1988. *Teaching Multilevel Classes in ESL.* Markham, ON: Pippin.

This handbook-sized paperback gives the new teacher many practical ideas on organizing activities for classes which have many different kinds and levels of students in one group, a situation more common than not.

Blair, Robert W., Ed. 1982. *Innovative Approaches to Language Teaching.* Rowley, MA: Newbury House.

This book is valuable to those who want to know about many popular approaches to teaching a second language. Some examples include Asher's *Total Physical Response*, Curran's *Community Language Learning*, Lozanov's *Suggestopedia*, Terrell's *Natural Approach*, and many more.

Hadfield, Charles and Jill Hadfield. 1990. *Writing Games.* Surrey: UK: Nelson Publishers.

While not useable in its exact form in all contexts, the pictures and ideas are great. This photocopiable book also contains a few lovely black and white pictures of a postcard size as well as some animated drawings which could stimulate story writing.

Hadfield, Jill. 1990. *Intermediate Communication Games.* Surrey, UK: Nelson Publishers.

———. 1987. *Advanced Communication Games.* Surrey, UK: Nelson Publishers.

———. 1984. *Elementary Communication Games.* Surrey, UK: Nelson Publishers.

These three books are all photocopiable and contain a good variety of games indexed to teach particular functions of the language. Although the terminology is British, much of the book is pictures which can be cut and pasted to make game cards, and in most cases, the lexicon is usable in all contexts.

Krashen, Stephen. 1982. *Principles and Practice in Second Language Acquisition.* Oxford: Pergamon.

No contemporary book for ESL/EFL teachers would be complete without reference to Stephen Krashen. He is considered to be one of the foremost theorists in the field today, in part for the distinctions he makes between *language learning* and *language acquisition*. This text is a must-read for teachers.

CHAPTER 9

The subject and the Subject

In this chapter, you will learn about:

- the difference between teaching subjects and Subjects
- the four skill areas which are part of language learning
- culture in the ESL/EFL classroom
- the value of real language in the classroom
- the place of healing and humour in the classroom
- the four Rs: respect, restore, review, renew
- teaching learning strategies
- Tools for Language Learning: a poster for the classroom.

Knowledge of one's subject is widely considered to be a prerequisite of teaching. What is less often considered is the knowledge of and attitude one has towards the *Subject* of learning: the student. We are teaching people first, and content second. Sometimes, we forget that and assume that it is the learner's job to learn the content, and ours to present it. I disagree with that perspective. Each of us needs to arrive at some balance between the subject and the Subject, as we plan and work through a program.

The Four Skill Areas of a Language

Traditionally, we have broken language learning down into four skill areas: listening, speaking, reading, and writing. Somewhere in the middle of all that, we also inject grammar, vocabulary, and pronunciation. These are components of the subject we call the English language. We know that for a learner to say he or she is fluent in a language, that learner needs to be able to understand what he or she hears, to speak meaningfully to another, to read what is written, and to write in a way that communicates meaning in the language.

Traditionally, most of the emphasis in teaching second languages in a foreign context has gone into reading and writing, primarily because the teachers of second languages have themselves often lacked confidence and/or skill in their own listening and speaking. Similarly, the theories of applied linguistics were also focused in that direction until more recently. Happily, that has changed as ESL has become part of the educational programming offered in our countries. Contemporary ESL programs are no longer limited to linguistic objectives. More and more, language is seen as the medium of content. Through their ESL curriculum, adult learners learn where to shop, how to find a job, and where to take further education. ESL children learn mathematics, social studies, and science in their new language.

We all know from having learned a language from birth, that the language lives first as it is heard and spoken. Many people throughout the world live out their lives never having learned to read and write and, whereas that would be difficult in North America, it is still true in many parts of the world.

Even having skill in all these four areas, however, does not mean one has *Voice*. To have Voice is to exercise one's personal power through the medium of a language. When we are teaching immigrants and refugees in particular, we have to teach with this in mind: that our job is to enable the learner to develop sufficient skill, knowledge, and confidence to exercise his or her rights and privileges in this society. We want the learner to be able to participate in what is going on around him or her in a way that gives the learner some control over his or her own life and that of his or her family.

What does this mean for the second language classroom? It means that it is as important for learners to learn how to ask questions, as it is to answer them. It is as important for them to give directions, as it is to follow them. It is as important for them to know their rights in the working world, as it is to know that it is important to come to work on time and to phone in sick if one is not feeling well. In the past, our classrooms have tended to produce passive followers rather than to encourage active leaders. There are times when most of us have to be both. Life is no different for the learners we teach.

Think about the normal classroom of your experience. Is it not usually the teacher who is asking the questions and the students who are answering them? Is it not the teacher who decides what is important to learn and what is not? Is it not the teacher who decides what is success and what is failure? I am suggesting an alternative. I am suggesting that we create classrooms in which everyone asks and everyone answers, in which everyone participates in the decisions as to what is important and what is not, and in which learners name what is success for them, which might be quite different from what we teachers would have imagined. There is no need for failure. What has been called failure in the past can easily be reborn as learning opportunities, both for the learner and for us.

In the next four chapters, we will be looking at ways of teaching the skill components of the language. For now, let us remember to put the first priority, not on *what* we are teaching, but on *whom*.

The Culture of the Language

Language and culture are as inseparable as seeing and hearing the world around us, providing we are blessed with all our senses. While it would be easy to say that language names our world, while culture defines and prescribes it, it is just not that simple. For one thing, language and culture are both imbued with values, and when we are teaching a language to someone who comes from another language and culture, I do not believe it is possible to do that without favouring values that may conflict to some degree with those of the learner.

Aspects of culture that are often considered by anthropologists include time, space, relationship with self, relationship with other, and relationship with the world. So, we teach learners that it is important to be on time, not only to work, but to social events as well. Have you ever been to an Ethiopian wedding reception? The invitation says 6:30 p.m. You and the kitchen staff are the only people there at that hour. The bride and groom arrive about 8:30, and the guests come between 9:00 and 9:30 and thereafter. North America is a continent of many cultures. Values and behaviors have to be contextualized. I was the one out of step in that context because I did not know the cultural norm in that regard. Have you ever been to a Cambodian wedding reception? I took a wrapped package as a gift. One other guest did the same. Everyone else brought an envelope of money, and gave it at the ritual moment for doing so in exchange for a cigarette.

In the classroom, whether we know it or not, we are teaching people about our cultural norms regarding time, space, and relationships. When we are conscious of differences, we talk about those differences and the consequences of non-compliance, but often we are not conscious. We simply expect things that others do not know we expect, and get angry or uncomfortable when those expectations are not met.

The learners rarely tell us when they are angry and upset or uncomfortable, because they do not want to admit to their vulnerability and lack of knowledge. Sometimes, they do not even know why they are uncomfortable or insulted, nor do they feel they have the power to do anything about it. If we want learners to feel comfortable talking about these things, we will ask real questions instead of meaningless questions (e.g., "Ask me my name," posed by the teacher who has taught the class for two weeks and been called by name that whole time). If we want genuine dialogue in the classroom, we must ourselves be genuine and we must inspire safety and trust.

I encourage people to ask *real* questions and make *real* statements when we are working, whether it is with vocabulary or grammar or whatever. Why waste our time on meaningless language when there is so much to be learned about one another and the world by using real language? A *real* question is one to which the learner does not know the answer and would genuinely like to know. A *real* statement is one that is true. It is the difference between my saying "I used to play racquetball until I hurt my knee," which is a fact that not only demonstrates a complex sentence using a modal, but also happens to be true, and "Mr. Smith can swim, but he swims poorly," which contains the same elements, but is meaningless because neither I nor anyone in the classroom has a clue who Mr. Smith is, nor cares!

Every time the teacher or a learner utters a true statement or asks a true question, our community is made stronger by the bonds of shared knowledge that are created. They understand me a little better and I understand them a little better. They understand one another better and that is more valuable than we may realize. When a class works together, caring about one another and supporting one another, everyone has a much more positive learning experience than when learners are actively competing with, ignoring, or insulting one another by making faces at someone's errors.

I watch people's faces and eyes when we are working. I try to pick up on unspoken questions, uncomfortable silences, laughter which has no apparent reason, and other body language which tells me that the "unspoken" needs some help to be spoken. I encourage people to talk about differences they see between their culture and ours. But I try not to be defensive when they are critical because, indeed, there are many aspects of our culture that not only *they* do not like, but that *I* too find wanting. It is not my job to impose cultural norms and values on anyone, but rather to inform them, to the best of my ability, what those norms and values are and what might be the consequences of choosing not to adhere to them. It is not my place to judge their decisions, although that can be very tempting when you see potential harm coming to them or to their children.

This is probably where there is the biggest difference between ESL and EFL. Students studying English as a Foreign Language, from within their own country especially, are at home in their own culture. Their being is in no serious way threatened by the study of this additional language. Immigrants and refugees, on the other hand, are trying to rebuild lives in a new country where everything seems strange, where the ground is no longer stable, and they do not know what to expect.

People want to be successful here, but it is hard to know how much to surrender and how much to hang on to, when to comply and when to stand one's ground. So many learners feel a loss of dignity and a sense of helplessness that they will never come to understand either this language or this people. They yearn to be understood, but few seem interested in understanding them because North Americans most often assume that in coming here, the other wants to become "like us." Some do; some do not. Surely, we have as much to learn from our newcomers, as they do from us.

The Person: The Place of Healing and Humour in the Classroom

I teach ESL because I have fun doing so. I like getting to know people, cultures, ideas, and events from so many different perspectives. I like the opportunity to know my own culture when it runs into the wall of one which is different. I make sure the classroom is fun, because I would not be happy being there if it were otherwise. I laugh at myself, I listen to others, I am silent when it is appropriate to be so, and I do not feel singularly responsible for everything that goes on in the classroom. I work at sharing that responsibility with everyone who is there. Like the learners, I learn vicariously. Because the differences between ways of seeing and being are so much greater in an ESL classroom than they are in other classrooms, I am afforded a kaleidoscope of opportunities to reflect upon aspects of myself which I would otherwise have few opportunities to even know exist. I tell you this not so that you will focus on yourself in the classroom—I do not—but so that you will recognize that if you are feeling happy, interested, and motivated, so will the students in your class. If you are bored, it is almost certain that the students will be more so.

While laughter is very important in teaching a second language, it is important to understand the difference between laughing *at* and laughing *with* a person. As language learners, we feel enormously vulnerable. We can feel stupid, helpless, and frustrated. In that state, we are supersensitive to criticism and allergic to anyone laughing at us. As a teacher, it is my job to create an atmosphere of lightness in the classroom, an atmosphere wherein we all expect to have fun, to laugh, to stumble, and to pick ourselves up and keep right on going. We have to shift that experience of shame to an experience of respectable persistence. Some teachers do this naturally, and know just when to be soft and when to be hard. Most of us have to work at it.

An atmosphere of lightness does not mean that serious work is not going on. Rather it means that that serious work is not going to weigh us down; it is not going to make us feel like a failure when we make mistakes or do not understand. I thank people for their questions, and I emphasize that I expect to hear the same question as many times as it takes for everyone in the class to understand the answer. I tell them that I have to hear something at least three times before I get it, and I expect that everyone is different, and that is okay.

You also get to know who can accept laughter when they say something hilarious, and who cannot. Respect those differences. Make it your job to ensure that everyone in that classroom feels respected. I have seriously misjudged learners on a couple of occasions, and I will be forever haunted by the consequences of my errors. One woman quit the class because she had thought I was laughing *at* her, when I had thought I was laughing *with* her. She and her whole family were very upset with me, but not nearly as upset as I was with myself. I cannot change what happened; I can make sure I learn from it and do not let it happen again.

Educator as Healer

Many people are very uncomfortable with the notion that educators are also healers. By that, I do not mean that we are psychologists or doctors or any other type of medical practitioner, or that we in any way substitute for the services these professionals provide. What I do mean is that most adult ESL learners are, to some extent, the walking wounded, in particular those learners who are trying to adapt to a very different language and culture. The traditional ESL classroom has failed formally, at least, to recognize this fact, and the result has been that the system finds casualties acceptable. The system says, "Some learners learn and others do not. Too bad." I cannot accept that. That may be the end result, but I can only accept that if I know I have done everything in my power to enable each and every person who enters my classroom to get everything he or she can from the experience. This means I must recognize wounds when they appear and must be prepared to work around them, with them, and through them. No one heals anyone else, but we do heal ourselves. Others can either enable that process, or add to the other's woundedness.

While I am very much a neophyte in understanding the world of energy, I recognize energy as a primary player in the ESL/EFL classroom. It is an energy which is somehow more than the energies of all those who are in the room. I am aware of the class picking up my energy when theirs flags, and of myself picking up theirs when mine flags. I am aware of some individuals who are like black holes, draining my and everyone else's energy. I am aware of activities which create high energy, and those which dispel or waste energy. I am aware of the need to consider the energies from which people have come, and to which they will go when they leave my classroom.

I know that the way I use my own energy in the classroom is important to the learners; they seem to take their cue from me. When I use a lot of energy in the classroom, it is not gone; rather, I am left with more than I had to begin with. That is the magic of a classroom in which focused energy abounds. All of us go away with energy to burn. And along with that is hope, confidence, faith, determination, accountability, and the ability to acknowledge and act responsibly towards others as we strengthen the communities in which we live. When I, as a teacher, use my energy in positive ways, I create an atmosphere in which the learner is free to relax and be who he or she is. In such an atmosphere, healing can take place.

The second book in the Voices and Visions series, *Issues, Challenges, and Alternatives in Teaching Adult ESL*, deals at greater length with the notion of educator as healer. For now, suffice it to say that it is an option we have and, along with that choice, we have to set boundaries to protect ourselves and the learners.

The Learning Environment: Respect, Restore, Review, Renew

Until a genuinely participatory classroom has been created in which every person takes accountability and responsibility for what goes on, the teacher, by nature of being the teacher, is expected to create a learning environment that works. Back in my early university days, I used to think that creating an effective learning environment meant making an attractive classroom by hanging appropriate posters, and having other interesting and relevant learning displays. (Personally, I have always thought plants were important, too.) When I began to teach ESL, I came to appreciate having a circle of chairs rather than a series of rows as a means of creating equality and closeness during communicative activities. However, as positive as those accoutrements may be, I think the learning environment is much more than the physical surroundings, and I am not undermining the importance of that aspect of environment.

I believe that a classroom environment also includes emotional, mental, and spiritual aspects. To create a desirable environment, I have identified four elements that I endeavour to keep at the forefront of my mind in the classroom. They are to respect, restore, review, and renew—the four Rs of a healthy learning environment.

Respect

I have emphasized this before, and I do apologize if I am seeming redundant, but respect is a concept I cannot emphasize enough because this quality is too often absent in many classrooms. Respect is the one experience that, above all else, language learners need to have if they are to overcome the fear of failure and embarrassment which so often accompanies language learning. Respect is not something we can fake. Either we genuinely respect the individuals we are teaching, or we do not. If we focus on what they do not know instead of what they do know and who they are, the learners will not easily feel respected because we are not seeing the whole picture. If we see our oneness with the learner, it is hard *not* to respect him or her, for we see each individual as a person, like ourselves, who is doing his or her best.

How do we demonstrate that respect? By listening, genuinely listening, and encouraging others to do likewise. By treating everyone fairly and insisting that others do likewise. By acknowledging one's effort as well as one's results. By not prying into experiences out of curiosity when those experiences are still raw and very personal. By respecting the priorities of the learners with whom we work, rather than imposing our priorities upon them. We demonstrate respect by not expecting the learners to do anything that we ourselves would feel uncomfortable doing, and by not making people feel guilty when they do not measure up to our idea of what the ideal learner is like.

You probably grew up with the Golden Rule as I did: do unto others as you would have others do unto you. That is a great rule when it applies to people in the same culture and circumstance as yourself, but it breaks down when you cross cultural lines. If you have ever formed a close relationship with anyone from another culture, you will know what I mean. Different cultures mean that we expect different things, that respect itself means different things. So, part of learning to respect those in other cultures is to become sensitive to the ways they need and like to be treated, which may be quite different in some ways from how we usually do things. It also means recognizing that what is experienced by ourselves as a personal affront, may not have been intended that way.

As an example, I have always been taught the importance of saying thank you when anyone does something for me. My children have obviously learned that from me and they get upset if I forget to say it. A good friend from another country scolded me a couple of months into our relationship for saying thank you too often. In her culture, she said, one says thank you to strangers and acquaintainces, but not to family and close friends. In close relationships, she said, one knows the other is grateful and it need not be said. For me to say it to her as often as I did was like asking her to keep her distance. How easily we judge others, I thought, without having any idea where they are coming from. Now, when students say or do things to which I am tempted to take affront, I try to ask myself if there is a cultural explanation which makes sense to them, if not to me.

Respect also means not judging, and that certainly presents a challenge because assessing results has always been part of what we do as teachers, and that borders very closely on judgment. When we have pass and fail grades, we, or someone else, has determined what is success or failure. When someone is terminated from a program of studies because she or he is not measuring up to someone's standards, that too is someone's judgment. However, this may bear little resemblance to the actual progress that a particular individual has made in conquering whatever barriers were present in his or her language learning. In this regard, I believe we must be always searching for new and more respectful ways of giving people helpful feedback on their learning, and of finding different ways to support non-traditional learners in overcoming the hurdles they experience on the path to success.

Restore

Restoration is another key component of building a positive learning environment and it is closely akin to respect. The difference lies in recognizing that, while teaching ESL learners a new language, we are also enabling them to find what many have lost. Most of our learners have experienced some measure of success and dignity in their lives. In becoming "an immigrant," however, many experience a severe loss of that sense of success and dignity.

In this instance, we need to enable learners to regain a sense of perspective, reminding them that while they may feel very inept in this new language and culture, they are still very capable, skilled individuals in their own language and culture. When they are feeling depressed about how hard it is, they need to remind themselves of what they *do* know and what they *can* do.

While having friends in the new language is definitely an asset to learning it, maintaining close ties with people in one's own community is, for many learners, an essential way of maintaining their identity and sense of who they are and who they have been. Ethnic communities which gather regularly, laugh together, dance together, discuss important issues, and help one another with day-to-day struggles, play a very important role in helping newcomers to survive the challenges of integration and adaptation to a new language and culture. Bilingual education for K-12 learners is one important support system for families who struggle with the cultural differences that children, and in particular teenagers, face in the new country. Without their ethnic communities, some individuals can and do experience mental illness, and some even commit suicide, because they find that there is no joy in life anymore.

We can support people in restoring their lost dignity by informing them about, and encouraging them to take part in, their own communities. Most people know how to locate these communities, but in instances where that community is small and these people do not yet know anyone here, they may need a little help.

It is also helpful to provide individuals with an opportunity to talk about their lives in their own country, if they want to do so, but not all are prepared to do that. When appropriate, some learners enjoy the chance to teach the class something about their people, their country, or the skill they practiced before.

It is also essential to assist individuals to make the connections they need to continue using their skills and experiences to their best advantage here. Linking learners with native-born people in their own or similar professions is much appreciated. Enabling learners to find out how to get their credentials evaluated here and how to get certification in their own occupations, are important steps in recovering from that sense of loss so many experience.

Review

It could be argued that review is purely and simply a good teaching strategy, and that is true, but I think review belongs in our section on creating an environment too because it creates a sense of security and trust. When learners think that they are only going to hear or see something once and then be expected to remember it, that creates stress for most people. Many of them become overwhelmed and give up, believing that they must be really stupid not to be able to do what is expected. Most of us need review. The secret of successful review is to make it just different enough each time to still be interesting. And for those who have understood and mastered whatever is being learned, review also has to provide an element of added complexity, such as new vocabulary, to keep those learners challenged and interested.

As I mentioned, I was trained to teach French as a Second Language. The audio-visual method they gave us translates roughly as Presentation, Explanation, Application, and Transition. We were to present a dialogue twice for the learners to listen to. Then, we explained the new structures and vocabulary in the lesson. Next, there were exercises in which the learners answered questions about the dialogue and practiced the new structures and vocabulary. Lastly, came the transition section. This was the section where the learners were expected to take the new components, use them in original dialogues, and integrate them into their existing body of French. As a learner, I found this part the scariest because I always felt that I was expected to know everything that had been taught by that point, and I did not. I was afraid to make mistakes, and so I was tempted either not to try at all, or to try things that were so simple that I knew I would get them right, which of course did not help me to advance my learning.

We need to encourage learners not to be afraid to ask the same question many times. And we need to find several ways to answer the same question, until one day, one way makes sense to the asker, and he or she has that "ah-ha" moment when it is clear, at least for the moment.

In my experience, the more relevant and meaningful the content is to the learners, the more easily they will learn. When they are experiencing learning as fun, they will learn. When they experience that what they are learning will make their lives easier, or richer, they will learn. When they have a good relationship with the teacher and with the other learners, they will learn well. And lastly, when they feel safe, when they feel that they can ask questions and no one will think they are stupid, they will ask those questions which further their own learning.

In some cultures, it would appear that review is the responsibility of the learner, not the teacher. I can remember the nightmare of trying to learn Korean at an evening class. Each night the teacher presented a vast array of new material, and no review, unless one considered a handed-in quiz on the previous week's material to be review. He was very unhappy with us because he concluded that we were not doing our homework, which, of course, most of us could not do. He expected us to behave like Korean students and study until we got it. He did not realize that we were mothers and fathers, wives and husbands, and workers who had many other responsibilities during the day. There was no way, for example, that I could learn the entire Korean alphabet in one week (how to say it and how to write it). My main difficulty with this task was that, until those symbols had meaning, as they did when they appeared in words and phrases, I had no mental hooks to hang them on. His teaching method did not conform to my learning method and, after two months of great frustration on both our parts, I dropped the class.

This is one reason why some of your learners will appear not to need review, and others will need a lot. The circumstances of their lives, and their cultural expectations about the classroom, are different.

Renew

One of the highest joys for me in teaching the second language class is the discovery that learners are learning more than a new language. In the medium of the new language, they are learning new ideas, new skills, things they never expected to learn in an ESL or EFL classroom. When learners realize this is happening and value this experience, it is like magic. The language is no longer just the object of learning but also the medium in which that learning happens. One's education continues and one's relationship to the dreaded new language is changed, as learners cease to see it as the enemy to be conquered and focus instead on what they are learning, which just happens to be *in* the new language. There is a letting go as people refocus on other learnings. The struggle now is to grasp the new ideas and connect them to their own, to express their own ideas, and claim that which makes sense in the new body of knowledge. Because it is not what they expected, the learners are often excited.

For example, when ESL learners are unemployed, finding a job is at the top of their list of priorities, even if they are in school at the time. Therefore, if they can learn things about how to find work, what employers in the new country expect of them, what their rights and responsibilities are by law, and what to do when those rights are violated, language is no longer the primary focus but rather the means of learning what they need to know. When parents are anxious to support their children in the school system, everything you can teach them which will help that process becomes important. For such parents, family literacy classes are an option. Here, they are learning to read stories to their children. Perhaps they are also learning some of the songs those children will learn in kindergarten. In that their priority is on being good parents, they are most happy learning how to support their children, but in the process, these learners too are learning.

The concept of Renew holds equally well for EFL learners. One of the greatest joys I had in working with successive groups of Korean teachers was in hearing the frequent refrain, "I came to Canada to learn English but I also find . . ," completed by a variety of learnings they had not expected. One woman found that, through journalling, she had learned a lot about herself. Another discovered that he was not alone in a rather unique hobby he enjoyed in secret. (He thought others would laugh at him if they knew he thought rocks could communicate.) Others found unexpected self-confidence through our drama activities. The program I had designed for the Korean teachers was an educational one in that they learned things which would advance, and make positive differences to, their lives.

Students I have taught through the years have expressed particular appreciation for a set of principles I teach them (e.g., accountability, truth, acknowledgement, etc.). These principles are woven into whatever context is most appropriate to a particular group. They might be defined as "Principles for Successful Employment," "Principles for Being in Charge of Your Life," or "Principles for Success in Life." The principles are almost the same in whatever context they are given, but the situations in which one learns them are different. I have always thought that the reason so many students have enjoyed these ideas is because they can apply them anywhere in their lives, not just in learning a language or finding a job.

One mother in a workplace program who was originally from Vietnam, recently told me that she was teaching her family the principles. For one thing, our discussions gave her a vocabulary to talk about the values of her culture in English, which made it easier for her to discuss them with her children, who had become more fluent in English than in Vietnamese. For another, she said she felt good to be learning something of value to offer to her children in Canada. In

Issues, Challenges, and Alternatives in Teaching Adult ESL, the second book in the Voices and Visions series, I have discussed these principles at greater length, for those who are interested.

Learning Strategies

How many of you discovered when you went to university that you had no idea how to write a term paper, to take the kind of notes that were easy to study from, or to do research? I think many of us had to learn these skills on our own, and the tragedy is that some students never did and failed as a result. Likewise, some of our learners come to class with excellent learning strategies in place for themselves, while others have no idea how to go about organizing their learning.

Part of enabling learners to get the most from their learning involves identifying who has what learning strategies, and who has none at all. Then we can build on those strategies people do have, and assist the learner who is new to formal education to develop some strategies which can work for him or her. These strategies will vary a great deal from person to person.

A person who has not had formal education before will more than likely not know what to do with the numerous papers most teachers dole out. Some learners will stuff handouts into a bag every which way, or even throw the papers away when they get home. Others will come to class with a binder, having seen their children organize materials that way. The learner new to formal education will be forever grateful to the teacher who takes time to help him or her set up a system for organizing materials: three-ring binder, dividers and notepaper, notebooks and memo pad for assignments. Work with such learners daily until they are able to use the system and, whatever you do, do not overload them with more paper than they can handle. That is the most frequent complaint I have heard from ESL learners.

Teach learners to keep personal vocabulary and spelling lists in their books, and to have a special place to make notes of important things they do not want to forget. Three-hole punch your handouts so that they are easy for students to put into their books. Give them some different ideas as to how to learn new vocabulary. One student of mine made cards for new words and posted them in her kitchen where she worked with them as she cooked and then changed to a new set when she had learned the old one. She created that system and it worked very well for her. Others keep personal lists in the back of their binders and study them in the evening.

Some learners do not learn well from paper, but learn wonderfully from sound. They are called *auditory learners*. Such learners may learn more from the soap operas on TV than they do in a classroom, depending on the kinds of activities available to them in that classroom. If a learner seems to learn well auditorially, see that he or she has tapes to listen to in class and at home. Encourage such learners to listen to the radio and watch TV.

Give the learners different strategies for different levels in their learning. In the beginning, learners listen only for meaning and the anxious ones will stop listening when they have understood one or two key words, which may leave them misunderstanding the whole communication. Teach them to listen for more and more of a communication as they gain in skill and to ask questions of clarification when they are unsure.

Post a poster in your classroom with appropriate questions that put learners in charge of their own learning:

Tools for Learning English

What does _____ mean?
I don't understand. Please say that again.
What is this?
What is that?
What are these?
What are those?
How do you say this word?
How do you spell _____?
What is he doing?
What is she doing?
What are they doing?

A more advanced class might have a poster reading something like this:

Tools for Clarification

Is it correct to say _____ in English?
I think I understand. Do you mean that you want me to
_____?
What is the difference between _____ and _____? They seem to mean the same thing to me.
Would you mind repeating that please? I want to make sure I understand.
Do you know a synonym for _____?
What is the correct pronunciation of _____?
Is it better to say _____ or _____?

By encouraging students to ask questions such as those suggested in the two posters on page 107, we are enabling students to ask for what they need. This is one of the best learning strategies I know. In using these posters, point to them when someone is struggling to understand something or is trying to ask a question, and help the students to get into the habit of using such questions often and correctly. This way, they will use them when they are in the community as well. If we simply see a question on someone's face and answer it before it is asked, that may be very welcome to the learner in that moment, but we are depriving the learner of the opportunity to develop the question skills he or she needs to be an independent learner.

I have found that it is wise to respect the strategies that people come with as much as that is possible in a diverse group of people. In my experience, Russians, Slavs, and Poles want dictations, spelling tests, grammar exercises, and tests. They are prepared to study hard for these activities, and they find that this is a system that works well for them. Whereas I might think that what they really need are communicative activities which will make them more comfortable in listening and speaking situations, I need to honour what this group of learners think they need. In return, they will generally give me a fair amount of latitude in trying new things with them. Such students will have little respect for a teacher who continually engages them in endless conversations, because they do not see that as a suitably structured course of teaching and learning.

A common technique in North American classrooms for enhancing the talk time that an individual gets is pair work and small group work. Some students welcome this type of work, and others feel their time is being wasted. They only want to listen to the *teacher* talk because, in their eyes, only the teacher has correct pronunciation and grammar. While I can see where such learners are coming from, I also teach them that, in this country, people speak with many accents and have different ways of speaking, and we have to get used to understanding and responding to all of them. I explain why I am doing what I am doing and, if they really do not like it, then I do something different. I also take time to build a sense of community in the classroom wherever that is possible. If there are large numbers of learners who are simply not open to that way of thinking, this can be difficult. However, I find it very desirable to work towards a feeling of community in the classroom, because then we are all teachers and we are all learners.

I believe there is a role for pair work in the EFL classroom too. Although learners from one native language will tend to reinforce one another's error patterns, if good material is given, pair work can give them the time to think through and practice what they are "learning in the class." Effective use of pair work in this situation, however, means the teacher must structure the activity carefully so that learners are not confronted with tasks beyond their ability.

Questions to Think about and Discuss

1. What do you remember most about Grade 3—the subjects you studied that year, or the teacher and how you felt about yourself in her presence? What do you think your students will remember about your classes 20 years from now? What do you want them to remember?

2. In your EFL class, you have a young man who is not well liked by his peers. He seems lonely and is visibly left out of conversations and extra-curricular activities. How might you use the English language curriculum as a way of showing off his strengths and of enabling the class as a whole to see the value of everyone belonging to a community of learners?

3. Imagine that you are teaching a workplace English class for eight sewing machine operators. You have heard the supervisors talking about Cheng, a newer worker who seems to have plateaued before getting up to the speed of the rest of her team. You know she really needs this job and are afraid that if she doesn't make a real effort, she might lose the job. Without betraying the confidence of the supervisor, how might you make her aware of the need to compare her output with that of her coworkers?

4. Imagine that in your class of refugees from four different countries, you have a young woman who tried to commit suicide in her country because she thought the soldiers were going to rape her. She took rat poison, which left her partially deaf and somewhat impaired mentally. There are no special education classes in the community for ESL learners, so she is in your class. She is very frustrated by her condition and loses her temper easily in the classroom. How can you attend to her needs while still addressing the needs of the other students?

CHAPTER 10

Teaching Listening, Speaking, and Pronunciation

In this chapter, you will learn about:

- principles for teaching listening and speaking
- responding (or not responding) to errors
- the priority of meaning
- listening for different things
- cloze exercises
- minimal pair exercises
- stress and intonation
- techniques for teaching speaking
- Medicine Bag stories
- making theatre in the classroom
- teaching pronunciation.

The biggest frustration I hear about from second language learners is that they do not understand what other people are saying. The second common frustration is that other people do not understand them and they get very tired of hearing, "Pardon me?"[1] These frustrations have been expressed by ESL learners who have been studying the language either for years of part-time work and study or after months of full-time study. Why is it that some people, who can with relative ease read everyday material, do grammar homework, and write what they need to write,

---

1 In a few cases, I suspect that the listener needs to take more responsibility for trying to understand a second language speaker. Some learners whom I have no difficulty whatsoever in understanding relate stories from the workplace or community of their listeners appearing to reject the words of people from a particular country or race. If we have done our jobs in availing learners of the opportunity to learn good listening and speaking skills, and we believe they have done so, it might be good to raise this subject, in class, of other possible reasons why people "do not understand."

have such difficulty with listening and speaking—the two skills which, in the natural order of things, come prior to reading and writing? This is the question we need to ask ourselves as educators. Could it be that we need to spend more time on these areas? Could it be that we need to find and/or create better ways of enabling people to learn these skills?

Many learners also struggle with pronunciation. Some learners have actually managed to acquire significant vocabulary and a sound working knowledge of the grammar, but still appear to native speakers to "need more English." The barriers created by significant problems with pronunciation prevent people from finding and keeping good jobs, from using their skills and experience to build financially secure lives in this country, and from communicating comfortably with others.

Principles for Teaching and Learning Listening and Speaking

1. While the beginning learner can find it helpful to listen to slowly spoken, clearly articulated speech, the progressing learner needs to learn to hear all kinds of speech: slow and fast, idiomatic and stripped down, educated and uneducated, accented and unaccented English. *Give learners a variety of listening and speaking experiences with diverse speakers of the language.* Working with more than one teacher is a start. Bringing in volunteers and frequent visitors is an asset. Taking students on field trips where they have to listen to others and ask questions to get information is helpful. Bringing in tapes of various radio and TV programs to listen to provides that diversity also. (This may not be possible in an EFL setting, but perhaps you have other alternatives: videotapes of English TV programs or movies, tapes made by friends back home, or recorded music.)

2. *Speak naturally.* New teachers may be forgiven for speaking loudly as if the learner were deaf, or for leaving out function words (e.g., the, some, have, did etc.) to simplify structures so that learners may more easily grasp the meaning. Good teachers do not do this. A good rule of thumb for me is, "Never say to a learner anything you could not imagine yourself saying to a native speaker." (This does not mean that you might not say it more slowly and clearly to a learner.)

   We do a disservice to learners if we teach them a baby-talk version of English just to make their initial understanding easier. More teachers than not have taught their students to say, "Repeat please" when they do not understand. A native-born English speaker would say, "Would you repeat that, please?" or "Sorry, I didn't catch that. Could you say it again, please." Whereas "Repeat please" works well in the classroom, what impression does it create in the community when people hear someone speaking in two- to five-word sound bytes? Learners trust their teachers to teach them what is right. They feel betrayed to learn later than they have been taught a form of the language that native speakers would never use.

Ironically, teachers often teach students to answer in full sentences when a native English speaker would answer in a phrase. For example, if I were to ask you, "What is your favourite kind of food?" You might answer, "Vietnamese." And yet, teachers expect their students to say, "My favourite kind of food is Vietnamese." They do this because it is a way of getting their students to practise saying the full structure, but there are other more appropriate ways to do that such as through dialogues.

3. *When you slow down or break down natural speech so that a learner can focus on one sound or word in order to understand it or say it, be sure you recontextualize that back into natural speech before going on.* Stress and intonation patterns change when we say words alone or when we emphasize something. If we do not recontextualize the point into natural speech, the learner has learned a stress and intonation pattern that only works if the word or phrase is being emphasized and does not work in regular speech.

Here's an example of what I mean. An Arabic speaker has trouble distinguishing between the sounds /p/ and /b/. She does not hear the difference and therefore makes mistakes in pronouncing these sounds as initial consonants. She is trying to ask her doctor for medication and says, "May I have a bill, please?" He says, "Oh, the nurse at the front will take care of that." She says "Thank you" and leaves, wondering why the nurse will not give her the paper she needs to get medication at the drugstore. So, as a teacher hearing this story, I want to remove the word < bill > from her utterance and teach her to say < pill >. I might do some minimal pair work (which is explained later) in which she learns to say < pill > correctly as an isolated word. When she has mastered both hearing and pronouncing these two sounds, I want to be sure to do the dialogue again. Better yet, I would prefer to teach her the word < prescription > which, if she pronounces as < brescription > will still be understood without confusion.

4. *Wherever possible, make real statements and ask real questions.* In our effort to focus on structure or pronunciation while we are teaching, we often forget that language is about meaning first. We have students answering questions that have no bearing on anything important, and we ask them to make up questions to which they either know the answer or could not care less about. We can, however, accomplish the task and, at the same time, be learning new things and enabling learners to do likewise. That is infinitely more interesting and valuable than practicing with artificial language.

For example, students are practicing new vocabulary. The word is "embarrassed." Which of the following sentences is more interesting to the student, to the class, and to you?

> A. Mr. Johnson was embarrassed when he forgot to pay for the cigarettes and got caught.
> B. I felt embarrassed when the alarm went off in the store as I was leaving with my new dress. I do not understand what happened.

No one has any idea who Mr. Johnson is, so they have no emotion one way or the other about this incident. When Marta, in Example B above, expresses her embarrassment at what happened in the store, not only does she have everyone's sympathy as the learners identify with her plight, but we also have an opportunity to explain how stores are working to prevent shoplifting and how we ourselves must watch to see that the little white security tags are removed when we purchase clothing. This can lead to discussions on personal honesty, the high cost of consumer goods, and various other topics, all of which just happen to be under discussion in English. The learners are learning so much more than just grammar and vocabulary. They are learning the culture, the challenges of living here, and ways to protect themselves from needless embarrassment. And, of course, they are also learning to speak and to listen.

As a teacher, I also want to give real examples to model this expectation of real language. Suppose our word is "incredible." I might say, "Mesfin, your wife says you have an incredible singing voice. Is this true?" The class now has a context for the word we are learning. They now know something about Mesfin they did not know before, and Mesfin feels respected for a gift he has, which, until that moment, no one knew about. By using real language in the classroom, we are teaching in a context of respect which says, "I am interested in you and what you think. I trust you with what I think."

Because learners are choosing to talk about topics that have meaning in their lives, they are learning language they can use to talk about their lives and to solve everyday problems they encounter in the real world. For example, as we practice various words which express emotion, Mrs. Thapar, an older learner, says, "I feel very upset my son no money me. I need little money live. I want buy grandchildren toy, candy. I buy stamps letters my sister India. No money, no letters." Through her real example, the whole class is exposed to an area we know as *elder abuse*, which is very common in some immigrant families. Parents have been sponsored to take care of grandchildren for working parents, and often that works out well for everyone. But in some cases, these grandparents feel like slaves. At that moment, Mrs. Thapar's well-being takes priority over the missing articles, verbs, and conjunctions in her utterance. She needs to know that there are choices if she chooses to exercise them.[2] This is the real curriculum of that classroom.

5. *In the beginning, keep it short and simple.* Beginning learners are easily overwhelmed by the sheer volume of discourse. They need to experience success early on if they are to continue to take the risk of embarrassment which so often accompanies language learning.

6. *Don't expect the same responses from all students.* Everyone is at a different place in his or her learning. Some learners are being successful if they can follow a polite command, while others are capable of composing elaborate descriptions.

7. *Let the learners decide when they are ready to speak. Do not force anyone to do what they do not yet feel comfortable doing.*

8. *Never laugh at mistakes unless that individual is already laughing, or you know that the individual appreciates how funny it can be when we are learning a new language.* Humiliation can be the single greatest barrier to learning a language, and we have to be very careful that we treat serious effort with respect and point out errors respectfully.

9. *Spend as much time teaching listening and speaking as you do teaching reading and writing.* We frequently err in thinking we are teaching listening and speaking when, in fact, we are really still teaching reading and writing. For example, if we give out written dialogues that people read and answer written questions about, this is reading and writing, not speaking and listening. Only if the learners have a chance to work with those dialogues aloud, without paper, until they are comfortable with the ideas in them, can we say these activities are about listening and speaking.

10. *Listen first to the content of what a person is saying rather than to how technically correct it is.* If a learner thinks that you are more interested in correcting her than you are in communicating with her, she will shut down quickly.

11. *Err on the side of caution in deciding whether to correct people or simply respond to them.* When a person is learning and making a lot of errors, he might be able to handle one kind of correction, the verb tense, for example, knowing that he will be more easily understood if he uses that correctly. But if you correct six different errors in one sentence, he is not

---

2 If she is not ready to talk about her personal situation, it may be inappropriate to do so, but she deserves the opportunity to know there are options.

likely to be able to hold all that in his head and will end up learning nothing from your corrections and feeling quite frustrated as well.

12.   *When a learner does want correction, teach her to stick with the correction until she understands it, and then to repeat the utterance using the correction.* Learners often listen to a correction and then dive right back into what they were saying as if the correction were an interruption. It may well have been just that. If a learner does this consistently, I will either stop making corrections, or I will point out to the learner that it seems to be very distracting for her if I interrupt with corrections. I then ask if she would prefer that I not do so. Some learners will say they want corrections when, in fact, their actions tell you they cannot handle them. There are ways of dealing with repeated errors other than by interrupting someone. (See the Ooops Sheets exercise in Chapter 12. This activity can also be done with verbal errors.)

Learning to Listen

The first thing a learner will do in learning the language is try to derive meaning from what is heard. Initially, this means grasping at the first recognizable word or phrase and letting that signal, along with body language, reveal the meaning of the entire utterance. Most learners gradually progress from this guessing stage to learning to listen to the whole of what is said to ensure that the derived meaning is the intended meaning. However, a few people, especially those who are very nervous and self-conscious about their learning, will get stuck in this earlier pattern and experience a lot of misunderstandings in their listening. It is helpful to the teacher to understand what is going on in a learner's mind in the activity of listening to a second language. If you have learned a second language yourself and have found yourself in the situation of trying to understand a native speaker when your vocabulary is minimal, this will be a helpful experience in understanding how the learner experiences this challenging time.

The first thing we must teach people to do is ask questions. "Would you repeat that, please?" "Could you say that again, please?" "What does _____ mean?" These expressions will help the learner to be accountable in coming to understand spoken English.

Secondly, we need to become conscious ourselves that we listen for different things. We listen first for meaning, for the main idea of the utterance. We also listen for details, facts, or information in the utterance. At the same time, we hear tone of voice, which expresses meanings that may not be in the words. Is the speaker happy with us, mad at us, or frustrated with us? For the learner, the tone is often heard before the words themselves. This is helpful when a speaker is very expressive, unless the meaning of the tone and/or body language is very different culturally than similar tones or gestures in the first language. When I am listening to people speak Chinese, I often have the feeling that the speakers are angry, but they tell me that they are not angry, just expressive. A person may sound abrupt just because of his or her accent and not because of any emotion behind the voice. Usually, however, body language and tone tell us a great deal when we are learning a language, and the listener usually picks up those clues readily.

We can also encourage learners to listen with the heart as well as the head. I have always been amazed when I have travelled to other countries where I spoke little or none of the language, to experience understanding between myself and the old women of the culture. They understood no English, and yet I felt they were understanding me, and vice versa. I experienced enormous empathy from these older women and felt that their intent to understand me, along with my intent to be understood, somehow transcended the linguistic tools we normally suppose to enable communication. I now believe that they were listening to me with their hearts, as I was to them. Our sense of connectedness as women was greater than our linguistic and cultural differences. I would be interested to learn if men have experienced this phenomenon in their travels.

We can encourage learners to listen with their hearts, first of all, by building their confidence and their expectation that they will under-stand and that they can learn, and are learning. If we can ourselves laugh at our mistakes and hapless efforts to learn a few words of the other's language, perhaps the learners will feel comfortable seeing that it is the *situation* which is funny and not the *person*, since feeling laughed at can be very discouraging.

Techniques for Teaching Listening

1. Tapes or passages read aloud

The learner can listen to these materials more than once for different purposes (e.g., to pick up or listen for the main idea, particular details, inference, and/or tone).

2. Dictations

Learners often enjoy short dictations of material they have studied because, in order to be able to write something, they have to first be able to hear it. This could be a list of words or it could be short sentences.

3. Cloze exercises

There are several kinds of cloze exercises one can do. The traditional cloze consists of a reading which has every 5th word whited out and a blank left for the learner to fill in the word as he or she listens to the tape. One can also develop cloze exercises for particular purposes, such as learning to hear articles, verb forms, or singular and plural nouns. This is a wonderful diagnostic tool as well because, as with dictations, you become very conscious of what people can and cannot hear and of what they do and do not know.

4. Minimal pair exercises

When I discover that learners cannot spell or pronounce something, I look first to see if they can hear it, and often they cannot. So I create instant mini-exercises of words on the board using the two sounds that are confusing. I number each word so that a learner can tell me, using the number, what I am saying.

Supposing I have some Amharic speakers who cannot hear the /ɛ/ in < bet >. Sometimes they think I am saying < bat > and sometimes < bit >. I will find all the simple words I can which are the same except for the vowels, and I will list them as follows:

	A /æ/	B /ɛ/	C /ɪ/
1	bat	bet	bit
2	mat	met	mitt
3	gnat	net	knit
4	brat	Brett	Brit.

I will then read a whole row aloud and then choose one word. For example, "In Row 1, 'bat.' Am I saying A, B, or C?" They will then guess, either as a whole class or as individuals. I generally let the whole group answer first and then, as they gain confidence, I ask individuals to try until everyone can hear the sound.

You will notice that in this exercise I use real words and not made-up syllables. I think that language learning is confusing enough without making up meaningless words to teach people. Mix the order up in choosing which word to ask so that the learners do not automatically guess based on which one you said last time. Note: Be sure to keep your intonation the same for each word. Usually, when we are reading lists, our voice rises for all but the last word (e.g., bát, bét, bìt.) If you do this, they will pick that up very quickly and you may think they are hearing the vowel when, in fact, they are hearing only your stress differential.

5. Real-life listening materials

Tape the morning news from the radio. This way the learners are listening to current events which are much more interesting to listen to than tapes that were made in a different country five years earlier.

Tape the recording from someone's answering machine or from a commercial voice mail message. Particularly challenging are the government messages that tell you to choose which number to push to find the service you want. By providing these real-life listening materials, not only are students practising their listening skills, but they are becoming familiar with a phone system they may need to use to get information about such topics as immigration, labour standards, and health and safety. Many telephone companies have numbers you can call to hear recorded messages with information about upcoming recreational events, news stories or various other information of interest to their customers. If you are planning to teach overseas, it might be a good idea to prepare beforehand real-life tapes of news broadcasts, recorded messages, or music.

6. Stress and intonation exercises

You can make up these kinds of exercises yourself or use any of the commercial materials available. It is important to know that learners are learning several different skills when they are learning to listen. Whereas distinguishing between various vowels or consonants teaches them that particular skill, learners must also learn the meanings transmitted by stress and by intonation. For example, < the white house > is pronounced very differently than < the White House >. Likewise, < greenhouse > is different from < green house >. These differences in meaning are only recognizable when the stress is said correctly.

Changes in intonation can change a statement into a question. Students of theatre will be familiar with the drills of changing meaning by changing stress and intonation, as illustrated below.

> The woman called my náme. (a statement of fact)
>
> Thé woman called my name. (This woman is of great importance and everyone knows who she is.)
>
> The wóman called my name. (as opposed to the man)
>
> The wóman called my náme? (as opposed to the man whom I would have expected to call my name.)
>
> The woman cálled my name. (I am justified in standing up because the woman did call my name after all.)
>
> The woman called mý name. (She did not call yours.)
>
> The woman called mý náme? (I can't imagine why she would have called my name.)
>
> The wóman called my náme. (I am surprised. I did not know she knew my name.)

7. Rapid speech exercises

Learners eventually need to be able to learn how to hear words whose sounds are pronounced very differently in the context of rapid discourse than when they are pronounced as individual words. Here are two examples:

- The < the > in "Give me the book" is very different from the word < the > when it is pronounced by itself.

- < want to > pronounced alone is very different from < want to > as we hear it when someone says, "Do you wanna come too?"

8 Listening for distinction in meaning between homonyms

Homonyms are words that sound the same or are spelled the same, but have different meanings. How does a new learner learn to hear the difference between < to >, < too >, and < two >?

- < To > is followed by a place (e.g., to the bank, to the store) or a person (e.g., to me, to him, to the man in the black suit.)
- < Too > is usually followed either by "much" or "many," or by an adjective (e.g., too hot, too cold, too heavy.)
- < Two > tells us *how many,* as in two dollars, or two pieces of pie.

With practice, understanding how these three words are used will become automatic but, in the beginning, it can be confusing. Analytical students will appreciate an explanation such as the following, together with examples:

```
To + |place  |
     |person |
Too + |much    |
      |many    |
      |adjective|
Two + noun + plural
```

Words like < here > and < hear >; < bear > and < bare >; < their >, < they're > and < there >; < whose > and < who's >; and many others can be very confusing to beginning learners whose logic tells them that if it sounds the same, it must be the same.

Part of learning to listen is learning to listen for the position a word takes in a clause and its relationship to other parts of that clause. Just as we saw with the < to >, < too >, and < two > example given above, so can each of the other words be distinguished by their function and position in relation to the rest of the sentence or clause. Learners who have some basic knowledge of grammar in any language will find it helpful to have this explained to them in these terms. The chart below shows how we could explain one set of homonyms, < here > and < hear >.

What is the difference between < here > and < hear >?
Here tells us where something or someone is. (It is an adverb.)
Please put the bag *here.*
Hear is a verb, which can be expressed in the present, past, or future.
I *hear* beautiful music. I *heard* it last night, and I hope I will *hear* it tomorrow, too.

Learning to Speak

Just as learning to listen involves several skills, so does learning to speak. The speaker must be conscious of more than the articulation of meaningful sounds. Just as we focused on those different areas in teaching listening, we must also do so in teaching speaking.

There are two personal traits that I believe are essential in becoming a fluent speaker of a language. The first is self-confidence, and the second is determination or perseverance. Confidence enables a person to learn by trial and error, without losing hope and feeling like a failure. We need to assess our classroom activities with the knowledge of which ones are likely to inspire confidence, and which ones may cause the learners to lose that confidence.

Perseverance is what keeps us going after we have learned to function in a language. Many learners stop when they have attained that functional level of competence. They do not care about correctness as long as they can understand and be understood with minimal difficulty. Few are the learners who have sufficient pride and determination to continue their learning until it is nearly native-speaker-like in quality. No one can expect to learn a language in a few months or a year. (To survive in it, yes, but to be really good at it, no.) In addition, individuals have very different rates and styles of learning, but what they have in common is the need to feel good about themselves, in spite of making errors.

Techniques for Learning to Speak

Several of the techniques in Chapter 8, the activities chapter, are very useful for teaching speaking: role-plays, dialogues, and problem-posing, for example. Please see that chapter if you have not done so already. Here are some other activities you might try:

1. One-Minute Speeches (and later two- and three-minute speeches)

In that practice makes perfect, the more opportunities one has to speak, the more confidence one builds in doing so. The one-minute speeches are intended to get people past the point of translating and editing everything they say, and encourage them to simply get the meanings out there without hesitation.

To do this activity, I prepare a set of index cards with a word or phrase printed on it (e.g., men, women, cooking, computers, holidays, work, etc.). Students can draw these topics randomly and talk about whatever is on the card or, if they are really uncomfortable with a topic, they can draw a second card or trade with someone. In addition, I tell them that it does not matter what they say, as long as they keep talking. So, a learner could spend the whole minute talking about why he or she does not want to talk about his or her topic, or why it is difficult to speak for one minute.

Someone is given the task of keeping the time, and no one is forced to do this until he or she is ready to do so. Rule: We all acknowledge the speaker with clapping when he or she is finished, but give no other reaction such as laughing, or asking questions, or adding our own stories. This is very important if people are to feel safe doing this activity, and to feel that the time is theirs alone, without interference.

I do not correct people. What I may do if the learners have done the exercise many times and are no longer paying attention to me, is to make notes as to the kinds of errors an individual is making most often so that I can later find ways of enabling the individual to address those gaps. (In the beginning, when learners speak, they watch the teacher for signs as to whether they are speaking correctly or not. I just listen, smile, and give no reaction to the content of what they are saying. I do not take notes at that point, because it would interfere with their speaking.)

2. Talking Stick

In some First Nations traditions, a talking stick is used to ensure that each member of the community gets equal time to talk about a community concern without domination by a few strong individuals in the group. In such traditions, the talking stick will be an artifact that has been made in the community, and has a history of problem-solving and group process behind it. The object is respected, and no one speaks out of turn as it is passed round the circle.

I originally used a talking stick in conflict resolution situations where emotions were running high, but I have since used a number of variations of the concept for different purposes. If you have time to make an artistic symbol of some kind for the class, perhaps a stick with everyone's name or symbol on it, fine. If you need something in a hurry, you can use a set of keys, or some other symbol that can be passed around the circle, to indicate that only the person with the symbol can speak, and that includes you.

If a person does not want to speak to an issue, he or she can simply pass the stick, or the keys, to the next person. If people are dying to speak again, they can wait until the stick comes their way a second or third time. There is no limit to the length of time a person can speak, as long as he or she does not speak outside his or her turn to do so, and in consideration of any other time limitations such as the length of the class. (For more information about the technique, see Smillie and Murphy in the bibliography at the end of the chapter.)

3. Medicine Bag Stories

Using Medicine Bag Stories has been one of my favourite activities for a number of reasons, only one of which is getting people to speak. Stories are a universal element in our life experience. Our lives, if you stop to think about it, are webs of stories joined together by the connections we make among them. People love to hear stories and they love to tell stories. I have been amazed at how fluent were the stories of learners whom I thought were severely limited in their language skills. They were motivated to share something with the group, and they did!

There are many ways to do this activity. I most often prepare a small duffel bag with a number of different objects from my home in it. I include things symbolic of childhood, marriage, recreation, household, and whatever else comes into my head. In the classroom, we form a circle with the bag in the centre, and we make a pact to hold in the circle that which is said in the circle. (No one goes outside and talks about what people have said.) I take this promise very seriously and ensure that others do as well.

Then, the bag is emptied onto a cloth in the centre of the room. I invite people to look at all the objects until one thing calls out to them to pick it up. They need not understand why; they just are more attracted to that object than to the others. Once an object is picked up, it is gone, and one must choose another. When everyone has an object, we begin.

I used to insist that anyone who listened also spoke but, in hindsight, I think it is better to let some learners pass. If people are not ready to tell a story and feel pressured to do so, it can be destructive. Anyone can begin with their story. If no one else wants to, I do. Sometimes, the stories are very funny; sometimes they are very sad. Almost always, they draw the group more closely together as they motivate people to speak and to listen.

Here is a story told by one Filipina woman whose English we had thought was very limited. She had seldom spoken.

> I take nice blue candle (said with tears in her eyes). I remember my country. Japanese in our country. No good. Everyone hard time. Husband—Japanese take, go work, carry heavy things. Husband very small. He fall down. They hit. He get up and he go. One day, soldiers take husband. Nighttime come, no husband. Take candle. Put in window—he find house. Sixty nights, candle, window. One night, he come. Blue candle, I remember.

As we listened to her story, we all had tears in our eyes (and yes, her husband did come home).

Not all the stories are this touching, but many are. I believe that people use the story circles to heal themselves when they are ready. Not everyone is willing to share such poignant stories of their lives with others, but I have found that when one shares something significant, it tends to lead others to do so. As long as no one feels pressured and as long as there are no questions, I see no problem. Some teachers are very uncomfortable with this kind of an exercise—either because they feel unprepared to deal with the depth of emotion it can evoke or because they consider it inappropriate to have that kind of emotion in the classroom. As with any activity, do not use it if you are not entirely comfortable with it. And if you do use it, follow the rules: invitation and confidentiality.

Others teachers have the students bring an object from home to talk about. This is a good way of sharing cultural differences and artifacts, but because the element of intuitive connection is lost when the learners have chosen the objects about which they will speak, you will not usually get the depth of story you did when the objects were unknown prior to the exercise. (Consult Smillie and Murphy, listed in the bibliography at the end of the chapter, to get more information about this type of activity.)

4. Presentations

At the late-beginner stage and up, students can do small presentations for the rest of the class where they either teach us about something they know well (e.g., their country, their job, a hobby or interest), or where they research something about the new community that will be of interest to everyone. It is good to have time guidelines for this activity so that no one who is passionate about his or her subject can bore everyone else. The key to success here lies in giving people choices, and in not doing the activity until there is a good spirit of community within the group, so that people are not only tolerant, but appreciative, of what one another contributes to the group. Because meaning is the priority, I will sometimes solicit bilingual help from classmates as the presenters need it.

5. Intermediate Taping Exercise

This particular exercise is a very time-consuming activity for intermediate-level learners, and especially for the teacher. But it is very useful if your object is to enable learners to become conscious of the errors they make in speaking. This exercise has several steps to it.

- *Step 1*: Students are paired off with someone who preferably does not speak the same language. (This ensures that the kinds of errors each learner makes are likely to be different and, therefore, more visible to the partner.)
- *Step 2*: Students are given a tape recorder and asked to have a conversation for no more than three minutes, or five minutes, or less if you think it prudent. They are instructed to try to give one another equal talking time. I often give a topic, but tell them they can choose another if they wish. For example, "Discuss your first impressions of this country when you arrived here."
- *Step 3*: After taping the conversation, both learners transcribe it, either separately or together. It is important that they write exactly what they have said, even when they are aware that they have made errors. Decide ahead of time. If the learners have a cassette recorder at home, it is easiest to assign this as homework or, if they are doing it together, the learners can do it in class time.

- *Step 4*: The learners are asked to circle any errors they see and then to make, in a different color of ink, any corrections they think are necessary. Next, they hand in the corrected transcript together with the original tape.
- *Step 5*: The teacher listens to the tape to ensure that the learners have transcribed and corrected it accurately. The teacher makes any additional corrections. (Sometimes, the students hear their errors when they first listen to the tape and, rather than transcribing them, they just make the corrections on the transcript. Where I see this happening, I mention to the students that they know the correct forms, but are not using them in their speaking. In this way, they can learn to work on self-editing their speech.)
- *Step 6*: The students rewrite the corrected version and select their priorities for working on the correction of habitual error patterns.
- *Step 7*: The students read the corrected version into the tape.

Step 7 is probably the most valuable as it is hard for people to read correctly what they have tended to say incorrectly. The whole class listens to the corrected version. The learners become aware of their own error patterns in this exercise, and this is helpful in setting priorities for the work they want to do to improve their language skills.

Because this activity is time-consuming, I do not usually do the whole class at once, but spread the activity over a two- to three-week period so I can handle the corrections. If you are fortunate enough to have a good educational assistant working in your program, or a capable volunteer, you might want to ask for their help with this project.

6. Making Theatre

Making theatre is a wonderfully fun activity which can be totally engaging of everyone in the class *if* you as the teacher are comfortable with it. It is not for everyone. I have had periods in my life where this worked very well for me, and other periods where I just was not in that space. It requires confidence on the part of the teacher, a high level of energy and focus, and a sense of fun and drama. As a medium for learning, this technique has a lot of possibilities, not only for language learning, but for giving voice to the other challenges of being in a new land: racism, integration, finding employment, working in culturally different situations, and resolving family tensions.

I have also used this a lot with the TEFL work I have done and found it surprisingly successful. This was largely due to the fact that the teachers with whom I was working did not know one another in their own country, and did not mind taking the risk of making fools of themselves in an environment that they knew would not affect them in any way in the future. In general, the more fun people are having with their learning, the more relaxed and engaged they are and the more they learn.

Theatre can be simple or elaborate. It can be done for the class only or for presentation to others. My only suggestion is that you not be presumptuous in diving right into this. Many of us are not comfortable with our bodies and need to ease into activities that call upon alternative styles of learning. We have to know it is safe.

I use *metaphor sculptures* as a technique for getting more in touch with our bodies and as a way of knowing, learning, and communicating. For this activity, we stand in a circle, and each person comes up with a metaphor that expresses how he or she feels at that moment. A learner who is tired, for example, might say, "I feel like a piece of cooked spaghetti." Someone who is overstimulated might say, "I feel like a balloon about to burst." The learners are normally very creative and once the ball gets rolling, there is no shortage of images, although it may take a few examples before they understand the "I feel like a _____" model. (One man said, "I feel like a hot person." This was no metaphor as the room was very hot, so we helped him to find a metaphor to say the same thing.)

The second step in the metaphor sculpture is to come up with a bodily sculpture to go with the words. A sculpture is a held body position. This activity by itself is a good evaluation tool to use at the end of a day to see how people are doing with what is going on. If everyone has metaphors of exhaustion and confusion, you will know that a change of pace is in order. If everyone has metaphors of joy and excitement, you will know you are on the right track.

When people are comfortable with this kind of work, they can then do group sculptures to explore experiences such as unemployment, being a newly arrived immigrant, racism, family violence, the first day in a new language, and other issues with which they can identify. In a group sculpture, one person starts with a position illustrative of some aspect of that experience and others join in, either enhancing that person's expression or creating some new aspect themselves. When the whole group is involved, each person takes time to go and inspect the whole, while the teacher holds that person's position until he or she comes back. You can then break for discussion. If you want to use this activity to explore solutions to problems, you can take it further. This technique is discussed further in the chapter on Participatory Education in the second book of the Voices and Visions series.

Teaching Pronunciation

If you have taken any linguistics courses, you will have learned a good set of *phonemes* to transcribe English orthography into its component sounds. Phonemes are minimal sound units in a given language (e.g., the sound of /n/, /t/, and /d/ as in < pen >, < pot >, and < pad >). Literacy-level ESL students may get very confused with a second set of symbols, but educated ESL/EFL learners often find it helpful to have symbols to write down the sounds of English because, unlike many of their languages, English is far from phonetic due to the many sources from which our words derive. Dictionaries use symbols, to denote various sounds, and you may wish to teach the class the same symbols that are in their dictionaries or, if they all have personal dictionaries which are different, you may wish to teach your own symbols. Appendix 3 of this book gives a complete set of common symbols for English consonants and vowels.

I only use phonemics when students have trouble hearing the differences in words. By my making the problem visual, many learners are able to persevere until they can hear the difference. Here is an example of what I might do:

bat	/bæt/
bit	/bɪt/
beet	/biyt/
bet	/bɛt/
bite	/bæyt/
bought	/bat/

When you use phonemics, teach the students that while the letters of English words may produce different sounds depending on the word, phonemics are consistent. One phoneme they need to learn is the *schwa*, /ə/, which represents the most commonly used vowel in English. It appears when a vowel is in the weak stressed position. For example, the sound of the "e" in the second syllable of the word "table"—/téybəl/.

Pronunciation Contrasts in English by Nilsen and Nilsen is a useful text to consult when a student needs to work on hearing the difference between two sounds. It is also a good teacher reference because each set of exercises comes with a list of the language groupings likely to have difficulty with that particular distinction.

Be wary of the growing number of computer programs on the market designed to teach pronunciation. Some of them look glossy and beautiful, but serve only to confuse learners unless they have a good deal of background to begin with. I believe that, like all other aspects of language, pronunciation is best learned in the context of real discussion and the effort to understand and be understood.

Questions to Think about and Discuss

1. When you are near people speaking a language you do not understand, what clues do you get as to what they are talking about?
2. Are there some people who, although they are speaking English, are

difficult to understand easily? What is it about their speaking that makes that so?

3. Because, generally speaking, listening is much less threatening for a learner than speaking, what kinds of activities can you think of in which people could enjoy themselves while listening to the English language? How would it be different for types of learners such as beginning adults, young people, or advanced university students?

4. Successful speaking (i.e., being understood when one is saying something that matters) does wonders to build a person's confidence. How could you ensure success for a group of learners just beginning to speak the language?

For Further Reading

Avery, Peter and Susan Ehrlich. 1992. *Teaching American English Pronunciation*. New York: Oxford University Press.

A good introduction to the teaching of pronunciation, this text is very readable and is formatted in an attractive manner with helpful graphics.

Kramsch, Claire. 1993. *Context and Culture in Language Teaching*. Oxford: Oxford University Press.

This book contains a good analysis of spoken language and suggests some practical ways of teaching speech in different contexts.

Nilsen, Don L.F. and Alleen Pace Nilsen. 1971. *Pronunciation Contrasts in English*. New York: Simon and Schuster.

This book is an old favourite amongst my generation of teachers, because the information is so useful. The material is organized around pairs of sounds that are often confused. A list of the languages that typically experience this confusion is followed by contextualized examples and lists of minimal pairs for practice. An excellent resource for teachers and good for some students.

Smillie, Ruth and Kelly Murphy. 1986. *Story Circles*. Saskatoon, SK: Saskatchewan Teachers' Federation.

This delightful resource was developed by two educators who use theatre to do education, in this case, with Native high school students. I find that immigrant students love the activities, in part because they are good activities and in part because I use the Native names to describe them. The learners with whom I've worked have been fascinated to learn more about First Nations peoples.

Teaching Reading, Writing, and Vocabulary

In this chapter, you will learn about:

- reading and writing as concepts
- guidelines for teaching reading, writing, and vocabulary
- techniques and resources
- error symbols for correction purposes
- portfolios
- journal writing
- teaching vocabulary.

Exploring the Concepts

While reading and writing have been the centre of what has been known as ESL and EFL for the better part of the last 50 years, the understandings behind both activities have been limited. We have concerned ourselves primarily with the technical aspects of both activities and largely ignored their emotional, political, and philosophical aspects. Just think, for example, about what a *word* is. It is the bounded naming of an experience of what we consider reality. Each language group bounds their experiences differently, thereby creating havoc and misunderstanding when we start to translate, as we do with bilingual dictionaries. When you start to teach vocabulary and students make up their own sentences, you realize how far short any dictionary falls in telling you what the real parameters of the word are.

Then there is the act of reading, a fascinating phenomenon, which differs considerably among readers, even within a culture. While one person enjoys being transported into a novel and losing all sense of the rest of the world, another reads for information and cannot identify with the other's experience of becoming the characters in a novel. Yet another finds any kind of reading to be pure pleasure and does not even understand why, until she explores her earliest memories of being read to on her grandfather's knee.

Similarly writing is defined for an individual, to some degree, by the context of that writer's beginning experiences with the activity of writing. Some people abhor writing and experience themselves as inept at writing, so strong is its association with childhood failure and criticism. Others love writing and find in it their freedom to explore themselves and the world without interference from anyone. Still others value the recognition they get from their writing, finding that that is the only place in their lives where they experience the value of their being. Just as you and I can find our places somewhere in the continua of both types of reading and writing experiences, so can the learners we teach. To approach such learners on purely a technical level, is to miss the deeper opportunity to enable the learners to enrich their lives by exploring and developing their own meanings and their own potential.

While we have seen reading and writing for the ways in which they are used to maintain the world in which we live, the average classroom has a long way to go in seeing how learners, individually and in community, can *reimage* and thereby *recreate* the world through their writing. Naming learners as *learners* promotes a tendency for us to forget that learners, as people, are also creators of our world. In that every writing is a naming and every naming has the potential to recreate the world, this is an important distinction, and we need to understand, as educators, whether we are opening up those possibilities or shutting them down by the ways in which we work with learners.

Reading is, as I have said, many things to many people. It is accessing information and knowledge, which means accessing power. It is allowing an author to entertain us, evoke our emotions, and challenge our ideas. Or, in the case of uninspired writing, it is allowing an author to lull us to sleep. Reading good writing is a way of coming to understand, not only the world, but also one's relationship to it. As an art, good writing (and our reading of it) can inspire, teach, challenge, entertain, and touch our souls. As educators, we want to introduce learners to good, relevant writing, and to enable them, through that writing, to see choices they had not considered before. We do this by respecting the capacity of the learner to understand the material, the background, and interests of the learner, and the needs of the moment and of the future for that learner in his or her new environment.

Writing is powerful in its implications for the individual. I am surprised at how many teachers of my acquaintance are uncomfortable with writing. I remember doing a workshop for teachers in Toronto some years ago that had been advertised as a "story workshop." The participants had misunderstood how the day would be spent and presumed I was going to be talking *about* stories and how to work with their learners' stories. The facilitator had neglected to tell them that it was a workshop where we would be working with *their* stories. At coffee time that morning, the organizer told me that, had the teachers not been paid to be there, they would probably all have left when I told them we would begin the day with the writing of four stories.

Their fear was tangible. A tall, elegant-looking principal brought his first story hesitantly to where I was sitting and asked humbly, "Is this what you want?" I explained to him that it was not what I want that mattered, but what he wanted, what he liked, that no one was going to correct his work or mock it or judge it in any way.

In spite of the initial fears, as the teachers got into their writing, one-by-one you could see the excitement take over. I could tell that most had never written their own meaningful experiences in story form before, and they liked the experience of doing so! By halfway through the morning, there was not one person who had not been totally claimed by what he or she was doing, and all were eagerly anticipating the afternoon to see what we would then do with the stories.

This was a very poignant experience for me because, although friends have told me how much they dislike writing and how incompetent they feel doing it, I had never seen such a large group of people feel the same way, without even having tried it. These were men and women who, for the most part, taught writing. I find this difficult to understand, in that I am one of those lucky people who engages in writing for many purposes, most of which I find purely pleasurable.

As teachers of writing, we have to come to terms with our own feelings about the genre. How can we teach others to write if we ourselves do not know why we feel incompetent or inept, if indeed some of us do? Most often, these feelings can be traced to our early experiences of writing. If we felt criticized and not appreciated, of course we will not enjoy the writing experience, until we recognize that the past is past and today is today, and we do not have to feel that way any longer. We know a lot more than we did then, and we are capable of learning more. Even more importantly, we can ensure that we learn from our own experience not to engender those same feelings of failure in the students we teach.

I also believe that poor writing is often indicative of unclear thinking. This is particularly true in the university students I have taught. Those students who understand their subject well, seldom have difficulty writing about it. Those who do not understand it at all, are most often ambiguous and frustratingly unclear in their writing.

When working with people in improving their writing, we need to ask ourselves what the real problem is and not make assumptions. Is it simply that the individual cannot spell and is embarrassed to write? Is it that the individual has had bad experiences with being criticized in the past and does not want to expose herself to humiliation now? Is it that the topic is completely foreign to the individual, and he has no idea what he is talking about? Is it that the individual's vocabulary is insufficient in English to address the topic? Is it that the individual is so depressed she simply cannot apply herself to the concentration required to write? Is it that the individual is distracted by more pressing concerns in life: a dying child, a brother in prison in the homeland, a wife who cries all day because she is so unhappy from being away from her family, the impossibility of paying bills with no money, and the list goes on?

For 30 ESL/EFL learners who struggle with writing, there could well be 30 reasons for that struggle. As educators, it behooves us to find out what those are, so that we can address the problem accordingly, which is not to say we need 30 different solutions. Very often, the utter joy of writing is the solution to a number of those problems, if one can inspire that joy amongst the learners. This I believe we can do, *if* we experience that joy in our own writing.

Writing is also the way people find and express their unique Voice in the world. Voice is about power. Voice is about naming *our* world, not someone else's world. When we read, we read the world of the Other. When we write, we can choose to name our world. This, Paolo Freire, a renowned literacy educator, understood well in his work. When people were learning to read, they learned those words which most powerfully described the pain and joy in their life experience as a community. When people began to write, they wrote first about those things which would make a difference, which would work to change their reality for the better. Whereas the majority of educators in ESL and EFL have not seen this as our responsibility, it is my hope that this is the vision which will inspire us in the future. Those learning English are seldom choosing to abandon all they value in their own cultures, languages, and lives. They simply are choosing a new medium in which to express it. We have not appeared to understand how smothering it must be for learners to spend all their time in pointless exercises which focus on grammar and have nothing whatsoever to do with life. As a teacher, you have the power to change that.

I am not going to deal with ESL literacy in this book as it is a very complex and difficult area. By ESL literacy, I mean basic literacy for those who do not read and write in their own language or who do so at minimal levels. The challenges around ESL literacy will be one of the topics addressed in the second book of this series *Issues, Challenges, and Alternatives in Teaching Adult ESL*. If you find yourself having to teach learners who are in this position, I suggest a book by Jill Bell and Barbara Burnaby called *A Handbook for ESL Literacy*. You may also find some useful resources in the Laubach Catalogue.

Guidelines for Teaching Reading, Writing, and Vocabulary

1. *Reading and writing activities should be selected on the basis of their relevance and appropriateness to the particular learners in a class.* Most often these activities are chosen because of the learners' level. While it is important that learners be able to access what is required in a reading or be able to do what is required in a writing assignment, in my experience, they will rise to enormous challenges *if* there is good reason to do so. If the learners want to learn about the information in an article, they are much more willing to spend time with a dictionary and ask questions, than if they have no interest at all in that article and see it as having no import for their lives.

2. *Be aware of what the reading (or writing) is for as well as about.* By that, I mean that we can read for pleasure, for knowledge, for instructions, or for learning the language (vocabulary and structure), among other things. The men and women who are thinking only about getting a job would be much more interested in reading a news article about the labour market in their province or state, than in reading about how Martha Stewart gets stains out of her clothing. On the other hand, the stay-at-home mother might be much more interested in the latter topic. Similarly, we can write to give information, to communicate with a loved one, to sway public opinion, or for numerous other reasons. Find writing activities which are of passionate interest to the learners.

3. *Provide choices for learners as often as possible.* This can be done either by allowing individuals to choose from a selection of topics, in the case of writing in particular, or by letting the class as a group negotiate with one another to choose readings which will be appropriate to the group as a whole.

4. *Teach contextualized vocabulary, as opposed to lists of words with no context.* It is much easier to remember meanings when they appear in the context of a story or short article.

5. *Allow regular times for reading and writing so that there is an energy allocated for those purposes.* Learners appear to value a certain measure of stability. If they know that they are going to be in a reading group for the first hour of every second class, for example, they are mentally prepared for that when they come into the classroom. This type of routine seems to create ease for learner and teacher alike.

6. *Share everyone's expertise in the classroom, not just your own.* Whereas you as the teacher are likely to have more experience in the language than do the learners, the learners may well have as much or more *life* experience than you do, and all of that is valuable in the experience of deriving meaning and making meaning. If you see

yourself as the *facilitator* of shared meanings, you will enable each person to give of their gifts and appreciate others for what they too can give to everyone's learning, including yours.

Techniques and Resources

Using Realia

Whereas textbooks have a certain convenience to them, and many learners like to have a textbook, in part, because it enables them to work to some degree at their own pace and at their own convenience, books are limited in time and perspective. *Even if you have a text, supplement it with current realia*: newspapers, notices, memos, signs, collective agreements, contracts, letters, phone messages, instruction manuals, offers of employment, and incident reports from places of employment, for example. It is in the real world that learners have to learn to function successfully, and these are the kinds of things they will need to learn to read. Try to use realia which is appropriate to your group of students. A Seniors Class would be interested in the recreational and educational programs in the community that are specifically designed for them. If these learners have money, they may be interested to know about Elderhostel, an international nonprofit organization which offers short-term educational programs to people aged 55 and older. (To find out more, visit their website or write for their brochures.) Learners in a Women's Program might be interested in recipes, health articles, the curriculum of K-12 programs, daycare brochures, state or provincial laws, and a variety of other topics, depending on who the women are.

Story Work

There is a place in most programs for both the reading and writing of stories. A story relates a series of incidents which have a beginning and an ending, and which contain the interesting details that bring an experience to life for the reader. A well-written story enables the reader to be there, to reexperience that event emotionally, visually, auditorially, tactilely, even as the author did. In reading another's story, we read through the eyes of our own experience, constantly comparing or identifying what the author is saying through similar experiences we have had. In doing so, we are valuing the other's experience and revaluing our own experience. We learn new perspectives that have an impact, not only on how we remember things in our own lives, but also on the choices we make in the future.

Writing stories can be even more valuable, in some instances, than reading them. In writing a story, we are naming our experience in a manner that captures aspects of that experience that seem important to us. We cannot write about an experience without evaluating it, choosing what to say and what not to say, deciding what is personal and what is public. In writing, we are exercising our power to evoke emotions in others, to elicit support for our causes, to teach or instruct (and there is a difference), to draw attention to that which we value. We can move others to laughter, to tears, and to action through our stories. And since stories reveal our world, they are also invitations to the reader to reveal his or her world to us in dialogue or in writing his or her own stories. In composing stories, we can heal ourselves. In reading our stories, others can find insight, hope, and possibility, among other things.

Work gently with stories that learners write. We expose ourselves when we write a story and, thus vulnerable, we are easily wounded by criticism or by being ignored. Respond to the meanings presented in stories, and negotiate with learners the kinds of corrections they are looking for. My suggestion is, if a learner does not ask for correction don't give it. (Just let him or her know that this is your policy.)

Comparison Correction by Learners

In correcting writing, an alternative to indicating errors and/or actually correcting them is to type the writing in its correct form and return it to the learner, who is then free to choose which differences he or she is ready to integrate into his or her own active knowledge of the language, and which errors he or she needs to ignore until another day. After getting back the typed version of his or her writing, the learner goes through it line by line while comparing it with the original version. I have found this technique to be very valuable for some learners, providing that I am very conscious of the degree of liberty I can take in the revisions. For some learners, I stick very close to their original, while for others, I go so far as to intuit what it is they are really trying to say and give them fresh new ways of saying it. For those for whom that is appropriate, I find that they love it and their writing really takes off after a period of time.

Peer Feedback

Another alternative is to have peer writing groups in which the learners respond to one another's writing in ways that make it stronger. Someone might say, "I don't understand what you mean here. Can you say it in a different way?" Or, "This is very interesting, but you have not given much information. Can you describe what happened so that we can actually imagine what it was like?" Or, "You have told us what happened, but you haven't said how you felt about it. How did you feel when this happened to you? What did you learn from this experience? How could others prevent a similar experience from happening to them?" By listening to their peers, learners are free to choose what to respond and how to do it in order to make their writing stronger.

The Internet

The Internet is a new and exciting resource to use in the second language classroom. One of our projects has just hooked up to Web, and the learners are looking forward to exchanging e-mail messages with students in the US. In addition, they have been invited to post some of their writings on a website where they can be shared with other learners like themselves.

I have observed in recent years that the computer is an incredible motivator and for a variety of interesting reasons. I sense that for women in particular, there is an energy in learning to use the computer that has not been there for other forms of language learning. In part, these women say they want to learn about using a computer so that they will not feel so stupid when their children and husbands know how, and they do not. Many are feeling left out of a significant activity in the family home and they want to change that. It is just one more example of the role reversal that so often happens when immigrant children learn the language more quickly than their parents, who then have to depend on them for many things. This situation creates some uncomfortable power imbalances in the home. Learning to use the computer and the Internet for their own purposes is a very empowering activity for these women.

Whereas I would not support a learning system which was 100% dependent on the Web if there were any other choices, I certainly see the computer as a valuable learning tool for many reasons, and it deserves exploration. There are ESL sites galore on the Web. Just use whatever search engine you like, and type in either English as a Second Language or English as a Foreign Language, and see what comes up. TESOL has a website for teachers with many interesting links, as does TESL Canada. A useful book you shouldn't miss is *The Internet Guide for English Language Teachers* by Dave Sperling. (See bibliography at the end of this chapter for more information.)

Symbols for Error Correction

Some teachers believe that students never look at their corrections and that it is largely a waste of their time to give them. There are ways, however, to make corrections more useful. One additional alternative to those already mentioned is to mark each error with a symbol which indicates what kind of error it is, and then let the learner correct his or her own errors. Encourage the learners to ask questions if they do not understand or know how to make the corrections. Here are a few samples of commonly used symbols. (It is better to use symbols which are common if possible so that learners do not have to learn a new set every time they get a new teacher.) Be sure learners have a copy of the symbols to begin with and that they have examples of how the symbols are used.

v.t.	verb tense
s/pl.	singular-plural error
art.	article missing or wrong article
sp.	spelling
voc.	wrong word (vocabulary error)
F.	wrong form (e.g., adjective instead of adverb form used)
P.	punctuation
W.O.	word order
∧	word missing
¶	new paragraph needed
prep.	wrong preposition or preposition needed
??	I don't understand. Try again please.
conj.	wrong conjunction or needs conjunction
RUN-ON	(I write this out in capital letters as it is a common error, and this causes people to pay attention and want to avoid this error in future.)
frag.	sentence fragment (incomplete sentence)

Using Portfolios

A portfolio is a file folder of learner-generated material through which a learner can see for himself or herself the progress he or she has made in writing over a period of time. This is an extremely useful tool for both learner and teacher alike, especially when one is looking to see real progress as opposed to test results. Portfolio entries should be dated and filed in chronological order, the most recent on top. Tests may tell us a learner's ability to memorize, or to manipulate words or ideas in a particular way, but few tests give us the well-rounded picture of progress the way a portfolio does.

In a portfolio, we can watch much more than the number of errors. We can see the length and difficulty of what a learner takes on. We can see how the complexity of vocabulary and sentence structure change over time. More importantly, we can see the changes in fluidity with which a person writes, and the comfort with which he or she does so. When students get discouraged and think they are not making progress, it is very helpful to pull out the portfolio and say, "Well let's see. I see progress here, don't you?" It is also helpful to identify the kinds of error patterns with which a learner struggles most often. It is helpful to have access to a photocopier to do this since learners may want to take their originals home. If that is not practical, the students can be invited to keep their work at school in the portfolio and take the whole file home at the end of their program.

Journal Writing

Journal writing has become very popular in ESL and EFL classrooms in the past 15 years. However, people mean very different things by the term. Journal writing for some means the keeping of a daily log where a short entry is made every day. These journals can be useful for learners who are in the workplace or on workplace training assignments, but they are not my favourite means of journal writing. My preference is that journal writing be optional, not compulsory, and the style of the writing be up to the individual as well as the type of desired response. Some learners may welcome the opportunity to have a one-on-one conversation with me, to explore feelings and ideas in a safe, nonpublic way. Others may want to use their journals as an opportunity to ask questions about things they want to know about our culture and our ways of doing things. If they do, I ask that they teach me about theirs at the same time. Some simply want another vehicle to practice their writing and get corrections. Whatever they want is fine. It provides an individualization within the program. In addition, the act of having to decide what one wants can be empowering to the individual who may feel very little other power in his or her life at that moment.

However, beware of writing personal information about yourself which you would not want shared with just anyone, for learners often share their journals with one another, and it contributes to community building when they do. In addition, beware of journals in which students are complaining about or reporting on other students with the expectation that you will act on those reports. I have learned the hard way to ask students to say nothing about other students, unless they are willing to have the issue addressed in the classroom. That stops the gossips and complainers. I feel very strongly that a grade should never be attached to a journal, nor do I believe that we should correct anything a learner has not specifically requested us to correct. I ask learners to tell me if they want corrections. Some say, "Correct everything" and others do not reply, in which case I respond, but do not correct. Some ask that I correct their spelling, while others want me to focus on verb tenses in one journal and on punctuation in another. I discourage most people from having everything corrected, for I have seen that this often takes away from the pleasure and feeling of success they have in working with the journals.

Writing for Special Purposes

There are many different genres of writing, and sometimes our students need to learn one or more of these for special purposes. For example, if a student is learning English to prepare to study at an English-speaking university, it is important to teach more than correctness in grammar. They also need an extensive vocabulary in the area of study and an awareness of what a term paper, an essay, and possibly a thesis are. They need to learn how to do references, footnotes, and a bibliography. The *American Psychology Association's Guide for Academic Reference* (*APA Guide*) is a good standard for academic writing in the humanities unless the student knows of another reference that is more appropriate for his or her purposes.

Professionals need to learn standard forms for business letters and should be reading in their fields to learn the professional vocabulary they need to understand and express themselves appropriately. I encourage professionals to purchase a text of some sort to work on while they are in an ESL program, as they can ask questions around meaning and pronunciation when they are unsure. Learners may also need to develop a résumé appropriate to their credentials and to practice writing cover letters for their job search.

In that many learners are looking for work, it is appropriate for ESL programs to assist them to develop good résumés, to learn how to fill out standard applications, to write effective covering letters, and to read collective agreements and labour standards for their province or state.

If you are doing English in the Workplace (EWP) or English for Special Purposes (ESP), you will want to build a strong collection of reading materials from that workplace. You will also want to learn what kinds of writing are required of the learners in the class and what kinds of writing would be required, should they be promoted into the next level in their work.

Life Story Writing

Whereas I have not done much of this work in the classroom myself, I know some teachers do so, and some students really want to begin what becomes for them a very long project—writing their autobiography. Learners often want to write it so that their children will know their roots and what brought their family to a new country. Writing an autobiography would be a wonderful specialized ESL class for someone to run for those learners who wanted to do it. I would not suggest doing it until the learners were fairly proficient with the language though, because it can be very time-consuming when an individual writes pages and pages of nearly unintelligible materials and wants you to correct them all.

Teaching Vocabulary

As I have said, vocabulary is best learned in context and, personally, I find newspapers, the *Readers' Digest*, and various other found books and magazines to be the best sources of such context. On occasion, I have created context in order to teach a particular collection of words, such as those in each *Reader's Digest,* if that is a resource students like. I will choose five words at a time, write a paragraph or story which collects those words into a coherent whole, and then provide definitions, parts of speech, and examples for each word. After that, there are fill-in-the-blanks sentences which help the learners to get an additional context for the words, and a word-family exercise so that they can see the related words with the same root. The word families I do in a table where one part is given, and they fill in the others. Spaces where you do not want a response should be filled in as below:

NOUN	VERB	ADJECTIVE	ADVERB
energy	*energize*	*energetic*	*energetically*
intelligence		intelligent	*intelligently*
frustration	frustrate	*frustrating*	*frustratingly*
relation	*relate*	*related*	

In class, we read the story together and go over the words. The learners have time to fill in the blanks and do the word-family exercise, and then we correct them together. Next, I invite the students to compose original sentences, and we discuss why the ones which do not work, do not. Then, the learners have the task of writing original sentences for each word and the option of doing the same thing for the other words in the word family. After four of such lessons, a total of 20 words, they get a quiz. Each quiz is cumulative: half of the test is about the last four lessons and the other half is about all those lessons that came before. (This review is necessary to keep what they are learning fresh in their minds.) I know that the words are really being learned when I see them appear in other writing the learners are doing.

When you are teaching vocabulary be aware that you are teaching many aspects of a word:
- the meaning,
- the usage or function (part of speech),
- the pronunciation,
- the spelling, and
- the tone or appropriateness of that word for specific contexts.

We know all of these things without thinking, and it can be confusing to learners if we are not conscious of teaching each aspect of a new word. For example, I remember teaching the word "morose" to a group of students when it appeared in a reading. After that, when I asked, "How are you?" I either got "Fine" or "Morose." The learners had no context by which to recognize that this word is not used often and that there are synonyms which would be much more appropriate for frequent use such as "down," "lonely," "sad," or "depressed." Traditional dictionaries do not explain the acceptable frequency of words, and yet native speakers are amused or irritated if a word is used by a speaker more often than is appropriate.

We also need to remember that there is a passive knowledge and an active knowledge of vocabulary. When a student can read a passage and answer questions about it, you know that the passive knowledge is there. This does not mean, however, that the learner can correctly use a specific word in a sentence or utterance. This takes much more skill and practice as learners feel out the word's parameters, qualities which the dictionary does not provide. For example, the word < diminish > means "to get smaller," but we do not say, "My dress diminished in the washing machine." We say, "My dress shrank in the washing machine" and yet these are exactly the kinds of errors learners will make until they become very familiar with words. It can be difficult at times to explain why a word is not right in a given situation when, by what the dictionary says, it appears that it should be. You can recommend that learners buy an ESL learner's dictionary which marks the core vocabulary in English that they need to be able to actively use.

When students tell me they want to learn vocabulary, I tell them to read, read, and read some more, because I believe that this is the best way to acquire new vocabulary. But language learners need to have reading materials which are highly motivating for them and not too difficult. A teacher in Vancouver surprised me by telling me she was using a text I had written that I thought would be much too difficult for the learners she was teaching. She said this book worked because the text was so well-presented by the publishers with coloured pictures and nice paper that the students felt very respected in reading it. They told her it was a *real* book, and she prepared them for it by giving them the needed vocabulary before they went into each chapter—a good reminder for me that choosing materials is about more than level and content. It is also about how the learner *feels* when he or she reads it. These learners felt the materials honoured them.

Questions to Think about and Discuss

1. What are your earliest memories of reading? Of writing?
2. How have those experiences effected your experience of being a reader? A writer?

3. What types of materials do you read? Which materials do you enjoy reading? Now, ask three or four friends the same questions. How do their answers differ from your own?

4. How do you feel when you write? When others read your writing?

5. If you enjoy having others read what you have written, why do you suppose that is? If you do not enjoy having your writing read by others, what would it take to change that?

6. How does your reflection on your own and others' experience of reading and writing inform your decisions around teaching those subjects to others?

For Further Reading

Allen, Virginia French. 1983. *Techniques in Teaching Vocabulary.* New York: Oxford University Press.

Teachers can use this practical book of ideas to vary their approaches to teaching vocabulary in all levels of ESL and EFL classrooms.

Raimes, Ann. 1983. *Techniques in Teaching Writing.* New York: Oxford University Press.

This useful tool box of activities for the writing classroom is an excellent resource. It is clearly formatted and includes many examples.

Silberstein, Sandra. 1994. *Techniques and Resources in Teaching Reading.* New York: Oxford University Press.

In keeping with the two previous titles, and part of the same series edited by Russell Campbell and William Rutherford, this book is organized around the genre of reading being taught. These genres include nonprose, expository prose, editorializing and opinion, fiction, poetry, and song. This text would be especially useful for teaching higher levels of reading.

Sperling, Dave. 1997. *The Internet Guide for English Language Teachers.* Upper Saddle River, NJ: Prentice Hall.

This useful book contains hundreds of ESL/EFL websites where you can share ideas with other language teachers, get free lesson plans, or even find an ESL/EFL training program or teaching job.

CHAPTER 12

Teaching Grammar

In this chapter, you will learn about:

- what grammar is
- parts of speech
- person, voice, mood, and tense
- linking verbs, modals, auxiliaries, and word order
- typical stumbling blocks for learners studying grammar
- activities for teaching grammar.

Grammar is simply a description of the way in which a group of people within a culture structure their naming of the world. Comparative linguistics is a fascinating field because when we compare the very different ways in which various languages name the world, we learn so much about what is possible and, therefore, about what choices our ancestors have made within that realm of possibility. As a small example, the English language places a lot of emphasis on time, as do all the European languages. Our verb tenses are essentially based on our need to situate experience on a timeline that is linear.

This does not mean that we do not have various other ways of experiencing time. When we say to our children "it is bedtime" or "it is time for breakfast," that is another sense of time. When I say, "I am getting old before my time," that is yet another. I am told that there are some aboriginal languages in which all time exists in the present. Other languages have far more complex understandings of our relationship to time than we do, such as *metaphysical time* in which one experiences that which has happened long ago, or that which has yet to happen. Such understandings of time are beyond my ability to comprehend, but remind me that the world is a much more complex place than what any one culture can know.

Language ensures that the *basic* experience of reality from one generation to the next does not suffer the same changes an individual would in moving from one culture to another which is radically different. It provides some continuity of experience. (That which is not named in a culture does not exist for that culture.)

Learners have difficulties with those aspects of grammar which are not present in the same form in their own languages. If the learner's native language does not use *articles* (e.g., a, an, the), the learner omits articles in English because he or she sees no need for them. If a language has *honorific* forms (a form of speech implying respect often used in South-East Asian languages like Korean or Japanese), it can be very difficult for learners who speak that language to know how to deal with this information in English. A Korean friend of mine did not feel comfortable speaking to other friends to whom I introduced him until he knew in what year they had graduated. I asked why and he told me he needed to know where they stood in relation to himself. I said, "But that it is not important in English." And he said, "I know. But it is important to my mind!"

The important thing to remember in teaching grammar is that we do not teach it for its own sake. We teach it to enable the learner to express himself or herself more precisely and effectively in English, to have Voice in this language. When we lose sight of that intention, we have forgotten the primacy of meaning in communication.

The balance of this chapter lies in two parts: a basic grammar for those who have never learned one, and techniques for teaching grammar. If your understanding of English grammar is solid and you do not need this review, I suggest you skip this basic grammar review and go to the second part of the chapter.

A Basic English Grammar: The Parts of Speech

My colleagues in the academic world may be disgusted with what I am about to do, which is to present a very old, traditional form of grammar to those who lack any system at all to name and explain the relationship between words in use. I am choosing the traditional route because I have found that it is the easiest and most familiar for the majority of students with whom I have worked. When I am with students who are comfortable with *transformational grammar*, however, I use it. Transformation grammar views human language as process oriented rather than form oriented. The whole point of being able to name grammatical terms, after all, is only so that we can explain how the language works to those who are struggling to understand it. Therefore, the simplest and shortest route to that end is the most justifiable. I know of no route that is perfect. Each approach has its own problems. However, we have to start somewhere and, for simplicity's sake, I am starting here. If you want alternatives to traditional grammar, I would recommend that you have a look at *The Grammar Book: An ESL/EFL Teacher's Course* by Marianne Celce-Murcia and Diane Larsen-Freeman, which gives a thorough, although complex, explanation of a transformational approach to teaching grammar.

Verbs

Verbs are one of the two most important types of words in English. Almost every complete utterance has one. In the case of commands, the verb may be the only word in the utterance (e.g., "Help!" or "Go!"). Verbs express an action or state of being. They are recognizable by the fact that they can be transformed by changing the ending, or by adding a word on at the front to indicate changes in the relationship between the present moment of speaking and the time the action or state of being happened.

> EXAMPLE I **live** in Alberta. I **lived** in Manitoba for a year. I **will live** in Mexico for two months this year.

In the examples given above, we see < live >, < lived >, and < will live > —three forms (*simple present, simple past,* and *future*) of the verb < to live >. This is considered to be a *regular verb*, although we do not repeat the letter < e > when we add < ed > to make the past tense. However, verbs can be *regular* or *irregular*. Students need to learn the irregular forms individually because they vary considerably (e.g., go, went, gone; have, had, had; throw, threw, thrown).

For a native speaker, verbs are easy. We speak and write them largely without any consciousness of the amount of information we need to know in order to do so. In fact, our choices take into consideration four elements: *person, voice, tense,* and *mood.*

1. Person

This designation goes with the subject of the verb.

First person singular: **I**   First person plural: **we**
Second person singular and plural: **you**
Third person singular: **he, she, it**   Third person plural: **they**

These are the *subject pronoun* forms. The same verb adjustment occurs with the noun forms: students need to learn that when speaking in the present tense, they must add the letter < s > to the ends of verbs in the third person singular.

2. Voice

Voice can be active or passive.

> Active voice: The subject of the sentence is the *agent* or *doer* of the action.
> **Fred** repaired the car.
> Passive voice: The subject of the sentence is the *receiver* of the action.
> **The car** was repaired by Fred.

3. Tense

This designation indicates *when* an action or situation occurred.

> *Simple tenses: present, past, future*
>
> Quebec **is** the largest province in Canada.
>
> Quebec **was** Lower Canada before Confederation.
>
> Quebec **will be** the subject of much discussion until the separation issue is resolved one way or another.

> *Perfect tenses: present perfect, past perfect, future perfect*
>
> I **have taken** a shower every morning for as long as I can remember. (*present perfect*)
>
> I **had started** my shower when the phone rang. (*past perfect*)
>
> I **will have completed** my writing before the deadline arrives. (*future perfect*)

> *Progressive or continuous tenses: present continuous, present perfect continuous, past perfect continuous, and future perfect continuous.*
>
> I **am doing** my homework. (*present continuous*)
>
> I **was doing** my homework when the phone rang. (*past continuous*)
>
> I **have been doing** my homework every night. (*present perfect continuous*)
>
> I **had been doing** my homework before dinner but found I ran out of time. (*past perfect continuous*)
>
> I **will have been doing** this homework for five nights by the time it is finished. (*future perfect continuous*)

4. Mood

This quality shows the speaker's or writer's intention: to tell or ask us something (*indicative* or *declarative mood*), to tell us to do something (*imperative*), or to express a wish, unreal condition, or request (*subjunctive*).

> Indicative: I **bought** my computer at Westworld.
>
>   **Did you buy** the computer you **wanted?**

Imperative: Please **take out** the garbage.

Subjunctive: I wish I **were** more energetic.

If I **were** a millionaire, I would continue to do the same work I do now, but I would not have to worry about money.

If I **(were to) take** the bus there, would you pick me up later?

Forms of Verbs

Infinitive and Participial forms:

When a learner is learning a new verb, especially an irregular one, it is useful to learn three forms: the *infinitive*, the *past tense*, and the *past participle*. Here are some examples:

Present	Past	Past Participle
see	saw	seen
go	went	gone
speak	spoke	spoken
forget	forgot	forgotten

Linking Verbs

There is a special group of verbs in English which are called *linking verbs*. They are called this because they link the subject and its complement. These verbs are special because they take *adjective modifiers* rather than *adverbs*. They are verbs that could be substituted by a form of < be >. For example, < feel >. I **feel** sleepy. I **am** sleepy. With verbs that are not linking verbs, we would say, for example, "The child wandered **sleepily** into his bedroom." But when we say the girl *appears* sleepy, we could also have said, < the sleepy girl > with a verb. When we can do this, we know a verb is a linking verb.

Linking verbs include the following: be, appear, seem, taste, feel, sound, look, smell, grow, and become. They can also function as action verbs, depending on their meaning.

The boy **is growing** very tall. (*linking verb*—the boy is *becoming* very tall.)

The old man **is growing** roses in the backyard. (*action verb*)

Linking verbs can be confusing for beginning learners.

Modals (Modal Auxiliary Verbs)

Modals are words used with the main verb to change some aspect of meaning.

I **may** go shopping this afternoon. (indicates uncertainty)

I **should** go shopping this afternoon. (indicates need)

I **have to** go shopping this afternoon. (indicates that there is no choice)

Modals include the following:
> be able to (can, could)
> be supposed to (shall, should)
> have to
> must
> had better
> may, might
> ought to
> have got to
> used to

Nonmodal Auxiliaries

These are words which are needed to accompany the main verb in the formation of the verb tense: be, have, do, will.

I **am** coming. (*present continuous*)

I **have** gone shopping already. (*present perfect*)

I **don't** know what you mean. (*present*)

I **will** be on time. (*future*)

Nouns

Nouns are the second most important words in our sentences. They are the subjects of our actions or states of being and the objects. In the sentence < Juan plays baseball >, Juan is the *subject* or *doer* of the action, and baseball is the *object* of his action. Nouns can be singular or plural, regular, or irregular and they can take articles or not. They often occur with descriptive words (*adjectives*) or phrases (*adjective phrases*) with them. Learners are challenged most by the differences between *count* and *noncount* or *mass nouns*. Observe how < pennies > and < money > are used in the following sentences:

Mary put **the pennies** in her change purse.

Mary put **the rest of the money** in her wallet.

Money is good to have.

A penny is rather useless nowadays.

In the above sentences, we see that <pennies> and <money> are both objects in the first two sentences and subjects in the second two. The word <the> precedes both <money> and <pennies> in the first two sentences. There is no article in front of <money> in the third sentence while the word <penny> is preceded by the article <a> in the last sentence. The reason for the difference is that <money> is a *noncount* or *mass noun* while <penny> is a *count noun.*

The differences in usage between count and noncount nouns are considerable and, for that, I will leave you to choose a good grammar reference. In the meantime, when you are teaching grammar, be sure to separate the two types of nouns initially, or the learners will become very confused. If you do not know which are which, you will discover that very quickly, I promise you.

Nouns often occur in the following pattern:

a the	} + adjective + noun (singular)	· a rusty **nail** · the right **answer**
some any the	} + adjective + noun (plural)	· some happy **children** · any new **changes**? · the wrong **answers**

Pronouns

Pronouns are words that stand in the place of nouns. For example, I can say, "The man bought the book" or if the person I am talking to knows that I am referring to a particular man whom I have already mentioned, I can say, "He bought the book."

There are five types of pronouns: *subject, object, possessive, reflexive,* and *relative.* Each type of pronoun is explained below. In the following lists, you will notice that the first column is for singular pronouns and the second is for plural pronouns with <you> taking the same form for both. The first row is *first person,* the second row is *second person,* and the third row is *third person.*

1. Subject Pronouns

I	we	I love reading! **We** read several books each week in our house.
you	you	**You** [one person] should come with us. **You** [more than one person] are all invited.
he/she/it	they	**She** made her sister a birthday cake. **They** ate it with her friends.

2. Object Pronouns

me	us	Please take **me** with you. In fact, take **us** all.
you	you	He gave **you** the biggest ice-cream.
		The teacher is giving **you** extra homework.
him/her/it	them	The teacher passed **him** the chalk.
		Where is the garbage? I took **it** out.
		We drove **them** to the mall to go shopping.

3. Possessive Pronouns

mine	ours	You need a pen? Here, take **mine**.
		You can't take that shovel. It's **ours**.
yours	yours	This plate is mine and that one is **yours**.
his/hers	theirs	**His** blanket is blue and **hers** is pink.
		Our room is next door to **theirs**.

4. Reflexive Pronouns

myself	ourselves
yourself	yourselves
himself/herself/itself	themselves

I bought **myself** a new dress to celebrate.
You should give **yourself** a holiday once in awhile.
He looked at **himself** in the mirror and realized he was getting old.
She looked at **herself** in the mirror and decided she looked terrific!
That in **itself** is not the problem.
We decided to pay **ourselves** a bonus at the end of the year.
Only you **yourselves** can make such an important decision about your futures.
The newlyweds treated **themselves** to a honeymoon in Bali.

You can see that reflexive pronouns can be used as objects of the verb which refer to the subject, objects of a preposition, or complements to the subject. Using a reflexive extra pronoun gives emphasis to the subject. For example, "I **myself** would rather not go to the party."

5. Relative Pronouns

The relative pronouns are < who >, < which >, and < that >. These words begin clauses within a sentence, and they refer to a noun that has been previously mentioned, usually the noun closest in proximity to the relative pronoun.

EXAMPLE: The teacher **who** was most popular was the one **who** showed genuine respect and caring for her students.

However, relative pronouns do not always refer to the closest noun, and one has to think about meaning because the verb which follows a relative pronoun must agree in number with the noun it refers to.

Sometimes this concept is a little confusing for students.

> EXAMPLE: Miss Nguyen is the one nurse among all the nurses on the ward who **is** truly dedicated to serving her patients.

We say "is" in this instance rather than "are" because the < who > refers to Miss Nguyen, not to the nurses on the ward.

Adjectives

Adjectives are words that give us more information about nouns, as do adjective phrases.

> EXAMPLES: The **intelligent young** woman won two scholarships. (*adjectives*)
> The man **in the black overcoat** is looking at you. (*adjective phrase*)

Adjectives are much easier to learn in English than they are in many languages because they hold the same form, regardless of gender or number. The only real challenge to learners in learning adjectives is word order when several adjectives are used together. A good grammar reference will give you categories of correct word order.

Articles

Articles are those little words which so often precede nouns: a, an, the, some, and any. (Some grammarians classify < some > and < any > differently, but the *Oxford Dictionary* includes them in modern usage as *determiners*, which is another word for articles.)

< A > and < an > are the *indefinite articles* used with singular nouns.

> EXAMPLES: Tetsuo wants **a** bicycle for Christmas.
> Chizuko wants **an** umbrella.

As you see in these examples, < a > is used in front of consonants and < an > in front of *vowels* (a, e, i, o, u, and sometimes y.) *Indefinite articles* are used when the noun is not specified as one particular item. *Definite articles* are used when it is clear which item or items the speaker is referring to.

> EXAMPLES: **The** key is on the table. (The speaker knows that the listener understands which key he is referring to.)
> **The** mail has not arrived yet. (We understand that it is *our* mail the speaker is referring to.)
> **The** bulletins will be ready for Sunday morning. (We understand that the speaker is referring to the printed bulletins with the order of service for Sunday church services.)

To return to our earlier examples of indefinite articles, if we say instead "Tetsuo wants **the** bicycle he saw in the store window," we know he will only be happy with one specific bicycle, not just any bicycle. Similarly, if we say "Chizuko wants **the** umbrella with the tiny red roses around the edge," we know she will not be happy with any other umbrella.

< Some > is the plural form of the indefinite article.

Give me **an** apple, please.	Give me **some** cherries, please.
There is **a** bus that goes to that park.	**Some** buses are painted with advertising, while others are not.

Adverbs

Adverbs are words which give us more information about verbs or adjectives. Adverb phrases do likewise. While many adverbs have a form which is entirely different from their adjective counterparts (e.g., < good > [adjective] and < well > [adverb]), some adverbs are easily recognizable by the fact that they have added "ly" after the adjective form (e.g., < quick > [adjective] and < quickly > [adverb]). Adverbs and adverb phrases answer the questions *how*, *where*, or *when*. Here are some examples of adverbs:

The little girl ate her dinner **quickly** so she could go outside to play.
Because she was tired, she did not do her homework very **well** that night.
The old man got a ticket because he was driving **too slowly**.
He stole the money from the bank **without thinking of the consequences**.
I will be **there in the morning**.
The letter was **absolutely** perfect!
That information is not **totally** accurate.
The diplomat was briefed **well** for his visit to our country.

Prepositions

Prepositions are words that begin phrases describing or giving more information about some other part of the sentences such as a noun or verb. There are prepositions of place and time, among others. Look at the following sentences.

The little girl **with Mrs. Botha** is her granddaughter. (This phrase tells us *which* little girl is being referred to.)
I will be there **at 10:00 a.m.** sharp. (This phrase tells us *when* the speaker will arrive.)
Please park the car **behind the garage**. (This phrase tells us *where* the speaker wants the driver to park his or her car.)

Thus, in the examples above, < with >, < at >, and < behind > are examples of prepositions.

When a sentence contains phrases of both time and place, place precedes time.

I put the groceries **on the counter last night**.

WHERE   WHEN

I am coming **into the office in the morning**.

WHERE   WHEN

Conjunctions

Conjunctions are words that join other words, phrases, or clauses together. Here are some examples:

Apples **and** oranges are fruits.

Canoeing on a quiet river **and** biking in the countryside are two of my favorite pastimes.

Whether you come with me **or** not does not matter.

There are *coordinating conjunctions* and *subordinating conjunctions*. The coordinating conjunctions join things of equal value or weight in a sentence, as we see in the examples above. The coordinating conjunctions are < and >, < but >, and < or >.

Mother is coming to our house for Thanksgiving **and** Father is going to your house.

I want to come **but** I don't have anything appropriate to wear.

We can either fly to Seattle **or** we can drive. Which do you prefer?

The subordinating conjunctions are words that join a main idea and a subordinating idea together. The subordinating idea gives more information about the main clause or limits it in some way. Look at these examples:

I can't come skiing with you **because** I hurt my leg playing racquetball.

Main   Subordinate

She won't visit us **until** she finishes her writing.

Main   Subordinate

Unless the car can be fixed by Friday, we will not be able to go to Calgary.

Subordinate   Main

Interjections

Interjections are words like "Oh!" which express a complete idea by themselves. Swear words would also fit into this category.

We have just seen a very, very brief introduction to the basic parts of speech in traditional English grammar. Because many learners no longer learn these terms in our schools, when those same learners become teachers, they often find themselves quite lost when teaching learners who learned grammar in their own countries and find it useful to use grammatical terms. If you are someone who has never studied grammar before, I hope you will have found this a useful introduction. I also recommend that you get yourself a good grammar reference, because you will most certainly need it.

English Word Order

Before we leave the basic grammar section, I would like to say something about English word order. Word order errors are among the most common errors made by second language learners, because each language has its own manner of ordering expression. Statement word order in English can most commonly, but not exclusively, be described as S-V-(O)-(P)-(T) or *Subject, Verb, Object, Place, Time*, with the latter three categories being optional. In addition, the Object category can be filled twice, once by a *direct object* and once by an *indirect object*. Here are some examples of this word order.

John flies. (This means that John is a licensed pilot.)

S   V

John flies a Cessna. (This is the kind of plane he flies.)

S   V   0

John flies a Cessna between London and Peterborough.

S   V   0

                                 P

John flies a Cessna between London and Peterborough every month.

S   V   O   P

(This adds information about how often he flies)   T

John gives flowers to his wife each Sunday.

S   V   O   T

               IO

This adds information about to whom or for whom the action was done (e.g., giving flowers).

Beginning students with little formal education may like to learn word order by using cards with the different components and laying them out in the correct order. With more advanced beginners, I might teach word order by asking questions which require the learner to add on the information for the piece requested.

EXAMPLES: **Where** do you want to work?
I want to work at a bakery.
When do you get to school each day?
I get here at 8:15 in the morning.

Teaching Grammar

Traditionally, grammar has been taught in a systematic order according to what grammatical points are perceived to be easiest and hardest, progressing from the former to the latter. If students have studied grammar in their own language, they may prefer this style of teaching and, if it works for them, that may be the appropriate way to organize your lessons. Students who have not studied grammar, however, or students who are more accustomed to learning from experience than from theory, can become very confused if taught in this manner. The fields of ESL and EFL have progressed from a grammatical organization of curriculum to *functional* and *situational* approaches, to the currently popular *communicative competence* approach. Others, like myself, prefer still another approach which we call *participatory* and most of us use an eclectic mix of several of these approaches, depending on who the students are and why they are studying the language. The important thing is to discover what works best for the learners with whom you are working and go with that.

If your students appear to want and learn well from a traditional grammar approach, there are many fine texts on the market which enable them to do that. The Azar books from Prentice-Hall Regents are a popular set. (See bibliography.) If you use grammar texts, however, be sure you supplement those with good listening, speaking, reading, and writing materials and activities.

Reality-Based Instruction

If the learners do not relate to grammar-based instruction, then I suggest you use a different approach, wherein you are teaching material in real situations and only introducing grammar as you need it to explain problems learners are having in expressing themselves. By "real," I do not mean "realistic," I mean *real*. In a beginners' class which is just starting, it is real to want to know the names of the other participants in the class, to learn what languages they speak, and where they are from, so that is a logical starting place. In a class of women with little formal education, it is real to want to learn about one another's families: spouses, children, and the ages of the children. In a class of employment-destined learners, it is real to want to be able to describe one's occupation, experience, and desires for employment in this country. Those topics become the foundation for instruction, and grammar is taught as the need for it arises.

For example, an early question in an ESL class is always, "How long have you lived in Canada?" The correct answer to that question is to say, for example, "six months," which does not pose a problem. If, however, a learner wants to introduce the subject and ask a question, he or she needs to say, "I have lived in Canada for six months. How long have you lived here?" Many learners struggle with the present perfect tense. I find with the verb tenses, the easiest way to teach them is to make them graphic on a timeline. Thus, the present perfect would look like this:

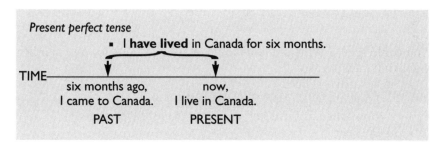

One way of practicing this structure in the classroom would be for the learners to ask one another two questions:

When did you come to Canada?   *I came in_____.*
                                   or
                                   I came_____ago.
How long have you been in Canada?   *I have been here for _____.*

Patterned Practice

We used to call this teaching technique *pattern drills*, and some people are anything but pleased when I say that I still use these on occasion. I do not deliberately set out to do pattern drills, but I do use them when it is apparent that learners are confused and need some security in their understanding. Yes, drills are very mechanical, but for some learners, this kind of repetitive application of a grammatical concept provides the security they need to "store" that concept to memory for when they need it. I would take time out of whatever we were doing to do this kind of practice and then return to the discussion or other activity at hand.

To follow through on the example given above, the present perfect, I might set up a pattern in this manner. If I can use real information about the people in the class, even better.

> Teacher: *Raisa is a salesperson. How long?*
>   Learner 1: *How long has Raisa been a salesperson?*
>   Learner 2: *She has been a salesperson for ten years.* or *(Since she came to Canada ten years ago.)*
> Teacher: *Solomon and Fikerte are married. How long?*
>   Learner 1: *How long have Solomon and Fikerte been married?*
>   Learner 2: *They have been married for twenty years.* or *(Since 1978.)*
> Teacher: *Shahin has a car. How long?*
>   Learner 1: *How long has Shahin had a car?*
>   Learner 2: *She has had a car since last week.* or *(For one week.)*
> Teacher: *I have a house near the university. How long?*
>   Learner 1: *How long have you had a house near the university?*
>   Me: *For twelve years.* or *(Since 1988.)*

You could then ask the students to generate questions for one another by giving them ideas:

- have a drivers' license
  Do you have a driver's license? (*Yes, I do.*)
  How long have you had a driver's license? (*Ten years.*)
- like pizza
  Do you like pizza? (*Yes, I do.*)
  How long have you liked pizza? (*Since I first tasted it.*)

(If the person says < no > to any of the first questions, the learner asking has to come up with a different question.)

- study English
  How long have you studied English? (*Since I was fourteen.*)

Ooops Sheets

One of my favourite teaching techniques is what I call "Ooops Sheets." These are exercises I make up based on student writing or, in some cases, on notes I have taken as I listen to students speaking. I take two errors from each student's work and put them into one exercise for the class to do. I change any personal information that would identify the student, and I do not identify learners when we are doing the exercises, although they sometimes volunteer when they recognize their error. The class is given time to identify and correct the errors, and then we go through the exercise together in class.

In the beginning, I suggest keeping these sheets to one error per sentence, and then you can add in complexity as the students become able to handle it. I find learners really like these exercises because they are so real to them. These exercises are focused on the actual errors that members of a particular *class* are making, rather than all the kinds of errors that one learner could be making. (Do not include sentences that are very confused in their wording; it is counterproductive.) The students learn from one another's errors, and it wakes up the editor in them. I try to choose errors that are made by several people in the class, not an error that only one person would make. Ooops Sheets are especially effective when we are working with homogenous groups, such as most EFL classes would be, because the kinds of errors the learners in one language group make tend to be very similar.

An option with this exercise is to put it on an overhead transparency and have everyone do it together. The advantage to doing it this way is for the learners to understand why an error is an error as you are doing it. The disadvantage is that students would not have a printed copy of this exercise to review later if they so wished. Nor would they have the opportunity to take however much time they need as individuals to sort out what is wrong and to correct it. (In class corrections, a few quick students have inevitably given the answer before some learners have even seen the error.) I prefer giving students the time to work through the exercise on their own or with a partner.

Strip Stories

Strip stories are not as wicked as the title might suggest, but they are fun to do and they really make the learners think about the ways in which ideas are connected in English. One takes a paragraph with enough sentences for each learner in the class to have one when they are cut into sentences, and retypes the passage with each sentence starting on a new line. (It is important to pick a well-written paragraph that has a logically presented sequence of ideas.) The passage is cut into strips and these are placed into an envelope from which each student draws one strip. Standing in a circle, everyone reads his or her sentence. As the others listen, the learners try to reposition themselves beside the appropriate individuals so that the story will make sense when everyone is standing in the right place. The more English the group has, the faster this activity will go.

Just to show you how it goes, I have included a short story of ten sentences, which could be broken down further into clauses if the class were bigger. See if you can put the sentences into the correct order. The bracketed information, which is not provided as part of the exercise is, of course, what I would hope students would be *thinking* as they heard each sentence read aloud.

A. **Whenever she could go to one, she did**. (Clue: The word < one > refers to something. Find that, and you know which sentence precedes this one.)

B. **On the way to the party, she stopped her car at a red light and waited**. (Clue: The word < the > in front of party refers to a specific party that has already been mentioned.)

C. **Joy loved parties!** (Clue: This could be an introduction. Is it?)

D. **One night, she went to a party where everyone had to dress up like an animal**. (Clue: This sentence could come right after the last one, but does it?)

E. **When she said she did not know where it was, they became quite annoyed**. (Clue: Both the < it > and the < they > refer to < something > and < someone > already mentioned. Look for that information and you will know what comes before this sentence.)

F. **That was when she decided never to be Big Bird again!** (Clue: This sounds like a conclusion. Could it be the last sentence?)

G. **She dressed up in a Big Bird costume she had bought at Halloween.** (Clue: We already know that she had to dress up like an animal. Could this sentence come after the sentence that told us that?)

H. **The two people in the car next to hers looked over and gestured for her to roll down her window**. (Clue: We know she stopped at a red light. This sentence must be after that one.)

I. **They thought she was advertising for the restaurant**. (Clue: We do not yet know what restaurant the speaker is referring to, so we are still waiting for a sentence to come.)

J. **They asked her for directions to the Chicken Delight restaurant**. (Clue: Ah-ha! There's the restaurant and we know the < they > must refer to the two people who stopped their car next to hers at the red light.)

Have you got it yet? (If you are still confused, it is: C, A, D, G, B, H, J, E, I, and F.) When you do this in a classroom, have the students arrange themselves in the correct order in a circle as they read their sentences aloud, and, after everyone has the correct order, ask them to tell you how they knew where to stand.

Modelled Composition

Students can be given a model written by the teacher which they can then change to include their own facts. Here is a sample:

My name is Virginia. I am a teacher. I like my job. I live in Edmonton. I have lived here since 1964. I have three daughters. In my free time, I like to travel, to read, and to visit with my friends.

My name is _____. I am a _____. I like/don't like _____. I live in _____. I have lived here since _____.

I have _____. In my free time, I like to _____.

Guided Composition

Another way of doing the previous activity would be by asking questions or giving key words. Here are samples of two different ways you could do this activity:

Write a paragraph by answering each of the following questions:
- What is your name?
- What is your job?
- Do you like your job?
- Where do you live?
- How long have you lived there?
- Describe your family.
- What do you like to do in your free time?

Write a paragraph by using the following key words:
- Name
- Job
- Like job/don't like job
- Live ... in
- Live ... since
- Married.....children
- Free time

The idea is to choose whatever stimulant or guide will best enable the learners to be successful.

Games

Many teachers like to use games to teach their students grammar. Some students will like this, while others will feel that their time is being wasted. It depends on the level of instruction, the educational background of the learners, and how much of a hurry they are in to learn what they need to know. You can make card games or board games to teach particular concepts, if this is a mode that works well for you, or you can use commercial games.

Question Practice

There are many ways to get students to ask questions. As you now know, I prefer that they ask real questions, namely, questions to which they do not already know the answers, but want to. I tell them I will answer almost any question *if* they ask it correctly. If a learner says, for example, "Where your house is?" I will gesture that he has the words backwards by crossing my forearms with the index fingers pointed up. The students quickly learn that this is my gesture for word order problems, and they will play with the sentence until they get it right. If they miss out a word, as in "Where you going after school?", I will say, "Where (and gesture a space with my right thumb and forefinger) you going after school?" The learners have come to know that this means "word missing" and, again, will experiment until they find the word.

Whereas I encourage learners to help one another to correct the questions, I always ask the original questioner to repeat the questions correctly. If the learner asks a question to which he or she knows the answer, such as "What is your name?", I say, "That is not a real question. You know my name. Ask me something else." If the learner asks a question which has obviously been created just for the sake of asking a question, such as "What colour is the mayor's hair?", I will ask, "Do you really want to know that?" Usually, he or she will laugh and say, "No."

When they tire of personal questions, which they always ask in the beginning, I give them ideas as to what they might want to ask about: history, geography, the city, the province, the government, politics, etc.

Questions to Think about and Discuss

1. Have you ever tried to learn a second language? If so, what was pleasant and enjoyable about that experience and what was frustrating and depressing? If you have never learned a second language, what language do you think you might like to learn and why? If you were studying the language you have chosen, how would you like to learn it? How would you want a teacher to teach you?

2. How can you use your experience as a language learner to inform your teaching?

For Further Reading

Azar, Betty Shrampfer. (1984, 1989, 1992.) *The Azar English Grammar Series.* Englewood Cliffs, NJ: Prentice-Hall Regents.

There are several books in this series, which has three levels. *The Basic English Grammar* books are the first level, then *The Fundamentals of English Grammar*, and finally *Understanding and Using English Grammar*. Each level has a text, workbook, and a teacher's guide. These books are widely used throughout North America and abroad.

Swan, Michael and Bernard Smith. 1987. *Learner English: A Teacher's Guide to Interference and Other Problems.* Cambridge, UK: Cambridge University Press.

This is a wonderful resource book if you are teaching any of the following groups: Dutch, Scandinavian, German, French, Italian, Spanish, Portuguese, Greek, Russian, Farsi, Arabic, Turkish, Indian. West African, Swahili, Japanese, Chinese, Vietnamese, or Thai. The author gives us typical areas of conflict for speakers of each language group when they are learning English in the areas of grammar, pronunciation, punctuation, and vocabulary. We even see the types of handwriting problems certain groups are likely to have. This is a very helpful, clearly laid out book.

See also the grammars mentioned in previous bibliographies and repeated in the back of the book.

CHAPTER 13

Accountability and Evaluation

In this chapter, you will learn about:

- accountability to learners, employers, funders, and yourself
- strategies for test-taking
- best practice guidelines and program standards
- Canadian Language Benchmarks Assessment (CLBA)
- standardized and teacher-made tests.

Any credible system of education and/or training is accountable to several sources including the learner, the funder, and the employer (provider). Evaluation is the means of discovering and demonstrating that accountability. Unfortunately, evaluation has all too often been interpreted as testing, but that is only a small part of valuing a learning program. In this chapter, we will explore some kinds of accountability and means of determining them to the three stakeholders mentioned, and to one more: yourself.

Accountability to the Learners

Learners entrust us with their time and sometimes with their tuition as well. We are accountable for ensuring that learners have the following information:

- what and how he or she can expect to learn in the program
- some sort of evidence that demonstrates the quality and quantity of progress he or she is making in the program.

Learners should also receive the following at the beginning of a program:

- information about the school, and its philosophy and way of teaching
- information concerning the roles of the staff and how to get help when they need it

- a student policy manual that spells out clearly the procedures as well as policies regarding such areas as attendance, punctuality, homework expectations, and the process for expressing dissatisfaction or handling problems
- information regarding how the students will be evaluated or assessed
- a copy of the general curriculum of the program and any costs which will be incurred for materials.

At least twice during a program, or more often if the program is a long one, learners should be given the opportunity to evaluate the following aspects of the program formally, usually in writing: the curriculum, the resources, the facility, the teacher(s), and the support systems in place. This evaluation can usually be done with a written questionnaire, and it is important that learners know that the teacher will not know what each individual said so that they will feel free to express their true feelings and opinions. (As an administrator, I usually went to the classes myself and had the learners put their questionnaires in an envelope when they were finished. The results were collated and given as a typed summary to the teacher. The teacher and I would then meet and discuss any concerns the students had expressed.)

However, this formal evaluation is, perhaps, not the most important one. The one that really counts is the ongoing evaluation that a teacher does daily and weekly with a class. This assessment enables him or her to change the direction or manner in which the program is moving in order to better accommodate the needs and abilities of learners as those surface. In order for this kind of evaluation to be successful, the learners must know that the teacher is open to criticism and ideas, and will not be offended by them. It only takes once for a teacher to react unkindly to a criticism, or condescendingly to a suggestion, after which it is quite possible that no one will ever make a suggestion or criticism again. As it is, we have to work very hard to build the level of trust that allows students to say they do not like doing something that we obviously think is great. We build that trust by respecting the feedback students give us, and acting on it wherever that is possible.

At the same time, we all work within parameters. If the students suggest cutting the classes from six to five hours a day, or increasing them to eight hours, for most of us, that would not be possible, as the funding has been set. If, however, the learners are finding that there is too much homework, and they are getting sick from lack of sleep, it is definitely possible to find other options for their learning.

Evaluation is more than just "Do you like this or that?" It is asking people, "What did you learn this week and why does that matter?" It is expecting them to continually challenge themselves to find their own real priorities and to make their own meanings. If you ask what someone learned and they say, "vocabulary," find out what specific words they learned—not all of them, just one or two really important ones. Then ask the learners why they value knowing those words. You will be surprised at what they tell you. Each round of this kind of evaluation informs our knowledge of who and what we are teaching, and why and how. Initially, students may be reluctant to do this kind of work. They may say to you that you are the teacher, and it is your job to decide what to teach them. In a training model, this is largely true. In an educational model, it is not. When learners are realizing their potential, which is the meaning of education, it requires a team effort to continually identify the best road for the journey to be taken.

Tests can be part of our accountability to learners as well as to our employer and funder. In fact, when tests are fair and not too onerous, learners often appreciate them because they can see what they have learned and, when learners are successful, they have pride in their results. This not only boosts their confidence, but also enhances their ability to learn.

I like to negotiate the number and kind of tests I do with learners. Some students want spelling tests and dictations. Others want fill-in-the-blanks, True or False quizzes, and/or compositions. I do find that it is helpful to make tests part of a pattern so that they are expected. Then students know what is coming and are not thrown off balance. Instead, many students can use tests as a way of consolidating and reviewing what they have learned.

In addition, many of our learners need to become test-savvy as we may use test formats quite different from those they are accustomed to in their own languages. It is not only in school that they will do tests. Tests are now used to screen job applicants or to assess applicants for training programs. Here are some of the different strategies you can suggest to your students for doing different types of tests:

- On timed tests, do the questions you know first and go back to the harder ones later.
- Sit near the tape recorder (as opposed to far from it) during a test that involves listening, such as the TOEFL. (This means arriving early to have a choice.)
- Know how the test will be marked beforehand (a point for each correct answer, a point deducted for each error, right minus wrong on multiple choice tests, etc.) so that you can adjust accordingly the number of guesses you are willing to make.
- On timed tests, calculate how much time you have for each question and pace yourself.

Personal interviews are also helpful in giving feedback to students, and listening to what they might not feel comfortable saying in class. In programs we have run, we have often done progress reports with the learners giving written feedback and suggestions, and noting their attendance and punctuality. Often, we follow those reports with a day of personal interviews where each learner gets anywhere from 20-45 minutes with the teacher. This practice is especially valuable for those learners who might be a little shy and do not get their fair share of time in the class.

Accountability to Funders

If you are teaching international students or EFL, this kind of accountability may not apply, as those programs are most often tuition-based. However, if you are teaching in a government-funded program, there will be particular expectations in place regarding accountability.

There are many changes taking place in both Canada and the United States at this time. Best Practice Guidelines and Program Standards, as well as certification and accreditation, are now terms which are familiar to most practicing teachers.

Best Practice Guidelines and Program Standards are terms that are used somewhat differently in different places, so don't be surprised if the definitions I am giving you are different from those in your context. Generally speaking, Best Practice Guidelines are statements indicative of the quality in a program that are used by the staff of that program to evaluate their own program and to make whatever changes are desirable. When we speak of Program Standards, however, we are talking about similar statements regarding program quality but, in this instance, they are being used by someone else to hold that program accountable. Program standards, therefore, tend to be somewhat more precise in their wording. Compare the following:

Best Practice Guideline: Staff shall be appropriately trained for the position for which they are hired.

Program Standard: Instructional staff shall have or be eligible for provincial accreditation from their professional association, and shall have a Bachelor of Education and/or TESL degree.

Another term that is heard in some areas is *key performance indicators*. These are measurable outcomes which can be converted into numbers for purposes of deciding who gets funding and who does not, and to what level. Sample key performance indicators are:

- the percentage of learners obtaining full-time employment (25 hours or more per week) at the end of a program that focused on employment needs.
- the percentage of learners who passed the TOEFL in a TOEFL preparation class.
- the percentage of learners who were accepted into an academic upgrading program following their language training.

In Canada, the preparation of the *Canadian Language Benchmarks* (CLB) has taken ESL practitioners a large step forward in finding a universal way to talk about language proficiency across the country. Learners going into many settlement programs are tested with the CLBA (Canadian Language Benchmarks Assessment) tool prior to their commencement and are assessed by the program using those benchmarks at the conclusion of the program.

Many of us see some problems with the current CLB system. The initial tests are standardized, take up to three hours per learner to do, and are done only by licensed practitioners across the country. The program provider, however, is supposed to make up the final tests but is not allowed to see the original assessment tools. Program providers do not have the time or expertise to make up the kinds of tests which would be regarded as equivalent. In spite of these problems, a good start has been made with the Benchmarks that should, in the long run, make it much easier for learners and providers alike when learners move from one province, centre, or program to another.

Accountability to the Employer

In that the employer is the bottom line for accountability to both the learner and the funder, you can be sure that the employer will have some system in place for evaluating the teaching quality in the program. Most programs have annual evaluations for everyone and three-month evaluations for new staff. Some have a written form that is used and, in some cases, both the teacher and the supervisor fill this out prior to sitting down together and having a discussion. Such evaluations generally look at planning, organization, curriculum, materials development, record-keeping, relationships with learners, atmosphere in the classroom, evaluation, professionalism and, of course, teaching ability. Very few ESL programs look at student results in the evaluation of their teachers, although most give students the opportunity to evaluate their program, which includes evaluating the teacher(s) either directly or indirectly.

Some EFL programs hire and fire staff on the basis of the results of their students. A teacher I knew in Saudi Arabia some years ago had to have a certain pass rate in his class to keep his job. In Kangwon-do, Korea, English teachers are categorized according to the final exam marks of their students. Teachers' ability to choose placements in an urban area over a rural one is conditioned by the category they are in. An "A" teacher can pretty well decide where he or she wants to be, whereas a "D" teacher will have to go wherever he or she is sent within the province. The final examination, for that and other reasons, therefore sets the tone for everything that happens in the classroom.

Accountability to Yourself

Most of us value success, and success in this occupation means that our students are learning and that we are learning. It means that, day-by-day, we learn from our mistakes. If we are serious about wanting to improve our understandings and our skills, we need to take the time to document our daily learnings in the form of reflections. Over time, these reflections are invaluable, especially when we read them over on completion of a program. Otherwise, we tend to forget things that potentially have great importance to us.

For some samples of daily reflections, see Appendix 1, Sample Lesson Plans. "Notes to Myself" at the end of each plan include sample reflections from the teacher.

In addition, it is important to mark changes on your curriculum as you use it so that when it comes time to revise the curriculum, you have all the information you need right at hand. Ideally, a curriculum should be formally revised annually, and informally adapted to each and every learner and group you have.

Part of your accountability to yourself is also to ensure that you are giving yourself ample opportunities to enhance your own knowledge by participating in conferences and through reading appropriate professional materials.

And, if you are a new instructor, don't burn yourself out. This field is so interesting, that it is easy to forget that you need a life outside the classroom and time to do things that have no connection with your work.

Tests

In that tests are what many teachers and students think evaluation is about, here are some of the kinds of tests which are common in our learning society. Students going on to other forms of education will no doubt encounter some or all of these.
- True-False
- multiple choice
- question-answer
- spelling
- homonyms and antonyms
- crosswords
- dictations
- fill-in-the-blanks (both spoken and written)
- compositions
- analogies (verbal reasoning)
    For example: slender is to_____as_____is to fat.
        a. skinny, thin

      b. skinny, plump

      c. thin, obese

(The underlying category of comparison in this analogy is the relationship of positive adjectives to their negative, or derogatory, counterparts. The correct answer is "b." Some university departments use these tests in their entrance examinations for certain programs.)

Using a variety of testing formats in the classroom will prepare your students to handle with greater ease the types of tests employers or educators may use with them in the future.

In addition, there is a need to distinguish between standardized and teacher-made tests. You can buy a variety of standardized tests from publishers. The advantage of standardized tests for assessment purposes is that they have been tried out with a large number of people and that the publishers have, at least in theory, worked out any problems. When a student gets a certain score, that is supposed to mean something to the person who hears that score in terms of his or her level of fluency in the language.

One disadvantage of standardized tests is that they are necessarily culture-bound to some extent. Tests made in Britain or the US are not as appropriate for Canadian students, as they are for students in the countries where they were prepared. A test that may reflect an accurate assessment for a well-educated student might be inappropriate for a student who does not have a formal education background. Even the region of the country could make quite a difference to the type of language a person has learned. My efforts to use most standardized tests in the past have not been satisfying, in spite of their obvious advantages.

Certain standardized tests are recognized for particular purposes. The TOEFL is the best known standardized test and is used almost universally for university entrance. Many students take TOEFL preparation courses to teach them specifically how to do well in this test, since it is not only one's language fluency that is being measured here but also one's ability to take the test. The TOEFL test measures a very formal English which is not used in everyday circles. For example, we would *say*, "Who did you give my pen to?" but on the test, that would be a wrong choice. On the test, one would have to choose, "To whom did you give my pen?" If your students are preparing for study in a university, even if you are not teaching a TOEFL class, it would be a good idea to acquaint yourself with this test and give your students some pointers. Most publishers of TESL materials have preparation manuals for the TOEFL.

Questions to Think about and Discuss

1. How do you respond to being tested? Do you know others who respond quite differently? If so, why do you suppose that is?

2. If you could choose a form of progress evaluation for something important you are learning, what would you choose and why? Which forms of evaluation discourage you, and which forms motivate you to do your best?

3. What ways have you observed testing to interfere with an individual's confidence in his or her learning?

4. In what ways can quantitative evaluation detract us from attending to the most important aspects of teaching an ESL learner?

For Further Reading

Madsen, Harold S. 1983. *Techniques in Testing.* New York: Oxford University Press.

This well-organized book provides a comprehensive introduction to all of the commonly used types of testing. The first section covers the language subskills: vocabulary, grammar, and pronunciation, and the second section covers communication skills: listening, speaking, reading, and writing. A very good resource for any teacher.

Being an Educator in ESL and EFL

Relationships

In this chapter, you will learn about:

- the importance of trust and commitment
- recognizing and preventing the abuse of power
- making the best interests of the learner our priority
- individualizing our response to learners
- avoiding the saviour routine
- building community in the classroom
- using conflict resolution
- seeing things from an administrator's point of view
- keeping our lives in balance

The essence of quality teaching lies, I believe, in the relationships we create in the classroom. In this chapter we will explore six different relationships: teacher to students as a group, teacher to student as individual, students amongst themselves, teacher to colleagues, teacher to supervisor, and teacher to self. Attention to all of these relationships will go a long way to ensuring healthy outcomes for everyone.

Teacher to Students as a Group

I distinguish between the teacher/*student* relationship and the teacher/*students* relationship because each person is an individual and, to some extent, that necessitates a difference in our relationship to each learner if we are at all authentic. Profound respect is the hallmark of a good teacher's attitude towards his or her students. I know I have emphasized this point many times, but it really is so very important. When a group of learners know that you are committed to their well-being and to enabling them to do what they need and want to do as learners, they will make a much greater effort than they would with someone who cannot relate to them at all and views teaching as a job rather than a vocation. Our respect for and understanding of the learners' challenges will bring out the best in each and will also encourage them to support one another's learning.

We must be cognizant of the difference in power between ourselves and the learners. Because we have the power to allow participation or deny it, and in many cases to name success and failure, we tend to neglect considerations of power. But you can be sure the learners think about it, especially if it is being in any way abused by the teacher. By "abuse," I mean using power towards some end other than that of the learner's learning.

As an employer, I have had occasion to regret hiring those teachers who had no compulsion about using their power for personal reasons. One very well-meaning teacher I have mentioned previously, saw nothing wrong with taking her students to her church for social events. She was very committed to her students and saw these outings as opportunities for them to practice their English with native speakers.

What this teacher did not realize was that some of the students felt very uncomfortable with this. They did not feel free to reject her hospitality, but also did not want to feel obligated to attend her church. Some learners belonged to other churches, some to other religions, and some to no religion at all. They privately felt that she would favour those learners who attended the events with her. When I discovered that she was doing this, I told her it had to stop, but for some students, the damage was already done.

Another teacher had a lot of personal problems which were not apparent in the beginning. He used his students as sounding boards for all his health and psychological problems. Again, these learners felt powerless to complain to him for fear that they would be treated differently if they did. And they felt uncomfortable complaining about him, because they did not want to be responsible for him losing his job, which he eventually did.

An administrator in another program was discovered to be manipulating the students into bringing her gifts. The learners quickly learned that if they wanted her intervention in solving problems with their funding support counsellors, they had better have it established that they would repay her in kind. When this was pointed out to her, she was unable to recognize it.

All of these situations are examples of abuse of power. In the first case, the teacher was well intentioned, but not conscious of the power issues existent in a classroom. In the second, the teacher was not fit to be in a classroom and needed to deal with his personal problems outside of class, since he was unable to leave them at the door when he entered. And in the third, the administrator had a lot of personal problems, and appeared to be unconscious of the ways in which she was manipulating the learners into boosting her sense of power and popularity by bringing her gifts.

Some people think that our students should never know if there is anything wrong in our lives. I don't go that far. That is not being authentic. If something terrible has happened in my life, my students may eventually know about it, but I do not dwell on it. The information is shared when appropriate and we move on. The male teacher and the administrator in those examples did not know how to move on with their students, because they did not know how to move on with their lives.

Learners do not expect us to be happy all the time. They do expect us, the majority of the time, to be fully present to the reason for which they are there: to learn. They expect us to *be* fair and to *appear to be* fair. They need us to be somewhat flexible in response to their needs. They may have registered for an English class, but what they might really need is information about dealing with an employer who is breaking labour laws, or assistance in dealing with a landlord who is not living up to his or her responsibilities in managing a building.

The learners also need us not to drown in their problems, but to be on solid ground when they reach to us for a hand. I found this particularly difficult when I was working with refugees. Their stories of loss, of injustice, even of torture were almost more than I could bear, and I felt helpless to ease their pain. What I have learned is that the world is a place of good and evil, and we can choose to focus on either. If I am to be a good classroom teacher, I believe I can do that best by living in the moment, making the best of it, and enabling learners to do likewise. I can be respectful of the other's pain, but I am not responsible for it (hopefully), and I do no one any good by wallowing in it.

Being sensitive to learners requires a particular form of balancing. On the one hand, we want to be close enough to them to earn their trust so that they will feel safe taking the risks inevitably involved in learning a new language. But, at the same time, we have to keep enough distance so that we are not, and are not seen as being, personally involved in the lives of our students. If you are, for example, socializing with one student and her family, think how the other students feel. They expect that you will do more for her than you would for them, and it does not matter if this is true or not; it matters that it is *perceived* to be true.

Lastly, it is unwise to date or become close friends with students whom you are teaching at the time you are teaching them. It is natural for men and women to be attracted one to another, and many ESL teachers of my acquaintance have ended up marrying former students, but it can cause untold problems if such relationships do not wait until a course is finished. Even then, think twice about the authenticity of a relationship in which one person has much more power than the other in the beginning.

Teacher to Student as Individual

While we certainly endeavour to treat all students fairly, we cannot possibly treat all students the same, nor would it be desirable to do so. Part of what it means to be respectful is to recognize each person's uniqueness. One of the things beginning teachers in particular must watch out for is giving more time to the students who demand it, who ask the most questions, who are the most charming, and who clearly know what they want and how to get it. (A colleague of mine would argue with my position saying that such students deserve more attention, and would get it in real life outside the classroom. She would simply draw the attention of the other students to the behaviour of those who were getting that attention so that, if others wanted it, they knew what they had to do to get it.)

While there is a lot to her approach, I don't think I am going to alter people's personalities in a major way in the length of an English course. I feel an obligation to each and every person in the class. This means that I respond differently to different people according to their needs. The student who is terribly shy does not get corrected in the same manner as the student who is very confident and asks me to correct his or her errors. The student who is suffering health problems does not have the same expectations around homework and energy in class as the student who is healthy and able to learn at a good pace.

I have found it useful to get to know people as individuals and then to negotiate, to a degree, what is practical for each person to enable him or her to get the most out of the course, whether that is in class or in doing homework. If someone has special needs not met by the course, and there is no other course more appropriate to his or her needs, it is important to create special learning opportunities for that person from time to time. For example, I had one ESL student who was not at all interested in the curriculum as a whole. All he wanted to learn was plumbing vocabulary so he would know what customers wanted when he went to work. For sure, the whole class did not want to learn the names of plumbing problems and tools. I found him a book with the names of the tools of his trade and gave him his own assignments in learning these names. At break times, I helped him with the pronunciation of these terms. In the meantime, he took in what we were doing in the classroom, or rather he tolerated it sufficiently to get something out of it, which he would not have done if he were not getting what he wanted as well.

Part of treating people as individuals is recognizing that they come from different cultural, racial, religious, and class backgrounds and have different personal interests. If someone is a musician with a beautiful singing voice, and the others want to hear him sing, invite him to do so. Celebrate his gift to the group and, hopefully, he will do the same for others in the group. If the Moslems in the group want time off to prepare their Eid feast, give it to them. The Buddhists in the group will then know that you will be equally respectful of their New Year festivities.

For the students who come across as particularly weak and wanting to lean on you, resist the urge to be the great saviour. When we see people in need, we have a tendency to do for them what it would be better for them to learn to do for themselves. We often help these weaker students, because it makes us feel good about ourselves. It may take longer to teach them to do it for themselves, but if that is at all practical, take the time. Not only will these learners become capable of taking care of themselves in the future, but they will also be able to help others in a similar situation.

When we have a particularly busy curriculum, we may want to make time to spend a few minutes with each individual in the class. If the administrator of the program is willing, you can do that by scheduling interviews at some point. If that is not possible, simply make a point of spending ten minutes talking to one person each day. Another way to get to know individuals is through journalling, for those learners who want to use the journal in that way.

Students amongst Themselves

Some students will naturally support one another's learning, while others want nothing to do with the other students and resent any effort on the part of the teacher to encourage cooperative learning.

It is my feeling that communities provide strength to their members and that a learning community enables everyone to get more out of a curriculum than if each individual is out for himself or herself alone. In addition, communities in which members get along with one another do not drain one another's energies, humiliate one another, or get into endless conflicts. It is, therefore, in everyone's interest to spend some time in getting to know one another and in finding a reason to like and help one another wherever possible.

Sometimes, it is easy to get this feeling of community, and other times it is anything but. The communication in a classroom cannot always be between a teacher and a student, or rather it should not be if students are to get an abundance of opportunities to practice listening and speaking. One technique that many teachers use is pairwork. This technique is valuable unless you get a few students who regard it as beneath them to waste time talking to anyone whose pronunciation is less than native-speaker-like. Such learners usually view themselves as better than the others in the class. I try to dispel that notion right away, partly by being respectful of all cultures, races, and individuals myself, and partly by not tolerating discriminatory behaviour from anyone.

Nonetheless, in any group together long enough, there is bound to be conflict of some kind. In a traditional classroom, conflicts are "resolved" by the teacher who imposes his or her solution upon the conflictive parties, and that practice is accepted by all and expected by most. I have learned that it is much more effective to have the entire group assume responsibility for the collective well-being of the group. Anyone who is witness to a conflict can choose to become accountable for the resolution of that conflict. This takes work and is not always popular with those students who see this as the teacher's job, but when a group gets to know one another, its members will usually see the logic in having everyone take responsibility for what is going on.

It is important to avoid gossip. Learners justifiably feel very angry if a teacher responds to one student's complaint about another with no idea as to what the truth is behind that conflict. Dealing with problems behind closed doors results in students telling other students their own personal versions of what happened, often making the problem worse than it was to begin with. That which is dealt with in the open by everyone, however, cannot be lied about. People can accept criticism if we are clear that it is a behaviour that we are criticizing, not the person. This means we have to be careful not to hold grudges. When a problem is dealt with, it is dealt with, and we move on, together. No one is perfect. Learners look to the teacher to set the tone for conflict resolution. As long as we are fair and are seen to be fair, and do not sit in judgment or act with favouritism, the learners will almost always support us in whatever methods we choose.

Teacher to Colleagues

Needless to say, everyone is better off when colleagues are collegial and share with one another. I remember years ago working in a school where the staff was a real team. If someone made up a handout and thought the other teachers could use it, he or she offered it to them. Then, it went into binders for anyone to use. When I did not know how to teach something, it was okay to ask, and no one treated me as if I were stupid. My fellow teachers made suggestions and I took them. So, when a new teacher was hired who had previously worked at a school which had obviously been very different, we were startled when, one day, she got very upset because someone had borrowed a spare handout from her desk to use in her own class. She said, "I worked very hard to prepare that and you have no right to use it." We were stunned that anyone could be so possessive about handouts, because we did not work that way.

Many of us form friendships with one or two colleagues, and there is nothing wrong with that. However, it is good to also be a community and to have common activities from time to time to which everyone is invited. This creates a positive working environment for everyone. It is in no one's interest to create little cliques where one group gossips about another, and becomes silent when someone not in their group walks by. This creates a negative atmosphere that affects everyone in the program, including the students. It is the responsibility of each of us to create the kind of atmosphere in which we want to work.

I also believe it is important to keep one's priorities straight. I mentioned the teacher who was exploiting his students for personal reasons. Other teachers knew about this long before I did, but no one said anything to him, and no one reported it to me. When I asked them about this later, they said, "Teachers don't rat on one another." My response to that was, "Even at the expense of the learners?" The learners in that class were suffering and were upset. They felt powerless to do anything. They had gone to the coordinator of the program and she had done nothing. I believe it is important to do what is best, not what is easiest. No one likes to get anyone in trouble, but if someone is doing something that is harmful to a learner or group of learners, their welfare takes precedence over the "not ratting" rule. If you see a colleague doing something that is clearly not right, speak first to that colleague and express your views. If that does not change the situation, consider your ability to initiate change in that situation.

Teacher to Supervisor

If it is difficult for you to see the significance of the power relationship between yourself and a learner, look at the relationship between yourself and your supervisor. Some of you are probably reluctant to say what you think to that individual, particularly if it is critical, and regardless of whether or not your supervisor would be open to your criticisms. It is natural to want to protect ourselves in relationships of unequal power.

My suggestion to you in regards to your relationship with your supervisor is to be accountable for it. Your supervisor is, like yourself, a person doing his or her best. The values and positions may be different, but both of you are living out of your own light, so to speak. I often used to feel frustration when, as a teacher, I was refused permission to do something that seemed very logical to me. Now, having been an employer, I can see things from a different perspective, and I have a lot more sympathy for the supervisors of my past, than I did at the time. Your supervisor has to think about the larger picture: implications for other students, financial liability, legal repercussions, public image, politics of the program, and many things which go beyond the needs of the immediate classroom. If you get permission to do something, what assumptions will the other teachers make about that? As an administrator, I remember once reimbursing a teacher for some refreshments she had bought for a class which had a guest speaker. The next thing I knew, everyone in the program was regularly submitting coffee, tea, and baked goods receipts, and the budget could not support that.

Try to empathize with your supervisor and it will be appreciated. Be forthright in expressing your ideas and in making suggestions and requests, but try also to see the other's perspective if those ideas are not accepted. And whatever you do, do not lie or try to cover up your actions, because once the trust is broken, your life will be considerably more difficult than it was before. When I trusted a teacher, I tended to give that person a lot of space to do what she wanted to do with her class. When I was given reason not to trust, I watched like a hawk. That was my job.

When your supervisor has done your job and has some expertise in the area, do not hesitate to ask questions. You can learn a lot by doing so. I respected those who asked questions when they did not know something, because it reassured me that they would learn. I was suspicious of those who appeared to know it all, because it has not been my experience that any of us do. I still have much to learn and I have to assume that is true of the majority. I respect those who approach their work with an attitude of curiosity and wonder.

Teacher to Self

You may think this is a rather bizarre topic to include in this chapter but it is, I believe, as important as the others. What I mean by our relationship to ourselves is our consciousness about who we are, why, how, and where we want to go in our life journey, particularly, but not exclusively, as it pertains to work. We are not automatons doing what we are programmed to do, or rather, we should not be. Yet all too often, we get so absorbed in what we are doing that we cease to be reflective about it. When that happens, we are no longer in control and no longer taking accountability for our experience. That lack of self-awareness not only affects our own lives in a negative way, it also affects those around us: the learners, the staff, and our families.

I think my dedication to the work I have done at various times in my life has blinded me to the need to have a life outside of work, and to attend as committedly to that life as to the work I was doing. We lose our perspective when we get too absorbed in our teaching. To get it back, we need to have activities that have nothing to do with our work and have friends who likewise are not attached in any way to that environment. Then we can restore (or keep) our sense of balance, and with that, our good health.

At the same time, I can truly say that I feel extremely fortunate to have a few very good friends whom I have met through my teaching. Working in ESL/EFL is like having a free ticket around the world. To get to know other cultures, languages, and ways of looking at life is a privilege which we ESL/EFL teachers are extremely fortunate to have. I can think of no career I would rather have had.

In conclusion, attention to the various relationships in and around our work will reward us many times over. Relationships lie at the centre of success in this work. Good relationships imply trust, mutuality, openness, and sharing. In that kind of environment, the learner is free to grow and so are we.

Questions to Think about and Discuss

1. Why do you (want to) teach ESL or EFL? What do you (want to) get out of it? What is your interest in this field?

2. What support systems do you have (or need) to meet your personal needs for acknowledgment, support, and friendship?

3. Do you have a clear sense of your own power to influence your environment in the best interests not only of yourself, but of those around you?

4. Think of one teacher you really liked in your schooling. Why is it that you really liked that person?

5. Have you experienced a community of people in which others supported the growth of your potential and you theirs? If so, what were the hallmarks of that community? What was it that made them special? If not, do you know anyone who is in such a community? If so, describe it.

6. Have you ever been the victim of someone's gossip? What did that feel like? How long has it affected you?

Exercise

If you are using this book in a class, or are working together with colleagues who are interested in doing this, work together to prepare a draft set of ethical guidelines. If you are working in an ESL/EFL program which does not already have one for use in your program, perhaps this is an activity you could work on at staff meetings.

CHAPTER 15

Professionalism: What It Means and Why It Is Important

In this chapter, you will learn about:

- professional associations
- the value of participation as a professional
- professional conferences
- the importance of staying up-to-date
- using the Internet for networking
- choosing the right TESL or TEFL program for you.

My Oxford dictionary lists over half a column of definitions for the word "professional." The meaning which comes closest to what I want to say is something like "of or pertaining to, proper to a profession," but the real meaning is much more than that. For me, the real meaning of professionalism has to do with excellence. That excellence is such that the learners recognize you as a professional and your colleagues likewise hold you in that light.

There are several aspects to professionalism. One is your behaviour. Do you act like a professional and, if so, what does that mean? At the obvious level, professionalism means coming to work on time; doing your job to the best of your ability; adhering to the policies and procedures of your employing organization; dressing, speaking and behaving appropriately for the job and the context in which you work; and not engaging in gossip, backbiting or other behaviours which would cause harm to those around you. At a less obvious level, it means setting yourself on a path to be not only continually learning what there is to learn about teaching ESL or EFL, but also working to actively contribute to that body of knowledge and practice.

Belonging to a Professional Association

I do not see belonging to a professional organization as an option for most teachers, but rather as an obligation and a privilege. Your professional association exists in order that its members may be the best they can be at what they do. It provides you with professional development opportunities through conferences, newsletters and/or journals, and participation in the politics of the profession. It offers a network of colleagues in the area of your specialization and with that, the opportunity to learn with and from them. Such an organization is always in need of good people to work on committees or the executive. By participating, that in turn provides you with an opportunity to exercise your voice for the good of everyone connected to the field and also gives you an opportunity to develop your leadership potential.

In that language is about voice, I do not believe we can fully claim to be teaching a language if we have not learned how to use our own voices. By that, I mean that when there are issues, one voice alone is limited in what it can do, whereas the collective voice of a whole organization carries a lot of weight and has a better chance of drawing attention to its concerns. If we want the learners we teach to become self-sufficient in English, we must ask ourselves if we are self-sufficient, if we are true participants in our own society. There are many issues in ESL and EFL. As you become aware of the issues pertinent to the work you are doing, or are about to do, ask yourself what you can do about those problems.

There are various professional associations. I belong to three: TESOL (Teachers of English to Speakers of Other Languages), TESL Canada, and ATESL (Alberta Teachers of English as a Second Language). TESOL is the international organization and provides quarterly journals with up-to-date research and theory in the field of English language instruction to speakers of other languages. They also have a very large annual conference which is located in a different city each year, most often in the United States, but sometimes in Canada. Thousands of professionals, both academics and classroom teachers, come to this conference every year. You will meet there the authors of the books you are using in your classrooms. You will attend the largest publishers' display you can imagine and find new materials you would like to use in your classrooms. Best of all, you will meet people from all over the world who are interested in the same things you are. You can now easily communicate with those colleagues through e-mail. While you may feel a little overwhelmed the first time you go to a TESOL conference, it is an experience you will want to repeat.

My provincial association is, in many ways, more significant to me. It is easier to become involved in an association close to home, and it is definitely cheaper to attend its annual conference. Our provincial association has the ear of politicians and can affect policy-setting in our province. It also has an excellent annual conference where speakers are invited in and where we as members all contribute to planning and giving workshops and papers for our colleagues. A newsletter keeps us all up-to-date on what is going on where and with whom. I have chosen to be very involved in this association in the past and have benefited tremendously from that choice. An association of any kind is only as strong as its members, and we need to commit to making our associations strong ones.

In Canada, most members of provincial associations are also automatically members of TESL Canada, the national association, the board of which is composed of representatives from each provincial association. TESL Canada's annual conference coincides with that of a provincial conference, each year moving to a different location across the country. In addition, they have a website which is kept up-to-date, but the most commonly appreciated aspect of TESL Canada is the *TESL Canada Journal*, a reviewed publication of articles and book reviews primarily written by Canadian authors.

Even after many years of teaching, you may feel that you are not good enough to offer to present a workshop or paper at a conference. If you think that way, it is unfortunate, because if it were not for colleagues just like you, there would be no conferences. It is people like you and I that plan and present at these events. None of us professes to be expert at what we do, only to share our thoughts and ideas with others who may be interested in doing so. I presented at my first conference in Vancouver in the late seventies. I had a little push to do so. The only way we could get paid time off to attend a conference in those days was to be invited to present at one. I wanted to learn so I submitted two responses to the call for papers, and was amazed to have both of them accepted.

I will never forget my first conference. To one of my workshops came Mary Selman, a well-known Canadian educator and author. I was so embarrassed that a woman of her calibre would come to my lowly workshop. She was, however, a very humble, pleasant person as eager to learn as I was, and we became good friends. In the second workshop, I had asked for volunteers who spoke uncommon languages to demonstrate a particular technique using their language. I was trying to prove a point. Two of the volunteers did exactly what I wanted them to and illustrated my point. The third did exactly what I wanted, but he did it so well that we learned *in spite of* the method. That was a very significant learning for me and was the beginning of my understanding that it is not the method that matters as much as it is the focus, energy, and relationships which exist in the learning moment. After that experience, I became a conference junkie, sharing my ideas and flourishing on those of others. I hope you will do likewise.

As for finding an association in your area, both TESOL and TESL Canada have websites that link to the websites of other associations.

You may wish to explore these and find the association that is most appropriate for you.

Staying Up-to-Date with Research and Reading

Our fields are changing continually. We have new understandings of what language is, how second languages are most effectively learned, and what methodologies are most effective. We cannot take a course of studies in TESL or TEFL and then assume that we know the field. We need to be forever updating ourselves by reading and listening to speakers.

It has been exciting for me to watch well-known Canadian theorists change and expand their thinking. I remember attending a workshop 20 years ago, by someone who is now a well-known and respected academic in the country. I did not find it helpful. The presentation was boring, filled with big words that I did not understand and complex computations of statistics to do with how learners read. I could not relate to the presenter at all. It has been with pleasure through the years that I have listened to that presenter several times since and found him to be continually discovering new and important things in his work; he has become a reasonably eloquent and entertaining speaker. We are all learning, or should be, and it is refreshing to see those we recognize as experts growing and changing even as we ourselves are.

We need to be critical readers of the theories presented to us, even as we need to encourage learners to be critical readers of the materials we give to them. A critical reader is one who reads in an identified context, asking himself or herself in whose interest materials are written. In that the majority of our theory comes to us from academics rather than classroom teachers, it is all the more important that we weigh these ideas against our own experience. If our "gut" tells us that something is not right, it probably isn't.

I think that when we can find the time to do so, we also need to become involved in the research that contributes to theorizing in our field. *Participatory research*, or *action research* as the Australians call it, is an approach to research in which practitioners research their own practice, or learners research their own learning. This type of research makes a great deal of sense and prevents the occasional problem of academics who are out of touch with the classroom posing false or trivial hypotheses that prevent them from seeing what is really happening in the classroom, and from discerning what is important and what is not. (This is not to say that all academics are out of touch with the classroom; many spend a lot of their time out in classrooms observing and working directly with teachers.)

To stay up-to-date with reading, I do two things. I read the articles in the two journals to which I subscribe, and I also read books, both those in the field and those in other fields which may have an impact on the work I do. Whereas authors in the ESL field tend to write most often about research and methodology, I find it is also important to stay current on social and cultural critiques, current and historical developments in the countries of the learners with whom we work, and curriculum theory in general. Others may find they want to stay up-to-date on linguistics, psychology, anthropology, or philosophy—all of which have something to say to us. David Mendelsohn has edited a book called *Expanding Our Vision: Insights for Language Teachers*, which looks at the influence of other fields and ideas on the work we do as professionals, with several authors contributing a chapter each on something which has had an impact on them. I believe this book to be a valuable contribution to our field, and one which opens our perspective to a wealth of ideas from different disciplines.

The Internet

The Internet is a relatively new resource and a very exciting one. Not only does it open up the possibility of inexpensive and regular communication with a network of colleagues all over the world, but it gives one immediate access to the most broad collection of ideas on every subject we could want to know about. There are ESL chat lines, networks, articles to read, and library resources. If you have any interest whatsoever in the World Wide Web, by all means, check out the ESL and/or EFL sites and consider the value of having students on the Web as well.

I have found that learners are very motivated by the computer as a learning tool. We had two writing programs which drew from the same pool of learners, and it was very interesting to see that the volume of writing produced by those students in the computerized writing course was considerably higher than the volume of writing produced by those students who had chosen to take the more conventional writing course. We were surprised because our original emphasis was on computer skills in the one course, not on writing skills. Adult learners want to learn how to use the computer. They are feeling left behind by their children who have become relative experts in a very short time.

Choosing the Right TESL or TEFL Program for You

If you are at a stage where you know you want to work in this area but do not have any training, research the various options before you choose one. Programs are by no means equal. There are increasing numbers of private organizations offering crash courses to prepare teachers to go abroad. It should be obvious that one cannot learn in a week what one would learn in a year-long program with assignments and time to read, observe, and practice teach. A good short course will give you an introduction to the field, but if at all possible, choose a program that has a variety of courses and instructors and that will present you with opportunities to work with students in real classrooms.

Not all of us have the option to travel to another location to learn, but if you do, there are a number of very interesting programs available. The School for International Living in Vermont is one such program and provides prospective teachers from all over the world with currently popular approaches to every aspect of the field. Universities throughout North America have programs of varying types, and you should talk to the professors and examine their calendars before you choose a program. I personally find that those programs which are housed in Linguistics Departments are limiting for the simple reason that linguistics is only one field of relevance to ESL and EFL. On the other hand, it matters less where a program is housed, than what concepts form the foundation for structuring a program and what type of staff are teaching it. You want to find professors who have themselves worked as teachers in the field, not someone who has read about it. You would be surprised how many academics have not themselves done the work they are teaching others to do. You also want to find professors who are open to a variety of perspectives and will support you in exploring things that are important to you. There is no single right way to do this work; there are many approaches and most have something of value to offer us.

When you are talking to instructors in these programs, they should be able to answer questions such as the following:

- What is your philosophy of education for ESL (or EFL) learners?
- What components are there in this course?
- What practicuum possibilities are there for participants in this course?
- How will I be evaluated?
- What is your preferred approach to ESL (or EFL) curriculum?
- What do you think the role of the teacher is in the ESL or EFL classroom?

Use your judgment to discern whether or not this TESL or TEFL program is where you want to commit your time and energy. If it is not, shop around and find a school that is right for you. Ask others who have taken programs what they liked and did not like. Ask graduates of those programs what they learned and what they wished they could have learned.

If you do not have contacts who work in ESL and EFL, offer your services as a volunteer for a few weeks in a program in your community. Most programs are eager to have volunteers who will commit to spending some time on a regular basis either in the classroom or with individuals. In this way, you will get to know experienced teachers and you can ask them to help you select a good program. You can ask them what they would like to have learned before they started working in ESL (or EFL).

You will see advertising from time to time about crash courses which promise to prepare you to teach in another country. A 25- or 30-hour course cannot possibly prepare you to do a good job of teaching in any context. You may wish to take it as an introduction, but hopefully, you will have more extensive learning opportunities to prepare you for a most rewarding career.

Questions to Think about and Discuss

1. Think of a person you consider to be highly professional and one whose actions you consider to be less than such. Now try to isolate what characteristics caused you to make those judgments.

2. What specific skills could you see yourself learning by volunteering to work with a professional association in some capacity?

3. What strengths and weaknesses do you offer an ESL or EFL class-room? Looking at your strengths, how could you see yourself sharing those with colleagues at a conference? What kinds of professional development could you seek out to address those areas of weakness you have identified?

For Further Reading

Mendelsohn, David, Ed. 1999. *Expanding Our Vision: Insights for Language Teachers.* Toronto: Oxford University Press.

> I have long awaited this kind of a book. I know that my key mentors in this work have not come from the field itself. Ten authors in this book describe how their favourite mentors from outside the field have influenced their work within it. It is a good read and suggests a valuable challenge for each one of us to find our mentors and apply their ideas to the enrichment of us all.

TESL Canada Journal. Published by the Teachers of English as a Second Language Federation of Canada, PO Box 44105, Burnaby, BC V5B 4Y2, 1-800-393-9199. E-mail: teslcanada@home.com http://www.tesl.ca

> Like the *TESOL Quarterly*, the *TESL Canada Journal* is a reviewed journal, which means that published articles have been screened by a review panel of people considered by the editors to have expertise in the area in which an author is writing. Articles address both ESL and EFL topics. Unlike the *Quarterly*, in addition to the academic articles, there is also a "Perspectives Section" which contains shorter articles giving

views on particular topics. Readers find it easy to relate to these articles in that they tend to address common themes for teachers everywhere.

TESOL Quarterly. Published by the Teachers of English to Speakers of Other Languages, Inc. 700 S. Washington Street, Ste. 200, Alexandria, VA 22314 USA, (703) 836-0774. E-mail: publications@tesol.org http://www. tesol.edu

This quality academic journal has set the pace for current theorizing worldwide. In addition, membership in TESOL gives you a choice of two other publications directed at more practical concerns in teaching as well as a newsletter in the field you have identified as your primary area of interest (e.g., adult education, EFL, computer-assisted learning, refugee concerns).

Check both of these websites for links to other sites of interest.

Discernment in Developing Voices and Creating Visions

In this, the concluding chapter, you will learn about:

- the meaning of discernment
- the importance of strengthening your own Voice
- ways of developing Voice in your students
- the importance of having your own clear vision
- ways of facilitating vision for your students.

What is Discernment?

In this book, you have seen *one* perspective on the teaching of English as an additional language, both within an English-speaking country and abroad, where English is studied for many reasons. The emphasis within my perspective has been on the importance of context, of understanding the nature of the learners whom you are teaching, and the nature of the situation in which you are teaching: the time, the place, the significant events of the day. While technical approaches to teaching provide us with ample tools to apply to our task, they do not give us the discernment to know when those tools are appropriate and when they are not. Nor do they enable us to adapt the tools to make them more appropriate, or give us the good sense to abandon them altogether when they are not. If I were to have a fairy godmother to whom I could make one wish for every teacher, it would be the gift of discernment that I would wish for.

Discernment comes with experience. It is the fruit of the wisdom that develops in those of us who are willing to admit we are wrong and who are willing to learn alternative ways of approaching things, not only from colleagues, theorists, and courses, but most of all from those whom we teach. Who knows better than learners do the effectiveness—or not—of what we have taught?

Discernment is also the ability to read a text and take from it that which fits and to set aside that which does not. I would hope that new readers to the field of *EFL* have not found it frustrating to read my numerous examples from *ESL*. I have simply spent more time in that aspect of English teaching and have a greater repertoire of stories there. Just because a story comes from that context, does not mean that it has nothing to offer other contexts. If you can look inside the story, to its essence, you can take that essence and apply it to many other contexts, including your own.

Discernment also strikes me as somewhat of a spiritual idea. It rises above the materiality of whatever we are talking about, into the realm of values, of *peoplemaking*, as Virginia Satir has called it in her book of the same title. Teaching is very much a peoplemaking activity, regardless of whether or not we are working with adults or children. We are not, as Paulo Freire reminded us, pouring information into people's empty heads, making bank deposits. Rather, we are meeting formed human beings and, through our interactions with those beings, we are reinforming, challenging, and enabling them to discover who they really are and who they can become. Too heady, you say, for the second language classroom? I beg to differ. Whether you intend this to happen or not, it does.

Learners will remember you, not for the material you taught them or the handouts you gave them, but for how they felt in your presence, and for how they came to feel about the subject matter because of the way you presented yourself to them within it. They will remember if the class was fun or boring, stimulating or tedious, clear or totally incomprehensible. They will be astounded when they realize they have learned more than language, they have learned about themselves and their potential. Language is, after all, the medium of learning, not the goal thereof. They will remember whether they felt stupid in this learning situation, or capable.

These experiences are not accidental. They do not just happen. They are within your control to the extent that you are conscious of what creates them. When you realize that humiliation shuts people down and prevents them from taking the risks they need to take as language learners, you will tread gently with corrections and ensure that you laugh *with* learners rather than *at* them. When you come to see the classroom bully or arrogant controller as a person with low self-esteem, who has not known the love and respect all human beings need and deserve if they are to thrive, you will replace harsh responses with attempts to find ways of giving this learner positive attention and recognition at any opportunity. When it dawns on you that we do not learn participation by following the orders of someone else, you will learn to stand aside and expect learners to make decisions in the classroom.

Similarly, we do not learn to *ask* questions by giving answers to the teacher's questions. These types of learnings will eventually come to most teachers. In the meantime, perhaps you can learn vicariously from one old hand who has learned many things the hard way. There is no point in you suffering the bruises, if you can learn from mine. I wish each of you the gift of discernment.

Developing Our Voices

We know that language learning is about voice, but what does that mean? Voice is more than sound forming intelligible words. Voice is about expression that makes a difference. We speak and write to be heard, to be understood, to have an impact on the world around us. As teachers in the second-language classroom, we can turn out robots who can conjugate verbs correctly and fill vocabulary into appropriate slots on demand, or we can facilitate speakers of other languages finding a voice in English that makes a difference in an English-speaking context. This latter approach is a political one. It is about power. In order to do this, we ourselves must be aware of what creates power and what destroys it. And we must be willing to share the natural power of the teacher in the traditional classroom with the learners who are in our classrooms. We must understand the effect on some learners we teach of having lived in oppressive regimes where one was not permitted free expression. We must learn to use our power wisely to enhance the coming to power and voice of the learners, and not to assert our dominance in this corner of the world.

Each learner who leaves our classroom goes into the world and has an effect on other people. It is my greatest hope that those whom I have taught might be a little more inclined towards respecting other people, tolerating those who are different, and finding more peaceful ways of being in the world than they might otherwise have experienced. I would like to think that those I have taught have learned, if they did not already know it, that learning can be fun, that it need not be confined to one topic or one textbook, but can be a serendipity experience of responding to all the elements in any given moment. Ultimately, I would like to leave my mark on the world by doing my best to make it a slightly better place. I suspect many of us would wish the same of our lives.

Sharing power does not mean that I surrender my voice, but rather that I identify it simply as *my* voice and not *the* voice. My voice counts as one voice in a group, as does that of each learner. Having a voice means that I know how to have an impact on my own environment, to effect change as I see it needed. It means that when I speak, others listen because they have come to expect that I have something worth saying. This means I participate in my professional association and I participate in my community. I vote when there is an election, and I ensure that I have done my homework, and know how to vote for the person who can best represent my interests and those of the people I care about.

Having a voice means knowing that I am respected by those around me. I know that from how others look at me and how they talk to me. This respect is earned by knowing what I am talking about and by not speaking ill of others, or stooping to spread destructive gossip about others.

I cannot expect learners I teach to develop their own voices when I have not taken care to develop my own. To be sure, this is not an easy task. If you were fortunate enough to have been born in a family where your parents were role models for strong, ethical voices, then you are many steps ahead of those who were not so blessed. My father was a municipal politician. I suspect a lot of my political awareness comes from growing up with him having an opinion about important issues and researching topics in order to have informed opinions. I have also had the good fortune of having a couple of teachers in my life who understood the importance of voice, and lived their beliefs in that regard. However, we can all develop our voices. The first step is to believe that it is important and the second to believe that it is possible. When we believe those two things, we are well on the road to developing strong voices.

Developing Voice in Others

This is not a unit in a curriculum. It is an approach to teaching in which we ask people what they think and we care about what they say. It means that in the classroom we take seriously what the learners want and need, like and dislike. Like anything else, voice is learned through practice and getting affirming responses. We ask, we listen, and we act on what we hear.

Critical to developing voice in second-language learners is understanding that *what* is being said is more important than *how* it is said. Technical approaches to teaching have left us correcting errors rather than caring what it is that people are saying to us. It is a finely attuned skill to be able to correct *in order to understand*, or in response to a person's desire to understand how the language works. When we correct learners at the expense of what they are saying, it is hurtful and discouraging. Some never recover from feelings of being stupid and incapable in second-language classrooms.

We are dealing with many personalities, many social identities, and many wounded psyches in our classrooms. It would be neither reasonable nor desirable to assume that everyone could develop equally strong voices. Our goal is to honour the individuals where they are and be present to them in their life journeys, whatever forms those might take. The teacher who does not respect his or her students genuinely is in the wrong profession.

Developing Our Own Vision

As children, we all had vision because we all had imaginations. It was parents and teachers, unfortunately, who destroyed imagination for many of us, or rather made it difficult to imagine, for I do not believe this ability can be totally destroyed. It has simply faded from disuse and needs some healthy encouragement to be regained. Do you remember yearning to be an adult so that no one could tell you what to do and when to do it? You could *see* yourself being a free agent. That was a form of vision. Vision is the ability to see what it is that we want to happen. By building a detailed picture of what it is that we want, we are actually creating the mental, if not the metaphysical, means of ensuring that what we want to happen does happen. Nothing has been intentionally created without first being envisioned by its creator. Inventors create first in their minds what it is that they want to create with their hands and their machines.

As teachers, we are called to envision the world and worlds into which the learners are likely to go, and into which it would be nice if they did go. If we see everyone as becoming a cleaner, sewing machine operator, or dishwasher, we have not served well those learners who are capable of so much more with a little encouragement and guidance. In addition, consciously or unconsciously, we create the expectations learners have for the way or ways in which the English-speaking world will receive them. When the teacher talks down to the learners, many of them will transfer that one experience into an assumption that all Canadians are like that, that this is what they have to expect in Canada. Conversely, when a teacher speaks with enthusiasm and respect to learners, they have every reason to believe that Canadians are enthusiastic and respectful.

In that we have a tendency to create our own experiences, learners' own expectations will have a lot to do with what happens when they begin to interact with people in the community. When they expect the worst, they are less than pleasant themselves and tend to draw unpleasant reactions from others, which confirms their worst expectation. When learners are friendly and eager, they tend to attract the same back, confirming their positive expectations. In other words, the actions of teachers tend to be magnified by the expectations they create, which in turn attract that which is expected.

Can we envision a world of hope and possibility for both immigrant learners and visiting learners? Can we teach to that vision of possibility, sending forth learners with the highest and best expectations of what they can be and can do in this place?

As a community of teachers, can we create together a vision of ideal learning and teaching contexts? Can we detail the ethical standards and approaches to teaching which are consistent with that vision and support it into being? Without a vision, we continue to reproduce the status quo. That is not only boring; it is less than what we are capable of, and less than the learners deserve.

Supporting the Development of Vision in Learners

Because immigrant learners are not visiting our country, but have chosen to make their lives here, it is particularly critical that they learn to envision the kind of life they want and are prepared to create. I hear and see too many immigrants who feel like victims in their new land. A few complain openly about the jobs available to them in spite of training and experience that would indicate far better possibilities. Some complain about the way they feel invisible in jobs such as cleaning hospitals and working in diet kitchens. But most suffer in silence and hope their children will do better in the new land than they are. What can become of any of us without dreams, and the faith that the best of those dreams can be made real by hard work and by believing in our own capabilities and in the goodness of those around us? We would not be doing what we were doing without at some point having the intention to do so, and the vision to make that intention real. So it is in our classrooms. We have both the opportunity and the obligation to encourage the learners to dream, to envision, and to strive for the life experiences they deserve.

We can do that by asking learners what they want their lives to be like, by acknowledging dreams that are do-able, and by pushing some a little harder when they are afraid to dream. We can make suggestions and point the way to resources and support systems which will enable them to identify, and take, whatever steps are necessary to make their dreams real. We can make their classroom experiences real, grounded in the reality of our communities rather than in the fiction of some textbook or workbook written in another country, another time. We can introduce them to people and places which will stimulate their own imaginations. And we can share our own stories of how we got to where we are and how others we know succeeded in achieving their dreams. It is especially important that ESL learners see the success stories of others like themselves, because some will have a tendency to dismiss anything *we* might say as belonging to English-speakers and not to people who learn the language as adults. They need to see people of many races and ethnic groups in positions of relative power, doing what they want to be doing and what they like doing. These are comparisons with which they may identify. "If he or she can do it, maybe I can too . . ."

In conclusion, may I extend to you my sincere wish that you may experience the joy, and the expansive growth in your teaching experiences, that I have enjoyed in mine. I consider myself richly blessed by those whom I have taught, and by those with whom I have taught and worked. I wish you no less.

APPENDIX I

Sample Lesson Plans

Sample 1: A Grammar-Based Lesson

This lesson plan is designed for a high beginner class of ESL students in about their 6th week of study. It presumes the ability to answer basic personal questions. The intents in this lesson are teacher intents and describe the behaviour of the teacher rather than the learner. The class is scheduled to be 50 minutes in length. Students are of varied backgrounds.)[1]

Monday, March 30

Intents:

1. To <u>assess</u> how everyone in the class is today.
2. To <u>introduce</u> learners to the use and form of the present perfect tense and enable them to see the connection it makes between two points in time.
3. To <u>have learners practice</u> questions and answers which use the present perfect tense.
4. To <u>review</u> past tense questions and answers, and ensure that people know when to use the past tense and when to use the present perfect with typical personal questions.

---

1 Some of you may look at these plans and say, "Nobody really does all this preparation." I have two comments in response to that thought. The first is, that after 30 years of teaching, I still make plans very much like this, even typed, when I am doing anything relatively new. These plans free my energies to be totally present to the learners in the moment I am with them. The second is that you will undoubtedly spend less time on planning after you have gained experience, but that is only because you will be doing a lot of this work in your head. Time spent on good planning now will serve you and your students for years to come.

Resources:

- Handout graphically illustrating the past tense and the present perfect tense with samples of both.

- Flashcards which give a phrase to elicit a corresponding question and answer:

time in Canada	*How long have you lived in Canada?* *I have lived here for _____ months.*
date of arrival	*When did you arrive in the United States?* *I arrived here in June of 1997.*
length of time married	*How long have you been married?* *I have been married since 1980.* or *I have been married for 18 years.* or *I am not married. I am single.* or *I am divorced.*
date of marriage	*When did you get married?* *I got married in 1980.*
time as a student in this school	*How long have you been a student in this school?* *I have been a student here for two months.*

- Workbook exercises for homework.

Activities:

10 minutes   1.   Ask how everyone is and what they did on the weekend. Use this warmup activity to review the past tense and to add any vocabulary people need to express their activities. If people did not do anything special, ask if they saw or heard anything special.

5 minutes   2.   Draw a straight line on the blackboard as follows:

Table A1: Present perfect tense

Present Perfect Tense
I have written you two letters this week.

_____Time

Before	Now
I wrote you a letter on Sunday and on Wednesday.	**I am talking** to you.
Past Tense	Present Continuous Tense

Use diagram to explain why we have the present perfect tense and give examples from my own life:
I have been a teacher for 30 years.
I have never been to China.
I have visited Korea twice and hope to do so again.
I have given birth to 4 children. That is enough!
I have lived in Alberta for 50 years.
Demonstrate each of these sentences on the diagram, showing where each activity started and how it has been true up to the present.

Give out the handout.

10 minutes   3.   Ask learners to make statements using the present perfect. If they need prompting, ask the following questions:
How long have you been away from your country?
How long have you studied English?
How long have you lived in (the name of your city)?

Teach when to use FOR and SINCE.
   FOR (the duration of time) e.g., six months, ten years
   SINCE (the date) e.g., January 1992

Have you ever seen a panda bear?
Have you ever tasted a mango?
Have you ever made pizza?

15 minutes   4.   Using the flashcards, have the learners make questions in the present perfect first and ask specific learners for answers. Make sure everyone gets a turn both asking and answering. When the learners seem clear on the present perfect, introduce the cards that require past tense answers, and mix them up with the others.

When they have gone through the flashcards, have students make up their own questions beginning with the following expressions:
How long _____?
Have you ever _____?
When did you _____?
Did you ever _____?

5.   Optional Activity (If there is time)

Have the students write a paragraph which begins:
There are many fun things I have done in my life and many fun things I have never done.

Provide some examples from your own experience to set them thinking:

- *I have canoed in lakes and rivers and been stopped by the wind.*
- *I have ridden my bicycle through the mountains with my baby.*
- *I have gone camping near the ocean and had the tide come in and knock us all down.*
- *I have lived through an earthquake in Chile and one of the biggest rainstorms in Korea's recorded history.*
- *I have never gone skydiving or hang gliding and I have never gone deep-sea fishing.*
- *I have never been to Europe and I have never piloted an airplane.*

6. Assign homework from pages 60-63 in their workbook.

7. Ask people what they learned today that mattered.

Notes to Myself:

Mei-Ling was a music teacher in her country. She plays the cello. Johanne plays the violin. They were both very excited to share their love of music. They said they would play something for the class one day.

The vocabulary I used in my sentence examples was too difficult for some. I need to bring in some pictures tomorrow of the sports (or draw them with stick figures!).

I was reminded today of why I always ask people to use real language in the classroom rather than artificial sentences. The learners were excited to hear that I liked canoeing and bicycling and asked me many questions about where they could go to do both and if they could rent canoes. I feel like we got to know one another better today.

Tesfai got very excited when he was asking people if they had ever climbed mountains. He told us about the mountains in his country and how beautiful they were. He said he would bring some pictures in tomorrow. He said people did not usually climb mountains for fun in his country, but often did so to visit one of the churches built high in the mountains. A couple of the women asked if it would be possible for a group of us to go to the Rockies for the day in the late spring. There seemed to be a lot of interest in that. I see no reason why we can't if there are enough cars. We could do a photostory of the experience and that would be a great souvenir of the class.

What they learned today that mattered: Most people named words or expressions that they learned from my sentences or someone else's. The most interesting thing someone said was that he learned that I rode a bike. He thought that was very funny!?

Sample 2: A Vocabulary Lesson

This lesson plan is designed for a women's class in a settlement education program. Most of the women have lived in the country for more than two years, but have not had the opportunity to attend English classes before. They have a basic functional vocabulary, but are very incorrect in their speaking and have a very limited vocabulary. Their educational background varies from well educated to Grade 4 education in their own languages. This is a one-and one half hour lesson.

Friday, April 2

Intents:

1. To <u>assess</u> how people are feeling about their week.
2. To <u>review</u> the weather vocabulary we worked on earlier this week.
3. To <u>introduce</u> a variety of words used to express emotions and have the learners use them to describe their feelings about a set of pictures provided.

Resources:

- Large laminated pictures of various weather conditions and seasons.
- Pictures of people in various situations with either clearly expressed emotions on their faces or situations which would themselves tend to produce certain emotions (e.g., car wreck, child's stained T-shirt).
- Flash cards with one feeling word written on each, enough for one for each student.
- Homework exercise modelled on "When _____ happens, I feel _____." (This will be given on paper and/or on tape for those who do not feel comfortable with reading and writing.)

Activities:

15 minutes   1.   Discuss what we have been learning this week and how people feel about it. List on a flipchart what people say they have learned, why it matters, and how they felt during the week. Generate a blackboard list of all the words people use to describe feelings.

20 minutes   2.   Have students choose one weather picture each and ask a question about the picture. For example,

What do you see in this picture?
What season is this?
What is the weather like in this picture?
Where do you think this picture was taken? Why?
How do you feel when you look at this picture?

Hold up one picture first after writing all the questions on the board. Ask different students to answer different questions. Then, when the students volunteer to ask the questions, have them choose different people to answer so that everyone gets a turn asking and answering.

Ask how each picture is similar to or different from the weather in the countries they came from. Ask if the pictures remind them of home or not.

15 minutes   3.   Introduce feeling words by role-playing various words and using vivid facial expressions and other body language. Use whatever words are necessary to convey what you feel. Encourage the women to interpret for one another if they get it and someone doesn't. Teach these words: happy, sad, depressed, frustrated, excited, homesick, upset, nervous, curious, bored, worried, contented, disappointed, proud, afraid, embarrassed.

Review each word several times until the majority get it just from your facial expression and body language.
Then let them practice the expressions and body language that go with each word.

15 minutes   4.   Play charades with the word cards. Each person draws a card out of a bag and acts out the card without naming the word. Be prepared to help anyone who has difficulty reading the words.

15 minutes   5.   If time permits, use pictures to explore the feelings of characters in the picture, and the feelings elicited by the pictures. Encourage learners to add words to their personal vocabulary lists as they come up in discussing the pictures.

10 minutes   6.   Have each person name their favourite feeling word that they learned that day and explain why it is an important word for them to know at this time. Be

sure to allow sufficient time for this last exercise as it will probably provide a good idea of what is going on in people's lives.

7. Optional homework: give out handout exercise and/or tape to those who want to practise at home.

8. If any time is leftover, ask what plans people have for the weekend and make suggestions for those who have no idea what to do with themselves.

Notes to Myself:

Jasmine said she was glad to learn the word "frustrated" because that is how she often felt when her in-laws expected her to do all the work in the house and did not help her.

Aurora quietly indicated that "afraid" was an important word to know. She did not want to explain it, but I am beginning to believe that she is suffering abuse. (She has come to school with bruises on her arms and face.) I will try to spend more time with her and make sure that all the women know about the women's shelters.²

Mai said she liked the word "excited" and was excited to be in the English class because it gave her hope for the future.

Enat said she was depressed and disappointed. She did not think her life in Canada would be this hard. She also said she was homesick.

Chanta said that her favourite word was also "frustrated" because that is how she felt trying to understand why we said things the way we did in English. She said it was much harder than Khmer.

I am surprised that the women did as well as they did with this lesson. I thought they might find it hard. I think they have a fair passive vocabulary just from the time they have been here and from watching some TV, but their active vocabulary is far less extensive. They need lots of opportunities to practise using new words. They also had a hard time in some cases, writing the words in their books. Literacy is a battle for about half of them. This is where it would be useful to have a volunteer spend some

---

2 By law, teachers of children are obliged to report suspected abuse. With adults, it is a little different, in that we hold adults capable of taking care of themselves and making their own decisions. I make a point of always teaching women in particular about the laws which protect them from abuse, and the support services available for immigrant women. Some immigrant women choose to stay in abusive relationships, because to do otherwise may cause them to become alienated from their communities, which in turn, affects the ability of their daughters to marry within that community.

extra time with those who are really struggling. I think I will make journaling an option for those who are interested.

Magda asked if I could leave the pictures and the flashcards in the classroom so that they could practise with them during break times. I thought that was a great idea and was glad she felt comfortable suggesting it. I also really like the way these women help each other. They seem to do a lot more of that than the mixed classes do.

Sample 3: A Functional Lesson

This lesson is designed for a group of mixed beginners with very low literacy skills. The learners have had some practice with simple telephone conversations. The class is one hour and twenty minutes in length. This lesson has been planned for April Fool's Day.

Wednesday, April 1

Intents:

1. To <u>introduce</u> learners to the idea of April Fools' Day.
2. To <u>introduce</u> them to the necessary components of a telephone message.
3. To <u>provide learners with opportunities to practice</u> writing telephone messages.
4. To <u>build their confidence</u> so that they are capable of taking a message and communicating it to someone in their family.

Resources:

- Sample telephone messages on a handout.

May 1, 2:30 pm.

Maria,
Your friend Lynn called. Please call her back. She will be home until 6 p.m.

Jorge

> *9:55 a.m.*
> *Mon. June 6*
> *John,*
> *Dr. Smith's office called.*
> *Your appointment today is*
> *cancelled. Please call the*
> *office to make another.*
> *The number is 327-4181*
> *Luis*

- Two telephones.
- Flipchart and pens.
- Exercise with essential parts missing from the message. The learners have to find the problem.

Activities:

5 minutes   1.   Announce that everyone in class has just won the lottery and will be getting one million dollars at noon. When people look at me like I am crazy, let them ask any questions they have and then say, "April Fools!" Tell them that this is April Fools' Day but that the jokes have to stop at noon. Ask if people in their countries like to play jokes on one another.

5 -10 minutes   2.   Ask them how they feel using the telephone. Ask how many take messages already and if they say yes, ask someone to role-play a scenario with you. You will call and ask for someone who is not there, and they will take the message and pass it on to someone else in the class to read. Use the two phones so that this role-play looks and feels real.

5 minutes	3.	If no one volunteers to do that, ask a learner to call and leave a message for someone. Write down the components on the blackboard. Be sure to include the following information: • time and date of call • name of caller • message with all important details • your name.
5 minutes	4.	Have the students copy the message from the blackboard.
10 minutes	5.	Role-play another phone call and have someone else write down the message on the flipchart. Have the group correct it together.
20 minutes	6.	Have the students divide themselves into pairs and give each pair two flipchart sheets and a pen. Let them work out two telephone conversations and write down the message from each. Have them practice until they feel comfortable, and go around to each group helping them to find the words they need.
15 minutes	7.	When they have finished, have them do their role-plays for the class, and show the class their telephone messages at the end of each role-play. Ask the class if there is any need for clarification. When they are doing the role-plays, ask them if they want correction of pronunciation problems or not. If they say yes, correct any mispronunciations that interfere with the communication. If they say no, tell them when you do not understand.
15 minutes	8.	Hand out written exercise which has phone messages with errors in them. Ask them to find the errors and to say what they would do if they received a message with that error.

FIND THE PROBLEM

1.

> 7 p.m.
>
>
> Lu-Chen,
> Please call Mr. Mah
> before 6:30 p.m.
>
>
> Shao-Li

2.

> 4:30 p.m.
>
>
> Danielle,
> Please call your
> friend back right
> away.
> It is urgent.

12 noon
Call the school.
There is a problem.
Gotta go. Bye.

Martha

4:30 pm.
Hi, Mom!
Mrs. Smith phoned
from your office. She
said she'd meet you at
some restaurant
at 8:00.
    Have fun!
        Sara

10 minutes   9. Correct handout together and challenge people to try answering the phone at home and taking messages. If you run out of time, correct the handout together the next day.

Note to Myself:

The Chinese speakers in the class had some major pronunciation problems which made it difficult for everyone else to understand what they were saying on the phone. A few people were embarrassed to ask others to repeat themselves more than once. Most are open to correction but cannot themselves hear the differences between certain sounds. Do some minimal pair exercises tomorrow to beef up their listening skills and then go to work on the articulation.

A couple of the older people were hesitant to commit to taking messages at home and said that, in any case, the only phone calls they got were in their own language. However, the parents with children who are always bawling them out for not taking messages, were quite eager to go home and try out what they had learned. Here's hoping it works!

Mr. Yee told us proudly today that he had answered the phone (which he had not been willing to do after a bad experience several months ago in which someone yelled at him) and told the caller that his son was not home. He asked the person who called to please call back later. The caller said thank you and Mr. Yee was very proud. (He will be even more proud when he can tell his son who called!)

Shiu-Yen is having trouble seeing the blackboard. I believe she needs glasses. I suggested to her that she go to the public health clinic or to the doctor to get her eyes checked, but she said she had no money for glasses, and that she knew she needed them. I asked if her son would not pay for glasses for her and she looked very embarrassed. She said she did not want to ask him. I said I knew someone who knew of an organization that paid for glasses for people who did not have money, and told her that I would make an appointment for her after she had a prescription for the glasses. She looked very happy.

Sample 4: A Situational Lesson Based on Cultural Differences

This lesson is to be taught to a group of 20 Korean teachers *in Korea* who are preparing to come to North America for summer school at a university. The group is mostly men with some women, and of mixed ages from 30-55. You have one hour to do this cultural orientation to customs surrounding eating in Canada and the US.

Monday, July 8

Intents:

1. To <u>encourage</u> people to feel relaxed about whatever mistakes they may make during their visit to North America.
2. To <u>provide</u> the learners with sufficient information about differences in eating habits so that they may avoid some of the more common faux pas, or at least be aware of them.
3. To <u>explore</u> the differences in how the two cultures view intercultural responsibility.

Resources:

- One or more menus from North America so that learners can see what kinds of foods are typically eaten in this country. Otherwise, make up a sample menu typical of what one might see at dinner in a North American restaurant.
- Pictures of table settings with and without food on the table.

Activities:

5 minutes   1.   Encourage the teachers who have gone abroad to discuss their experiences and observations around food in the countries they have visited. Elicit any differences of which they are already aware and list them.
- Kimchee is not standard fare in most households.
- Rice is not a staple in the way it is in Korea, although some form of it is available in most restaurants.

10 min.   2.   Pass around the pictures of table settings with and without food and ask people what they see. Encourage them to talk about which foods they like and don't like, which ones they recognize and

which they do not. Encourage learners them to ask questions about anything they see in the pictures.

10 minutes 3. Ask them to identify habits of foreigners to Korea which they find personally offensive (e.g., blowing one's nose at the table, talking at the table, leaving rice in the bowl while eagerly eating everything else in sight, etc.).

10 minutes 4. Tell them about some Korean habits which North Americans may find offensive or remarkable. For example,
1. slurping noodles
2. burping at the table
3. eating before the hostess has sat down and begun to eat
4. just eating rather than engaging in conversation
5. leaving the table before everyone has finished eating.

10 minutes 5. Discuss why customs may have developed differently in the different countries. For example, noodles were not part of our diet; potatoes were. Slurping noodles is logical in that it prevents a person from splattering them all over. However, we took our table manners from Britain in which there was no need to slurp anything and in which eating quietly while talking politely was considered good manners. While eating in Korea is primarily a functional necessity, eating in Europe was a social act requiring a lengthy amount of time, which is still the case in high society.

10 minutes 6. Compare two intercultural rules:
In Korea, one does everything one can to make the guest feel at home.
In North America, the rule is "when in Rome, do as the Romans do."
This difference in expectation has led to many hurt feelings and misunderstandings, particularly for the Koreans. Give them a chance to talk about their feelings and thoughts in regard to these two rules and how they might be played out in practice.

5 minutes 7. Ask the learners how they are feeling about all these cultural differences and reassure them that the onus is also on the hosts to make adjustments

to their visit. And that, indeed, North American people will be oriented to their visit even as they are being oriented to being in North America.

Notes to Myself:

The Koreans seemed to find it all quite amusing. I suspect the young people will really make an effort to follow the customs of where they are going and to try out new foods and have new experiences. The older people, however, seem to vary in their reactions, which ranged from amusement to offense, that some of these things are even mentioned. Korean culture seems like a very monoethnic culture, but then they do not have the cultural mix that we have in North America, so I guess that is not too surprising.

A number of people have travelled to the States at least once before, but they do not seem to have learned much there. It was mostly a set of photo ops for most of them.

It was very interesting to hear them talk about what they consider offensive in our behaviours. In fact, I suspect there is probably a lot more that they did not say due to the fact that I am North American. In any case, we all have a lot to learn from one another. I wish I were going with them when they go to North America. I would love to see if this orientation makes a difference to their experience.

Must remember to tell Mr. Choi that I think Mrs. Park is going to have some problems. She does not seem keen to go on this trip and her English skills are far more limited than anyone else's. I wonder why she is going?

Sample 5: An Introductory Participatory Lesson

This class is an English for Special Purposes class designed for people who are studying to become accountants. Some have a background in finance and others do not. Most have been in the country for more than five years, while about five have arrived within the last year and have not had much time to settle. All have high intermediate to advanced English language skills, although most have some area of weakness such as pronunciation or writing. The class has been together for one day, during which time they have gotten to know one another and the instructors somewhat, and have had an orientation to what the program includes and what will be expected of them in terms of time and results.

One of the courses in their program is called Canadian Experience and is intended to fill in the blanks between the other courses which are highly specialized (e.g., Accounts Payable, Computerized Accounting, etc.). The course is to be team-taught by the administrator of the program and an instructor, a refugee herself who has successfully settled in the country. The course has a good deal of flexibility. There are 20 students in the program and this class is two hours in length.

Intents:

1. To <u>convey</u> to the learners that, of all their courses, this one is the most flexible to their needs and the most needful of their active participation.
2. To <u>explore</u> with learners various areas of possibility for the curriculum of the course.
3. To <u>listen</u> to what learners have experienced as most problematic in their time in Canada.
4. To <u>communicate</u> to learners our agenda for the course, which is that people will be self-confident and be able to stand up appropriately for their rights on the job and in the community, and that they will know what their rights and responsibilities are before going into the workplace.
5. To <u>negotiate</u> with learners both what they want to learn in terms of priorities and what learning strategies they have found most effective.
6. To <u>demonstrate</u> that what the learners think and want matters, and will make a difference to what we do in this course.
7. <u>To be honest</u> about what is not negotiable (e.g., money available, length of the program, hours of classtime).

Resources:

- A draft curriculum of the course with intents, tentative resource materials, and possible activities.
- Flipchart paper and pens to record learners' ideas.

Activities:

20 minutes	1.	Discuss with the learners what learning has been like for them in the past, what they liked and did not like, what they found difficult, and what kinds of things helped them to learn. Let them know that no one need speak until he or she is ready, and ask people to be patient with one another as some find speaking more difficult than others. Make a note of things people like and don't like, and see what agreement there is on these things. Use the flipchart to record their responses.
20 minutes	2.	Give everyone a copy of the draft curriculum and go through it with them, assuring them that this is a draft and that it is very open to changes according to what they perceive as their needs. Ensure that they know that we are open to their ideas and suggestions and that we genuinely want to know what they think. Ask which of the items they find most appealing and which they find unappealing. Ask what they think is missing. Let them know that, while we will make sure that their suggestions for today are incorporated into the next draft, we can make changes at any time. Tell them what the fixed parameters are for our program.

- The hours per day are governed by our contract with the government.
- The money available for the program is likewise fixed.
- The hours the learners have with the technical institute are fixed, and the institute sets the program.[3]

---

3 This proved to be a problem in the actual program, as the institute was not allowing for the extra time it would take second language learners to work with their material and understand it. We addressed that by hiring a student tutor who gave several hours a week in additional class time to those who needed it. We took the money from our materials budget to do so.

1 hour 10 minutes	3.	Give each person up to five minutes to talk about their experiences of being in Canada which have been the most difficult and how they have addressed those challenges. For those who are willing, try to discover which areas they still find challenging and what they need to meet those challenges. Let them know we are there to assist them in any way we can to find the resources and the strength they need to make the adjustments they choose to make here.

If people have difficulty getting started with this discussion, A. will speak of her experiences and the things she found difficult. This usually frees people up to realize that everyone faces similar difficulties.

Try to elicit experiences of work, of consumer difficulties, of language and cultural difference, of communities, of health, finance, dealing with schools, and consumer goods and services.

10 minutes	4.	Give each person a chance to express how he or she feels about the session. If time allows, summarize the main things we have learned from them today.

Notes to Myself:

This is going to be a great group to work with. There is a lot of energy and excitement in the group and they are very eager to gain the credentials they need to work in a decent occupation here. Some of them have been driving taxis, cleaning offices, or working in fast food joints. One has been washing dishes. The fact that the three courses they do at the technical institute will count towards their CGA designation is a real plus.

The one Vietnamese and two Chinese speakers have major pronunciation problems which, if we do not help them to do something about, will surely prevent these students from finding employment, regardless of what kinds of credentials they have. We must discuss this at the staff meeting and see what strategies might be most effective in working with these problems.

Two of the women in the group feel quite outclassed by the others, if one can judge by their demeanour. One is here by virtue of her bookkeeping experience and the other by work she did in her country. The first has very little formal education as compared to everyone else. The second seems very fearful of everything and everyone. Both are going to need a lot of encouragement and positive experiences in the program.

The two Syrian bankers have had very little time in the country and are very depressed about their losses here. (They came as entrepreneurs and lost everything in a short period of time.) The woman in particular is very high-strung and emotional. I hope she relaxes as she gets to know people and begins to see a brighter future for herself. It is beyond my imagination to know how awful it must feel to lose one's life savings like that.

The Egyptian man is behaving rather badly towards the two Egyptian women in the class. He seems to need to be dominating at all times, even to the point of sabotaging them if necessary. Is this just male ego or something more? Will have to keep an eye on this and try to understand what it is about. I think the women are behaving very well under the circumstances, but it is unhealthy nonetheless.

Maria seems to be a real leader. She not only takes initiative in saying what she thinks, but she gives a lot of encouragement to others to do so and is very good at acknowledging their efforts and achievements.

Sue is an absolute whiz as a learner! She has learning strategies that I can learn from and does not miss a thing. If we can just identify what she is doing and help others to do it too, everyone will gain so much. She will be very easy to place when the time comes.

Janusz is a funny, endearing personality. He acts the clown to cover his own embarrassments, but is a most capable person. I am betting that when A. does the camera work with him, he will blossom.

As for our draft curriculum, the learners all seemed to be quite enthusiastic and interested to learn what we had outlined. It was helpful to hear their experiences so that we know where to put our emphasis. One woman said in leaving, that A. and I are the curriculum for this course. From the looks on their faces as they watched us working together, our complementarity gives them all a sense of hope and possibility for the future.

Writing Intents—Answer Key

Topic 1: *Asking information questions (who, what, when, where, why.)*

Teacher Intent:

To enable learners to correctly form real questions which begin with <u>who</u> and <u>what</u> (subject and object questions), <u>where</u>, <u>when</u>, and <u>why</u>.

Learner Intent:

To be able to form correct questions beginning with <u>who</u> and <u>what</u> as subject and object, as well as questions beginning with <u>where</u>, <u>when</u>, and <u>why</u>.

Intended Learning Outcome:

Learners shall be able to ask information questions in the simple present and simple past tenses as illustrated:

Who took the money? (who-subject)
Who is the money for? (who-object)
What happened yesterday? (what-subject)
What is the announcer saying on the radio? (what-object)
When are you leaving?
Where are you going?
Why can't I come?

Topic 2: *Vocabulary required to describe to a medical doctor the location and circumstances of a persistent headache.*

Teacher Intent:

To introduce and practice with the learners the vocabulary needed to describe to a doctor the location and circumstances of a persistent headache.

Learner Intent:

To be able to tell a doctor where the pain of a persistent headache is, what it is like, and when I get it so that he (or she) can understand me and help me.

Intended Learning Outcome:

The learner shall be able to verbally describe the location and circumstances of a persistent headache to a doctor in such a way that the doctor has sufficient information to prescribe either medication or treatment and/or recommend further tests. The learner shall also be able to understand how to follow the doctor's directions for care.

Specifically, the learner shall understand and be able to answer the following questions:

Where do you feel pain?
—*in the right temple, in the left temple, across the forehead, down the right/left side of my head, up the centre from the back of my neck, across my shoulders and up my neck, etc.*

Is this pain throbbing or steady?
—*It is throbbing. It is steady. It comes and goes.*

How often do you get this headache and when?
—*At the time of my period or if I eat chocolate or drink red wine. Maybe once every two weeks or so. Every second day. Every morning I wake up with a headache.*

Do you have any visual disturbances before or during your headache?
—*Sometimes my vision is a little blurry during and after the headache. Sometimes I get a ring of light around objects before the headache.*

Topic 3: *Refusing to do work that is dangerous.*

Teacher Intent:

To prepare learners to refuse dangerous work politely, but firmly, in whatever setting they may work.

Learner Intent:

To refuse to work in dangerous settings, but to do so politely and firmly

Intended Learning Outcome:

The learner shall be willing and able to refuse work which is clearly unsafe or unhealthy in any workplace. He/she shall state the reason for thus refusing and the conditions for returning to work. For example,

1 – *Mr. Smith, that platform is cracked and looks very unsafe. I'm sorry, but I am not willing to go up there until it is replaced.*

2 – *Mary, the exhaust fumes in that room are very strong. We are not willing to work in that room until they have dispersed. Something should be done to prevent this situation. Could the air intake not be moved away from the helipad?*

3 – *Joe, it is against safety regulations for us to carry more than one bundle of shingles to the roof at a time. I will not carry two, as I am not willing to hurt my back.*

Topic 4: *Questions one does not ask a new acquaintance.*

Teacher intent:

To show learners that Canadians may be offended if they are asked personal questions about their age, their weight, or their income.

Learner intent:

To learn which questions are offensive to native English speakers and in which circumstances.

Intended learning outcome:

The learners shall recognize that personal questions concerning one's age, weight, and income are inappropriate in casual conversation with new acquaintances.

Topic 5: *Deciding which candidate to vote for in an election.*

Teacher intent:

To introduce learners to the main political parties and give samples of their primary platforms.

Learner intent:

To learn about the main political parties and their primary issues, so that I will feel comfortable deciding who to vote for in the next election.

Intended learning outcome:

Learners shall know the names of the leaders of each of the four main parties in the federal election as well as the names of the representatives running in their constituency, and shall be able to state succinctly two of the main platform positions for each.

List of Phonetic Symbols

Consonants

Stops	/p/	pot
	/b/	bought
	/t/	taught
	/d/	dot
	/k/	caught
	/g/	got
Fricatives	/f/	fail
	/v/	veil
	/θ/	thigh
	/ð/	thy
	/s/	sue
	/z/	zoo
	/ʃ/	shoot
	/ʒ/	pleasure
Affricates	/tʃ/	church
	/dʒ/	judge
Nasals	/m/	ram
	/n/	ran
	/ŋ/	rang
Liquids	/l/	lice
	/r/	rice
Semi-vowels	/y/	your
	/w/	war
	/h/	heart

Vowels

Front	/iy/	beat
	/ɪ/	bit
	/ey/	bait
	/ɛ/	bet
	/æ/	bat
Back	/uw/	boot
	/ʊ/	book
	/ow/	boat
	/a/	bought
Central	/ʌ/	but
	/ə/	about
Diphthongs	/ay/	buy
	/aw/	bough
	/oy/	boy
	/ər/	bird

Source: Avery, Peter and Ehrlich, Susan (eds.). *The Teaching of Pronunciation: An Introduction for Teachers of English as a Second Language* in *TESL Talk*, 17 (1) 1987.

Bibliography

ESL/EFL Titles

Allen, Virginia French. 1983. *Techniques in Teaching Vocabulary*. New York: Oxford University Press.

Ashworth, Mary. 1985. *Beyond Methodology: Second Language Teaching and the Community*. Cambridge: Cambridge University Press.

Avery, Peter and Susan Ehrlich. 1992. *Teaching American English Pronunciation*. New York: Oxford University Press.

Azar, Betty Schrampfer. 1992. *The Fundamentals of English Grammar*. Englewood Cliffs, NJ: Prentice-Hall Regents.

_____. 1989. *Understanding and Using English Grammar*. Englewood Cliffs, NJ: Prentice-Hall Regents.

_____. 1984. *Basic English Grammar*. Englewood Cliffs, NJ: Prentice-Hall Regents.

Barndt, Deborah, Ferne Cristall, and dian marino. 1982. *Getting There: Producing Photostories with Immigrant Women*. Toronto: Between the Lines Press.

Bell, Jill. 1988. *Teaching Multilevel Classes in ESL*. Markham, ON: Pippin.

Bell, Jill and Barbara Burnaby. 1984. *A Handbook for ESL Literacy*. Toronto: OISE Press.

Blair, Robert W., Ed. 1982. *Innovative Approaches to Language Teaching*. Rowley, MA: Newbury House.

Canadian Congress for Learning Opportunities for Women (CCLOW). 1996. *Making Connections: Literacy and EAL Curriculum from a Feminist Perspective*. Toronto: CCLOW.

Celce-Murcia, Marianne and Diane Larsen-Freeman. 1983. *The Grammar Book: An ESL/EFL Teacher's Course*. Rowley, MA: Newbury House.

Hadfield, Charles and Jill Hadfield. 1990. *Writing Games*. Surrey, UK: Nelson Publishers.

Hadfield, Jill. 1990. *Intermediate Communication Games*. Surrey, UK: Nelson Publishers.

_____. 1987. *Advanced Communication Games*. Surrey, UK: Nelson Publishers.

_____. 1984. *Elementary Communication Games*. Surrey, UK: Nelson Publishers.

Helmer, Sylvia and Catherine Eddy. 1996. *Look at Me When I Talk to You: ESL Learners in Non-ESL Classrooms*. Toronto: Pippin.

Kramsch, Claire. 1993. *Context and Culture in Language Teaching*. Oxford: Oxford University Press.

Krashen, Stephen. 1982. *Principles and Practice in Second Language Acquisitions*. Oxford: Pergamon.

Kress, Jacqueline E. 1993. *The ESL Teacher's Book of Lists*. West Nyack, NY: The Center for Applied Research in Education. (Distributed through Pearson Education.)

Lightbown, Patsy and Nina Spada. 1993. *How Languages are Learned*. Oxford: Oxford University Press.

Madsen, Harold S. 1983. *Techniques in Testing*. New York: Oxford University Press.

McKay, Sandra Lee. 1992. *Teaching English Overseas: An Introduction*. Oxford: Oxford University Press.

Mendelsohn, David, Ed. 1999. *Expanding Our Vision: Insights for Language Teachers*. Toronto: Oxford University Press.

Moskowitz, Gertrude. 1978. *Caring and Sharing in the Foreign Language Class: A Sourcebook on Humanistic Techniques*. Rowley, MA: Newbury House.

Nilsen, Don L.F. and Alleen Pace Nilsen. 1971. *Pronunciation Contrasts in English*. New York: Simon and Schuster.

Quirk, Randolph, Geoffrey Leech, Sidney Greenbaum, and Jan Svartvik. 1985. *A Comprehensive Grammar of the English Language*. London: Longman.

Raimes, Ann. 1983. *Techniques in Teaching Writing*. New York: Oxford University Press.

Robinson, Julia and Mary Selman. 1996. *Partnerships in Learning: Teaching ESL to Adults*. Toronto: Pippin.

Sauvé, Virginia. 1991. *Windows of Meaning in Adult ESL*. Unpublished doctoral dissertation. Edmonton: University of Alberta.

Silberstein, Sandra. 1994. *Techniques and Resources in Teaching Reading*. New York: Oxford University Press.

Sperling, Dave. 1997. *The Internet Guide for English Language Teachers*. Upper Saddle River, NJ: Prentice-Hall.

Stevick, Earl W. 1990. *Humanism in Language Teaching*. Oxford: Oxford University Press.

Swan, Michael and Bernard Smith. 1987. *Learner English: A Teacher's Guide to Interference and Other Problems*. Cambridge, UK: Cambridge University Press.

TESL Canada Journal. Published by the Teachers of English as a Second Language Federation of Canada, PO Box 44105, Burnaby, BC V5B 4Y2, 1-800-393-9199, E-mail: teslcanada@home.com
http://www.tesl.ca

TESOL Quarterly. Published by the Teachers of English to Speakers of Other Languages, Inc. 700 S. Washington Sreet., Ste. 200, Alexandria, VA 22314 USA, (703) 836-0774. E-mail: publications@tesol.org
http://www.tesol.edu

Voices. Issue 18. V.8, No. 2, Fall 1997. Available at leegee@radiant.net

Wallerstein, Nina. 1983. *Language and Culture in Conflict: Problem-Posing in the ESL Classroom.* Reading, MA: Addison-Wesley.

Wright, Andrew. 1984. *1000 Pictures for Teachers to Copy.* London: HarperCollins Publishers.

Titles from Related Disciplines

Boud, David, Rosemary Keogh, and David Walker, Ed. 1985. *Reflection: Turning Experience into Learning.* London: Kogan Page.

Dalton, Harlon L. 1995. *Racial Healing: Confronting the Fear Between Blacks and Whites.* New York: Doubleday.

Giroux, Henry A. 1983. *Theory and Resistance in Education: A Pedagogy for the Opposition.* South Hadley, MA: Bergin and Garvey Publishers.

Gusdorf, Georges. 1965. *Speaking (La Parole).* Translated by Paul Brockelman.

Evanston, IL.: Northwestern University Press.

Hall, Edward. 1983. *The Dance of Life: The Other Dimension of Time.* Garden City, NY: Anchor Press/ Doubleday.

_____. 1973. *The Silent Language.* Garden City, NY: Doubleday Anchor.

_____. 1969. *The Hidden Dimension.* Garden City, NY: Doubleday Anchor.

Nozick, Robert. 1989. *The Examined Life: Philosophical Meditations.* New York: Simon and Schuster.

Satir, Virginia M. 1976. *Making Contact.* Millbrae, CA: Celestial Press.

_____. 1972. *Peoplemaking.* Palo Alto, CA: Science and Behavior Books.

Sennett, Richard and Jonathan Cobb. 1973. *The Hidden Injuries of Class.* New York: Vintage Books, Random House.

Smillie, Ruth and Kelly Murphy. 1986. *Story Circles.* Saskatoon, SK: Saskatchewan Teachers' Federation.

West, Cornel. 1993. *Race Matters.* Boston: Beacon Press.

Zukav, Gary. 1990. *The Seat of the Soul.* New York: Simon and Schuster.

Index

abuse of power 51, 174–5
accountability 31, 100
 to employer 166
 to funders 165–6
 to learners 162–5
 to yourself 167
action research
 (participatory research)
 185
active voice (grammar)
 145
activities, classroom
 appropriate 68–70,
 78–9, 82–3
 basic guidelines 82–4
 Dress-up Bag 86–7
 field trips 91–2
 Mystery Box 84–5
 photostories 90–1
 pictures 89–91
 posters 85–6
 problem-posing 87–9
adjective phrases 147
adjectives 147, 150
adverbs 151
articles 142, 150–1
auditory learners 106–7

Bell, Jill 131
Best Practice Guidelines
 165
bilingual instruction 22
body language 97, 116
Burnaby, Barbara 131

Canadian Language
 Benchmarks
 Assessment (CLBA) 166
classroom relationships
 conflict resolution 178
 human element in
 viii–ix
 husband-wife learners
 22
 intervening in personal
 problems 18, 175

mono-ethnic group 23–4
 power 38, 192
 students amongst
 themselves 177–8
 teacher/individual
 student 176–7
 teacher/students 173–5
 trust and mutual liking
 17–8, 44–5, 96–7
community
 classroom 108, 177–8
 ethnic 102
 global 57–8
 local 54–6
 national 56–7
 regional 56
conjunctions 152
coordinating conjunctions
 152
count nouns 147
culture
 behaviour and context
 96
 and gender 21–2
 meaning and language
 4–8
 sensitivity to 24, 29–30,
 42, 55–6, 101, 176–7
 shock 31–32

declarative (indicative)
 mood 145
discernment 39, 190–2
disrespect, and self-
 esteem 30
Dress-up Bag 86–7

education
 bilingual 102
 dictionary definition 9
 participatory 38, 50
 and peoplemaking 191
 settlement 55
 success in, notion of 52
educational approach
 9–10

educator, as healer
 99–100
EFL learners
 goal of ix, 55
 special purpose
 programs for 10, 20
employment preparation
 20–1
empowerment and life
 skills, teaching 18,
 56–7, 88–9, 191
English for Special
 Purposes (ESP) 20
English in the Workplace
 (EWP) 20
ESL learners
 and adaptation to new
 culture 97
 attitude 7–8
 classroom needs and
 expectations 18–9
 illiterate and
 semi-literate 10, 19
 and loss of status 31–32
 mental and emotional
 pain, effects of 26–7
 personal circumstances
 17, 18, 22–3
 purpose of learning
 English ix, 19–20
 settlement issues 16
 special needs 176–7
 see also refugees
ESL Teacher's Book of
 Lists 76–7
evaluation 70–71, 101–2
 by employer 166
 by students 163–4

field trips 91–2
Freire, Paulo 131, 191
functional approach, to
 grammar 154

gender, and mixed classes
 21–2

grammar
  function 142
  parts of speech 143–54
  teaching approaches
    154
  transformational 143
grammar, teaching
  techniques
  games 159
  guided composition 159
  modelled composition
    158
  patterned practice
    155–6
  question practice
    159–60
  reality-based instruction
    154–5
  Strip Stories 157–8
grammatical intent 65
guests, classroom 92
guided composition 159

Hall, Edward 42
homework 23
  optional 20
homonyms 119
honorific forms 142

imperative mood 145
indicative (declarative)
  mood 145
intents 64–6
interjections 153
Internet 135, 186
intonation
  exercises 118
  meaning and culture
    115–6

journal writing 137
joy, in learning 98–9

key performance
  indicators 165

labelling, slow learners
  33
language
  function 142–3
  as medium of human
    experience 4–8
  teaching through

content 20–1, 95–6,
    104, 106
  transmission theory of
    3–4
Language Master 79
language training 9–10
laughter. See joy, in
  learning
learner intents 65–6
learning environment
  renew 104–6
  respect 100–2
  restore 102–3
  review 103–4
learning, factors of
  age 25
  culture and language
    29–30
  degree of integration
    22–3, 31–2
  educational background
    18–9
  family relationships 23
  gender 20–21
  intelligence 32–3
  job and employment
    situation 19–21
  life experience 25–6
  marital status 22–3
  mental and emotional
    pain 26–7
  personality 28
  physical health 26
  politics 33–4
  race 30–1
  religion 33–4
  spiritual health 27–8
learning outcomes
  intended 66–8
  measurable 52
learning strategies 106–9
lesson plan
  components 64
  functional lesson 206–11
  grammar-based 197–201
  optional (extra)
    activities 71
  participatory lesson
    215–8
  situational lesson 212–4
  time allocation 71
  uses 63
  vocabulary lesson 202–5

lexical intent 65
life story writing 138
linear teaching approach
  71
linguistics, university
  courses 187
linking verbs 146
listening and speaking
  skills, improving
  content of message 114,
    115
  correcting mistakes 114
  intonation 115–6
  meaning of message
    115–6
  natural speech, using
    111–1
  principles for 111–5
listening techniques
  audio tapes, use of 116
  cloze exercises 116–7
  dictation 116
  homonyms 119
  minimal pair exercises
    117
  rapid speech exercises
    118–9
  real-life listening
    materials 117–8
  stress and intonation
    exercises 118
literacy, ESL 131

mass (noncount) nouns
  147–8
measurable learning
  outcomes 52, 165
Medicine Bag Stories
  121–3
Mendelsohn, David 186
metaphysical time 142
modals 147
modelled composition
  158
mono-ethnic classroom
  23–4
Mystery Box 84–5

natural speech, in
  improving listening and
  speaking skills 111–2
noncount (mass) nouns
  147–8

nonmodal auxiliaries 147
"Notes to Myself" 71
nouns 147

object 147
office politics 52
Ooops Sheets 156–7

pair work 108–9, 177
participatory approach, to
  grammar 154
participatory education
  38, 50, 91, 100
participatory intent 65
participatory research
  (action research) 185
passive voice (grammar)
  145
peoplemaking 191
personal interviews
  164–5
phonemics 125–6
portfolio, student writing
  136–7
power
  sharing 192
  traditional classroom 38
  see also abuse of power
prepositions 151–2
professional associations
  182–5
professional development
  185–6
professional relationships
  teacher to colleagues
    178–9
  teacher to supervisor
    52, 179–80
program
  accountability
    structures 51–2
  community-linked 58
  constraints 48–9
  flexibility 50–1
  priorities 49–50
  supervisor 52
Program Standards 165
pronunciation 125–6
pronouns
  possessive 149
  reflexive 149
  subject 148–9
pronouns, relative 149–50

questions
  learning through asking
    95–6, 102, 115
  meaningful 112–4

race, racism 30–1, 42–43,
  55
reading 128–9
  teaching guidelines
    132–3
  techniques and
    resources 133–8
real statement 97
recontextualization, stress
  and intonation patterns
  112
refugees, and wounds of
  the past 7–8, 57–8
religion 33–4
Renew, concept 104–6
research work 185–6
resources
  appropriate 69–70, 78–9
  cassette 77–8
  community links 58
  dictionaries 76
  games 78
  grammar references
    75–6
  household and found 77
  inclusive 76
  Language Master 79
  maps 77
  online 186
  pictures 73–5
  and teacher intents
    68–70
  textbooks 79–80
  thesauri 76
  workbooks 79–80
respect 100–2
restoration 102–3
review, lesson 71, 83
role-plays 87
romance, teacher-learner
  23, 175
Rule of Invitation 83–4

Satir, Virginia 28, 191
School for International
  Living 187
self-awareness 37–38, 40,
  180–1

settlement education 55
single (unmarried)
  students 22–3
situational approach, to
  grammar 154
situational intent 65
social activities, after
  class 49, 50
speaking skills
  determination and
    perseverance 120
  pronunciation 125–6
  self-confidence and 120
  see also listening and
    speaking skills,
    improving
speaking techniques
  intermediate taking
    exercises 123–4
  making theatre 124–5
  Medicine Bag Stories
    121–3
  one-minute speeches
    120–21
  presentations 123
  talking stick 121
spiral teaching approach
  71, 84
spirituality 27–8
story work 133–4
Strip Stories 157–8
subject 147
subjective mood 145
subordinating
  conjunctions 152

Talking Stick 121
teacher intents 65
teacher preparation
  programs 186–8
  recipe approach vi
teaching
  commitment and 38–9
  cultural/racial
    sensitivity and 42–3
  discernment and 39
  life experience and 44–5
  maturity and 41
  multilingualism and 41
  personality and 40–1
  social class and 43–4
  social skills and 41
  support systems and 40

training and experience and 45
underlying motivation for teaching and 37–8
teaching style, individual vii–iv
tenses 142
TESL Canada 183, 184
TESL/TEFL programs 186–8
TESOL 183–4, 184
tests 164, 167–8
theatre 124–5
TOEFL 168
Total Physical Responses (TPRs) 83
translations and interpretations 6

values
culture, language and 96
imposition of 12–3, 51, 97
North American cultural 12–3

valuing, process of 70–71
verbs
forms 146–7
linking 146
modals 157
mood 145
person 144
tense 145
voice 144
vision
defined v–vi, 194
in learners 195–6
of society, teaching and 11–3, 194–5
vocabulary 128
active and passive knowledge of 140
aspects of 139–40
contextualized 132, 138–9
teaching guidelines 132–3
voice v
effecting change 192–3
exercising personal power 95, 131

of learners 193–4

word order 153–4
writing 129–31
teaching guidelines 132–3
writing, techniques and resources for
comparison correction 134
Internet, use of 135
journal writing 137
life story writing 138
peer feedback 134–5
realia, use of 133
story work 133–4
student portfolios 136–7
symbols for error correction 135–6
writing for special purposes 137–8